Acclaim

"This book is not just a travel memoir, it's a life manual."

Keith Moen
Author and publisher of Hopeace Press

"A book for young and old alike, *Trekking the Globe with Mostly Gentle Footsteps* takes you on an incredible trip around the world—a dream shared by many, yet only pursued by few. As you travel in the comfort of Irene's backpack, this book will give you the inspiration to map your own itinerary, to 'Expect the unexpected,' and before you know it, you too will be exploring the world with mostly gentle footsteps!"

Sean Aiken
Author of *The One-Week Job Project: 1 Man, 1 Year, 52 Jobs*

"What an exhilarating read. You will feel like you are on the adventure with them. It is packed full of travel tips and life lessons learned along the way. This book is a great reminder that it is never too late to follow any dream no matter where it might take you."

Dr. Carolyn Anderson MD
Eye surgeon
Founder of the online senior's magazine *Impowerage.com*

"A remarkable, readable, vivid account of an ambitious adventure filled with joy, struggle, insights, and respect for the world that binds us all together. In Kathmandu, Irene and Rick declare: 'Our perspective on everything we thought we knew was in flux; all we knew for sure was that we would never be the same.' Ample reason for readers to share this journey."

Mike Keenan
whattravelwriterssay.com

"This book is a must-read. Irene's vast travel experience and her writing style make you feel like you are a hitchhiker on one of her trips. It is absolutely fantastic ... well written, very impressive."

Laurel D'Andrea
Publisher of *Beyond 50 Magazine*

"This journey in words will have retirees rushing to stuff backpacks and lace up hiking boots for their first globe-trotting marathon. Amid tantalizing descriptions, humour, and sound advice, Butler shows travellers how to afford their dream destinations without sacrificing too much comfort."

Julie H. Ferguson
Author and addicted traveller, beaconlit.com

"*Trekking the Globe* is the grown-up version of the '60s backpackers *Europe on $10 a Day*. But it's much more than a book on travelling. Poignantly written, *Trekking the Globe* reflects the dreams and aspirations of many of the boomer generation. It offers insight into the relationship of the authors with unfamiliar cultures—and with each other. A great read that encourages us all to find our passports and get on the road."

Terry Ohman
Travel & Tourism Solutions (TTS) Inc.
**Contributor to *Steps to Success: Global Good Practices*
*in Tourism Human Resources***

"An engaging blend of history, geography, and human interest. Makes me want to pack my bags."

Janice Strong
Editor of *Canadian Traveller*

"Retired, rejuvenated, and ready to ride. Irene and Rick Butler prove that—armed with an around-the-world airline ticket—advancing years can't quench the irresistible adrenaline of adventure. Where the Butlers are concerned, time is for travelling; and when a destination like Kathmandu calls, there's no time like the present. Rule out the rocking chair: they've got a lot of living to do. This book may tempt you to do the same."

Ursula Maxwell-Lewis
Travel columnist and founder of the *Cloverdale Reporter News*

"This is a great read. Irene's compelling narrative will inspire more than a few would-be adventurers. She has a talent for serving up just the right amount of information. I plan to keep this book on hand, as her thorough research on a myriad of cities and sights will be a valuable resource for my own round-the-world trip."

Leigh McAdam
hikebiketravel.com

TREKKING THE GLOBE
WITH mostly GENTLE FOOTSTEPS
Twelve Countries in Twelve Months

by
IRENE BUTLER

Granville Island
PUBLISHING

Library and Archives Canada Cataloguing in Publication

Butler, Irene, 1944-

Trekking the globe : with mostly gentle footsteps : twelve countries in twelve months / Irene Butler.

ISBN 978-1-894694-79-7

1. Butler, Irene, 1944- —Travel. 2. Butler, Rick, 1949- —Travel. 3. Voyages and travels. I. Title.

G465.B88 2010   910.4   C2010-900932-0

Editors: Meg Taylor, Adriana Van Leeuwen

Proofreader: Renate Preuss

Book Designer: Omar Gallegos

Satellite images from: maps-for-free.com

Granville Island Publishing Ltd.
212–1656 Duranleau St · Granville Island
Vancouver BC · Canada · V6H 3S4

604 688 0320
1 877 688 0320

info@granvilleislandpublishing.com
www.granvilleislandpublishing.com

First Published May 2010 · Printed in Canada on recycled paper

This book is dedicated with love to our grandchildren: Brittany, Ruby, Breanna, Terrance, Dylan, Leif & Liam

Acknowledgements

Thanks to Ruth Kozak, my first travel writing instructor, friend, colleague, and mentor, for doing the initial read of my manuscript and offering many great suggestions. Thanks to Margaret Deefholts and Jane Cassie, the owners and editors of Travel Writers Tales, for which I've been a contributing writer since its inception. I learned a lot from you both over the past four years.

Much appreciation goes to Jo Blackmore and her team at Granville Island Publishing—Vici Johnstone, Adriana Van Leeuwen, Meg Taylor, Omar Gallegos, Renate Preuss—for all their excellent work. Thanks also to my publicist, David Litvak.

Most of all, I owe special thanks to Rick—my best friend, lover, husband, travel partner, chief editor, and finance minister—who was by my side almost every minute throughout this year of travel, and who encouraged me every step of the way in writing this book.

Rick and I would like to extend our heartfelt thanks and our gratitude to all the people who crossed our paths and enriched our lives during our 12-month trek through 12 countries. For more of our gypsy travel experiences go to our website: **www.globaltrekkers.ca**

Contents

Foreword

Irene and Rick Butler are not of my generation. Yet, as a devoted traveller, it's easy to recognize fellow members of the tribe. We share a strong desire to explore our planet's beauty, people, creatures, and culture—and to tell others about what we find.

I, too, have packed up my things, picked up a backpack, and set out to see the world. I have walked some of the same paths as these two travellers, although my relative youth and insignificant budget restricted me to sleeping in places I really wouldn't wish on anyone. Five years later, I'm still on the road for half the year and am approaching the 100-country milestone.

What the Butlers prove, so ably, is that global adventures are not limited to young kids postponing the "real world" after college, transients incapable of stability, or the handful of travel writers lucky enough to make a living at it.

Just about everyone dreams of seeing the world, on their terms, and at a leisurely pace; to see landmarks like the Taj Mahal or Tower of Pisa, and to meet the kind of unforgettable challenges that only arise when you truly expect the unexpected. Yet very few people actually do, especially once the responsibilities of life come knocking. We allow dream adventures to be reduced to two-week holidays. Well, this book is proof that, with a little elbow grease, anything is possible.

Irene and Rick must have had their friends voice concerns for their well-being, both physical and mental. After all, can you imagine your grandparents backpacking to India, Nepal, and China? What are you guys ... nuts? I often give thanks to the nutty people in the world, for without them, who would have the courage to just go for it, and in doing so inspire the rest of us?

Where would we learn such vital information as that one should leave a water bottle behind when visiting the corpse of Chairman Mao, or get a visa before taking the train to Poland? Where would we learn about the beauty and magic of a world that, despite the best attempts of newspapers to convince otherwise, is not out to get you?

Irene repeatedly shows us that we live on a beautiful blue ball, full of people quick to open their hearts and homes. Her chapters are filled with interesting facts and practical advice, so that we learn something about each destination along with the experience that comes with it.

The adventures and misadventures of the Butlers on their epic journey are an inspiration to readers and travellers of all ages. They knew, out the gate, that their travels needn't take them too far out of their comfort zone, and that sticking to Rick's budget was crucial for them to reach their goals— and crucial to ignore on occasion too. Their gentle footsteps remind us that humour, enthusiasm, and attitude go a long way in the world of hardcore travel.

Robin Esrock
Travel writer and star of the TV series *Word Travels*
Broadcast on OLN, City TV, and National Geographic International

Prologue

I can barely breathe with the exhilaration of it all. Rick and I bounce along atop a camel named Moses, our eyes transfixed by the Great Pyramids of Giza. Our turbaned guide ambles alongside and occasionally tugs at Moses' reins to change directions. An hour of circumnavigating these wondrous monuments passes as quickly as a desert breeze.

In the distance we see the patch of camel wranglers that had been our starting point and where our ride was to end... but we are veering away.

"Where are you taking us?" I call down. No response. My heart takes a small tumble, the feeling like when a fire truck with sirens blaring races ahead of you down your street.

"Hey, we are going in the wrong direction!" I yell. He says nothing. He leads the camel to the peak of a steep sand dune, then stops so we can appreciate the drop on the other side.

"Baksheesh," he says, his grin exposing brown stumps for teeth.

"Nooo, we already paid you."

"Baksheesh," he repeats.

"No way," Rick pipes up. Our antsy camel shifts under his weight. I cling white-knuckled to the saddle-horn. Sand cascades down the embankment from under the camel's feet.

"You want down? Then give baksheesh."

We part with an American 10-dollar bill....

In Morocco, the Sahara's dunes beckon us. On a camel again—this time in a caravan—we cross the desert to spend a night with Berber tribesmen.

Although we had waited to start out until our guide, Hamzal, said, "The storm has almost blown itself out," the swirling grains filter through my makeshift turban and face scarf. I squint out at the wave of dunes in the sea of grit, feeling like a flinty salt trader of old.

The wind abates and four tall, striped tents come into view. A steaming kettle of chicken tajine awaits us. Sitting cross-legged in the dining tent, we sup royally on the hardy stew along with chunks of bread, followed by cinnamon-doused slices of the sweetest, juiciest oranges in the entire world.

Stars rule the heavens as we move outside to sit around a blazing campfire. With heavy eyes, albeit mostly from the sandman, it is off to the sleeping tent to swaddle ourselves in thick woollen blankets against the crisp night air.

* * *

We were hooked! Our trips to Egypt and Morocco had been short in duration due to the demands of running a large retail store, but there was no holding us back now. A craving for travel had entered our bloodstream and each experience was a fix for our addiction.

We began squeezing in trips between our business month-ends. Before leaving on these whirlwind stints, we would put in sweatshop hours to leave affairs in good order. Then we'd head off for two- or three-week adventures so chock full of activities that we needed rest-breaks upon our return. Of course, those were not to be: our desks were always bowed from the weight of paperwork waiting for us. But to us, it was always worth it. Our passion for travel only deepened. We kept it up for our first 10 years together as a couple.

Chapter One
Beginnings

And Then ...

Ask me if I believe in miracles, I thought. I rubbed my hand over the airline tickets again and again, but we did not need a genie to appear to grant us our wish. Our dream had already come true and was about to begin the following day (July 1). Rick and I were to embark on a journey around the world lasting a year.

Exactly six months earlier, we had been offered an opportunity to sell our business. It took us 10 minutes to decide: we said "Yes." After 35 years of being bound to the rigours of the work-world, we made a decision to retire—or "restyle our lives," as we called it.

Rewarding our retirement with a year away was such a radical move for us it was difficult to get our heads around actually doing it. We vacillated between anticipation and uncertainty as we whirled like dervishes to get things in order before leaving. Was it too much, too soon? I was often heard mumbling things like, "Could we not have started out our new life with a month on a luxury cruise?"

Taking Care of Business

As I sat giddily fondling the tickets, my mind flashed back to the frenzied past half-year.

First we had plodded through the forest of legalities around selling our business. As we dealt with the seemingly endless loose ends, we wondered what government bureau would eventually hunt us down for some forgotten procedure in the paper blizzard of closing our company.

Then there had been the formulation of plans to take care of a year's worth of personal matters such as income taxes, medical and insurance payments, and the payment of other bills that would come due while we were away.

Fortunately, one of our sons and his partner took on the responsibility of being the recipients of all mail while we were gone and letting us know about any unanticipated things which might crop up. Alas, no matter how you pre-plan, there is always a bumper crop of those.

Luckily, we had not yet bought a home since relocating to Vancouver a year before our retirement, which eliminated the need for a house-sitter. Being renters meant we could simply give notice to our landlord and pack up our belongings to be put into storage.

Then, unexpectedly, the whole high-rise complex where we were renting came on the market a month before our departure date. We squeezed in time to purchase a unit complete with tenants; a mutually beneficial arrangement, as they would not have to relocate, and we would have our costs of ownership covered while away.

Letting friends know "what's up" was easier: we sent them all a letter or e-mail announcing our plans.

Most important were our children and grandchildren. I worried that a molehill-sized problem might seem like a mountain from halfway around the world. With worldwide internet access, e-mailing would be key. It was also essential to actually hear their voices and feel from their words and tone that they were okay. We devised a rotating phone schedule to keep in touch.

Then, of course, there was our travel research. We split the list of countries we planned to visit between us, and with the aid of guidebooks charted out a tentative course, making note of prominent sites we did not want to miss. Pulling out our backpacks and giddily puzzling over what to pack for a whole year into a single backpack was our watershed moment, coupled with the ritualistic burning of our completed "Things to do before we go" checklist. Between them, even the slightest misgivings were swept away by the thrill of adventure ahead.

Our Travel Trails So Far

If we knew more about our ancestry, Rick and I are convinced a good shake of our family trees would produce a number of gypsies. He has always been drawn like a magnet to new trails, and as long as I can remember I have wanted to see the world. I always admired those who took sabbaticals, travelled between career changes, or just plain quit their jobs and took to the road.

Aside from Egypt and Morocco, during the past decade and a half we have whisked away to Mexico, Greece, Turkey, England, France, Portugal, Spain, Monte Carlo, the Bahamas, Cuba, and Jamaica. Those destinations were interspersed with visits to our neighbour to the south. Some of our favourite American spots included Las Vegas, New Orleans, Arizona, Florida, New York, and Hawaii.

In tandem with those trips, a preferred method of travel evolved. When we first started holidaying together, we were tourists. At some point during those excursions we became travellers.

On our first trips, we had suitcases like trunks, each filled with colour-coordinated shoes for each outfit and a different bathing suit for every day of the week. We have since learned that if we pack what we think are necessities, then cut that in half, we have everything we need.

Our first trip abroad—to Egypt—was a package deal with a planned itinerary. On the one hand, with our limited time it made sense to be escorted from highlight to highlight without having to invest the time to figure out how to get from A to B. But even on that first trip, a few negatives crept in; our main gripe was the rigid schedule. I could have lingered in the Valley of the Kings for a whole day; it was painful to leave after the four hours allotted. To make matters worse, our tour bus unexpectedly turned off to a merchant's shop selling paintings on papyrus, and then to a manufacturing plant of alabaster jars; on these time-wasting diversions my impulse shopper mode kicked in, and I came away with two paintings and three jars.

During our next phase, we booked a two-week travel package, then spent a week discovering the country on our own.

Our first trip totally sans tour was to Morocco. We just bought airline tickets and had not so much as a hotel room booked. We were amazed at our evolution. After landing in the capital, Rabat, we took a bus to the small town of Chefchaouen in the Rif Mountains. Then we headed down to Fez and Meknes, worked our way over to Merzouga for our excursion into the Sahara, across to Marrakesh and on to Casablanca. We hit every mosque, kasbah, and ancient ruin along the way; quite a feat in only three weeks. We loved the freedom and the challenge of going it on our own. The exposure to the culture was so different and real that we knew we would hang up our tourist hats forever and become travellers.

A Oneworld Ticket Is the Way to Go

Oneworld is an alliance of many of the world's airlines. The price of a Oneworld ticket is gauged by how many continents you plan to visit. There is also the option of one additional flight within each continent, which we mostly chose not to use (in order to see more of each country with overland travel).

So that we would not have to backtrack, we chose to fly out of a different city or country than we landed in each time. With the exception of the departure date, we took advantage of the option to leave most of the flight dates from continent to continent open. We were to call or visit the partner airline at least 48 hours in advance to set the date for these open flights. Of course, we had to commit to the countries beforehand in order to determine the ticket price, and so that we would be in the airline's computer data for each country.

Our flight itinerary was as follows:
1. Vancouver to Australia;
2. Australia to Hong Kong (from there we would proceed overland through mainland China, Tibet, Nepal, and India);
3. Mumbai (Bombay) to Rome (from there we would travel overland through various countries to Paris);
4. Paris to New York;
5. New York to Vancouver.

Budget?

Details firm as concrete became like asphalt on a sweltering summer day when Rick asked, "What if we could travel for a year for the same amount of money as if we stayed home sitting on our couch?"

"What? You've got to be kidding," was my response. "I realize we can't stay in as posh accommodations as on a three-week vacation, but come on, if we are going to be tightwads we may as well stay sitting on our couch and watch the travel channel."

He began to calculate our Canadian cost of living and formulated "The Budget," taking into consideration the exchange rate for the various countries we would be visiting. Then, through guidebook pricing, he figured out the average cost of mid-range accommodations, food, and sightseeing along our loosely defined route and proudly came up with an estimate of expenditures based on the approximate number of days in each country. He said he left some wiggle room.

I was willing to go along with this challenge, but being of the female gender, I intuitively could see it would be wise to have some agreed-upon modus operandi, which led to the development of ...

OUR TRAVEL MOTTOES

- **We are not here to suffer**
  Our comfort range is to be adhered to in accommodations and eateries (realizing different cultures have different standards), and we'll never be chintzy when it comes to visiting the sights we travelled so far to see. (In short, a counter-balance to Rick's budget.)

- **Expect the unexpected**
  Don't get hung up on preconceived notions of how things should be from our own societal perspective. Don't get stressed out. If plan A doesn't pan out, go on to plan B or C.

- **Travel at a leisurely pace**
  Take rest times between excursions for good health maintenance and in order to absorb our experiences to the fullest.

- **Follow the sun**
  Let spring precede us in countries that have bone-chilling winters.

- **Find ways to maintain our own breathing space**
  Being together 24/7 would be a major adjustment. Solitude needs must be respected so that abundant togetherness does not end in divorce.

We were about to test the theory that being away from familiar surroundings and old habits is a perfect transitional setting. It would be an opportunity to let go of old patterns and, we hoped, see more clearly where we wanted to channel our energies during the next segment of our lives.

Our title—*Trekking the Globe with Mostly Gentle Footsteps*—follows our longstanding creed of leaving behind favourable impressions wherever our world journeys take us: how we touch others, our dress, our demeanour, our respect for their country and culture. The "Mostly" engages a retrospective look at our 12 months of trekking the globe. Given our human foibles, our idealistic footsteps intent on fun, frivolity, and brotherly love were instead often clumsy, confused, anxious, and vexed. In fact, it's a wonder we are still here to tell about it, but since we are, here goes ...

AUSTRALIA

Tennant Creek

Alice Springs

Kings Canyon

Ayers Rock

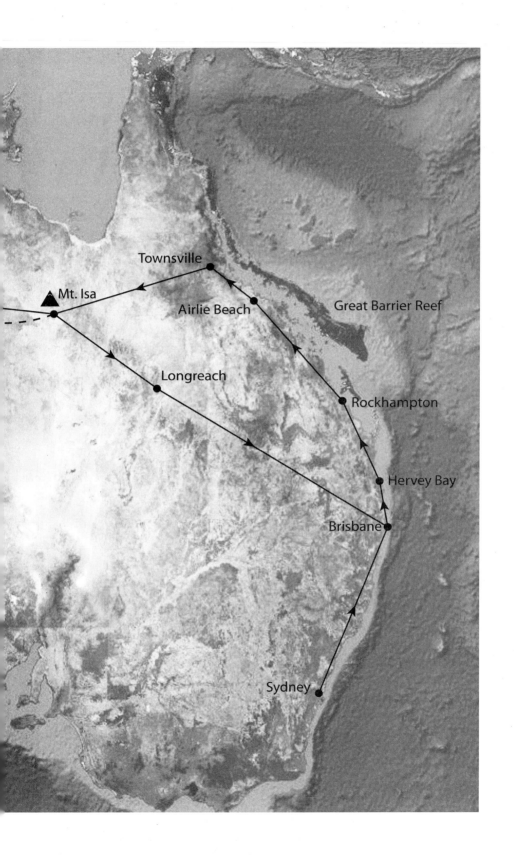

Chapter Two
Australia

Australia was the perfect place to kick off our year: no language barrier, friendly and welcoming people, relaxed atmosphere, unique fauna, and incredible geographical phenomena.

Bonus: our Canadian dollars were worth $1.20 Australian. Regardless of that, Australia was expensive (realizing that expensive is a relative term). When Rick did his pre-trip research, he found that even the "cheapie" hotels in the country were costly; and to our chagrin, the prices in actuality were even steeper than our guidebook quotes. We decided to stay in hostels, but would choose the top category for hostels—meaning private rooms instead of dorms. Knowing our year of travel had just begun made us super-conscientious about costs and ready to look at serious budgeting pronto.

Another perk to beginning Down Under was getting the longest flight we would have during the next 12 months over with upfront. From Vancouver, we flew to Dallas, Texas, then on to Sydney. (With a Oneworld bargain package, I suppose one should not expect a direct route.) The 25 hours from start to finish were surprisingly painless, and our jet lag was not nearly as severe as on previous trips abroad. Since we kept flying into night, the black sky outside for over 15 hours made sleep easier than on the other trips overseas, when we kept flying into daylight and never had more than a few hours of darkness.

We arrived in Sydney at 6:00 a.m. and made our way over to the handy accommodation board at the airport.

"The hotel listings are on the next board," a young girl standing beside us pointed out.

"We're looking for backpackers' hostels, like you. Or won't they let us in?" I joked, knowing I was old enough to be her grandmother.

"Where are you from?" she asked.

"Vancouver," I responded. "Canada," I added.

"I don't believe it. So are we. I'm Bonnie." A flurry of handshakes and introductions were in order as her friend, Angie, joined us.

"The Boomerang is the best," Bonnie offered. "We're staying around here for the day to meet friends, but we'll be going there tonight."

Off we went to the Boomerang. The girls were right: a sparkling-clean private room with a good shower was everything we could want for less than half the price of a hotel.

After a full night's sleep, we were ready to take in the iconic images associated with both the city and country: the Sydney Harbour Bridge and the Opera House.

The panoramic view of the massive steel-arch bridge spanning the sapphire water is no less then spectacular. Excavation for the bridge began in 1925 and construction on the arch commenced in 1929, the shape prompting locals to nickname it "the coat hanger." Formally opened in 1932, the Sydney Harbour Bridge is the fourth-longest span bridge in the world; it takes first place for the widest bridge (according to Guinness World Records) with eight lanes for vehicles and two for trains, as well as pedestrian and bicycle lanes.

The Opera House's immense concrete form appeared to the right of where we stood. The soaring roof of interlocking vaulted shells clad in white tile evoked the image of a giant ship in full sail (and full sail can also describe the 3,000 events held here each year).

This distinctive structure was designed by Danish architect Jørn Utzon. The engineering skills of Ove Arup transformed Utzon's dream into a reality, but the process was anything but smooth sailing. Built in three stages between 1959 and 1973, it became one of the longest contractual sagas of the century. Before the second phase was completed, the Minister of Public Works and Utzon argued over cost and interior design. The lack of collaboration (dubbed Malice in Blunderland) caused Utzon to quit the project. The interior was completed without him. It was not until the late 1990s that the Opera House Trust reconciled with Utzon and agreed to involve him in future changes to the building.

We left the harbour with the heady feeling that comes from seeing world-renowned sites and forevermore being able to say, "We were there."

* * *

The sunny day was rapidly being displaced by ominous black clouds, but fearlessly we forged ahead to another famous landmark: St. Mary's Cathedral. The seat of Catholicism in Sydney loomed against the sombre sky. After the original church on this site was consumed by fire, construction of this grey sandstone Gothic Revival cathedral began in 1865 and has continued in phases, with still more plans for the future. As we climbed the long flight of stairs and entered the great doors, it was interesting to note that the tall spires guarding each side were recent additions, started in 1998 and completed in 2000.

The soft light of the interior reflected off golden walls. This mellow illumination brought out the radiance of the multitude of stained-glass pictorial windows. We moved along the aisles absorbing the window themes, such as Mary enthroned by her Son as He sits in judgment, the lives of saints, and the mysteries of the rosary. The 22-metre (74-ft) vaulted ceiling of red cedar makes the cathedral seem immense. The Tomb of the Unknown Soldier lies in the aisle; this moving depiction in slate-grey of a dead soldier was sculpted by G.W. Lambert (1873–1930), an Australian known for his war art during World War I.

A frigid, wind-driven rain blasted us as we left the church. I could barely see through the sheet of water streaming from my hair onto my face as we made a beeline for our cozy room at the Boomerang.

The weatherman forecasting the wicked cold snap lasting another week sealed our decision not to tarry in Sydney. It being July—the mid-winter season when the weather is more severe in southern Australia—we set our sights northward up the Sunshine Coast. Paying homage to our motto "Follow the sun," we flew to Brisbane the very next day.

Brisbane

"Still a bit chilly, but at least it's bright," Rick happily noted as we deplaned. Eyeing other backpackers, we ventured over and asked where they were headed. A young English bloke, Tony, told us about the YHA—a hostel belonging to the Youth Hostel Association. These hostels adhere to set standards, and there are publications for finding out where they are located in almost every country around the world. For a minimal fee, we had become members before leaving Canada, and so were eligible for a small discount (which tickled Rick's fancy). We agreed to share a taxi with Tony and headed to the Brisbane YHA. Upon our arrival we found that they only had one double room available, and only for one night. We offered the room to Tony, but the private room was too rich for his budget, so he moved on to find a dorm at another hostel.

The room was superb, with a springy mattress, loads of fluffy pillows, and several fleecy blankets. After dropping our packs in a corner, we zeroed in on the hostel's amply stocked cafeteria.

"Who said hostels are only frequented by youth?" Rick said. A sea of grey spread from wall to wall, as well as more wrinkles than handwashed and wrung-out 100-percent cotton. It was not long before we scooped the particulars: the World Veterans' Athletics Championships were currently taking place in Brisbane, with over 6,000 age 50-plus participants from 79 countries attending. We blended in well.

Since we only had one night's stay at this hostel, our first priority of business after lunch was to find a bed for our next two nights in Brisbane. There was a small hostel right next door and a larger one farther down the street.

Deciding to give the smaller one a go, I entered a 2 x 2 metre (6.5 x 6.5 ft) room with a counter across the back. The counter's side was covered in the same green shag rug as the floor, and there was a curtained doorway to the left. A young woman's head popped up from behind the counter, and she asked in a singsong voice, "How can I help you?"

"Are there any rooms available for two nights, starting tomorrow?" I asked.

The curtain flew wildly toward the ceiling. An old man charged out, hollering in a heavily accented voice, "Where you stay this night?"

"The YHA—"

Before I could finish the sentence, he yelled, "Get out! You not my customer! Out!"

"I am trying to be your customer," I retaliated. "You sure won't get many customers this way."

The short, stocky, bullish codger got louder and redder, arms waving, spit flying as he moved menacingly in my direction. "Out! Son's a bitch! Get out! You not my customer!"

I bolted for the door, and tore up the sidewalk to where Rick was waiting for me. I attempted to relate what just transpired, but just sputtered, unable to find the words. Once I was able to compose myself, I approached the City Backpackers' Hostel next door, with Rick in tow just in case. Our room booking for the next two nights went off without a hitch.

Later that afternoon, while walking into town, we ran into Tony, who said he was also staying at City Backpackers. I started to tell him about the episode with the nasty old man.

"Me darlin', you're not alone. After leavin' you folks at the YHA, I went o'er to the small hostel," he rambled in his Cockney manner, "and same thing, the 'bastards' and 'son's a bitches' were fook'en flying thicker than molasses. I coun't remove meself fast enough." His animated and comical account drained the tension of my own encounter. I broke into laughter.

"Why did he attack you? You had your backpack on. Not having ours on was a dead giveaway that we were staying elsewhere."

"The old coot must watch the comin's and goin's to and from the hostels on each side, and he prob'ly saw I tried ta'other first. By the way," he continued, "didya notice the printing on the walk in front of the place?"

"No."

"Well, it says 'STAY HERE' in faded black paint. An' someone chalked in 'DON'T' in front of it," he said, grinning like the Cheshire Cat.

Instead of recognizing that being flanked on either side by larger hostels could be a drawing card to fill his establishment with the overflow, this foolish fellow was fouling this opportunity by word of mouth. Hostellers are always comparing notes, and the grapevine is thick and far-reaching.

* * *

Soaking up sunshine became a priority for the rest of the day. We sauntered up and down streets filled with shops. The constant flow of traffic and modern buildings created a big-city facade, behind which there was a laid-back quality to the capital of Queensland, with its nearly 2 million residents. Its somnolent nature might have had something to do with its subtropical climate.

I found the colloquialisms on the signage amusing, such as "bottle shop" for what we call a liquor store, "post shop" for post offices, and "chemist" for drugstores. Take Over lanes are equivalent to our passing lanes. We must have stood out as visitors, judging from the looks and smiles of passersby.

The next day was our first Friday away from home. We were pleased to come across a theatre, and noted the show times for that evening. Friday has always been our "party night," which translates to a movie, super-sized popcorn, chocolate-covered almonds, and possibly a decaf latte nightcap.

The movie playing was a musical. Although not our favourite genre, it felt good to sink down into a darkened theatre and munch our treats while the actors warbled out the plot. We decided to uphold our Friday-night movie tradition whenever possible.

En Route to Hervey Bay

Before we left Canada we had bought a Greyhound Pioneer Australia 11,000-kilometre (6,835 mi) bus pass. Now it was time to plot our tentative route. The passes were slick; we were supposed to book each leg of our trip a day or two before our desired travel date, and the number of kilometres on each segment would be deducted from our total amount until the pass was used up.

Our first bus destination was Hervey Bay, six hours from Brisbane.

Three quarters of the passengers that day were from families belonging to a particular clan, bound for a reunion at Hervey Bay. The Brisbane stop added 11 km to the 30 already on the bus from other cities along the route. Almost all had on a lime-green T-shirt with a stylized Smith across the back and first names on the front. They were operating in hyper-mode. I was not surprised when, a dozen kilometres down the road, these kindred souls broke out into the strains of "Waltzing Matilda."

I had always known this to be an Australian ditty, and had sung it myself a few times, but the meaning of the lyrics escaped me. With schoolteachers of the Smith clan Mick and Fanny sitting directly in front of us, I could not pass up the opportunity to ask, "Who is Matilda?"

With much enthusiasm they had the group sing the song again, and then translated the colloquialisms for us foreigners.

Once a jolly swagman camped by a billabong
Under the shade of a coolibah tree
And he sang as he watched and waited 'til his billy boiled
You'll come a-waltzing matilda with me.

***Waltzing matilda, waltzing matilda.
You'll come a-waltzing matilda with me.
And he sang as he watched and waited 'til his billy boiled.
You'll come a-waltzing matilda with me.

Down came a jumbuck to drink at that billabong
Up jumped the swagman and grabbed him with glee
And he sang as he stuffed that jumbuck in his tucker-bag
You'll come a-waltzing matilda with me.

***(Refrain—vary by using the third line of the verse)

Up rode the squatter, mounted on his thoroughbred
Up rode the troopers, one, two, three
"Where's that jolly jumbuck you've got in your tucker-bag?"
You'll come a-waltzing matilda with me.

***(Refrain)

Up jumped the swagman and sprang into that billabong
"You'll never take me alive!" said he
And his ghost may be heard as you pass by that billabong
You'll come a-waltzing matilda with me!

Swagman—tough and tattered man who lived on the road carrying his *swag* or tucker-bag containing all his possessions: blanket, provisions, and a billy (can with handle for boiling tea).

In Australian bushman lingo, *matilda* refers to the tucker-bag, a de facto wife supplying his needs and swaying to the rhythm of his walk like an intimate waltz partner.

While the swagman was resting under a *coolibah* (eucalyptus) tree, the *squatter* (ranch owner) caught the swagman for stealing his *jumbuck* (sheep).

The culprit in the song jumped into the *billabong*, a river backwash or waterhole—Mick gave me a thumbs-up for knowing this term—where the swagman drowned rather than be arrested for theft.

"We just sang the third and most popular version, written by Marie Cowen in 1903," said Fanny. "A second version by Harry Nathan also appeared around the turn of the century."

"The original author of this lore was poet and nationalist Andrew 'Banjo' Paterson," Mick added, "way back in 1895. Banjo grew up on a ranch in New South Wales, where he became a skilled horseman. Later, as a lawyer, journalist, and soldier, he wrote profusely about what he loved and knew best—the outback."

Mick told us how the song took on an intensified import during the depression of the early 1930s. A swagman probably thought nothing of pinching a sheep off a rancher, as during this period there was much conflict between the two groups. The ranchers refused to pay these transient workers better wages.

Known as the unofficial national anthem, "Waltzing Matilda" has a special place in the hearts of citizens of this great rugged country (or at least in most of them). In recent years, controversy has erupted over its appropriateness at sporting events. Some feel that only the country's official national anthem—"Advance Australia Fair"—should be allowed. When the controversy reached the legislative level several years ago, the public outcry quashed the banning of this spirited song.

I could now see how "Waltzing Matilda" held a reservoir of emotion and embodied the resourcefulness, defiance of authority, and free spirit associated with Aussie pride. It is sung for prime ministers, during backyard barbies (barbeques), during sporting events and celebrations of every nature, and for marching soldiers to and from wars.

I liked Fanny's summation: "It is said to be the only thing that can bring even the biggest, burliest Aussie bloke to tears."

We had asked the bus driver to drop us off near the Colonial Backpackers' Resort at the edge of town. Instead, our gallant driver drove us right up to the door. The well-wishes reached a crescendo as we exited. Left in the dust and silence, we waved goodbye to the Smiths.

* * *

Our choice of the Colonial as the place to hang our hats turned out to be a good one. Our room was bright and spotless. A small kitchen churned out homey fare. A gorgeous outdoor pool was an added fillip. Though we hadn't found bathing-suit weather yet, we could finally shed our jackets and lounge on the deck chairs in T-shirts and shorts.

"What's there to do in Hervey Bay?" I asked the manager. It was a bit too early in the year for whale-watching, for which Hervey Bay is renowned. The mighty humpbacks, migrating from their breeding grounds with their newborn calves, stop in at the bay during September and October to rest before continuing their journey back to Antarctica. The total distance of their journey is an amazing 12,000 kilometres (7,456 mi). Though the whale-watching tours had already commenced, the reports were that no one had yet seen a single hump, let alone any flukes.

"You don't want to miss Nature World," said everyone we surveyed. We were told it was brimming with fauna unique to this part of the world. Molly, our chauffeur and guide for the excursion, stuffed us and six other enthusiasts into the Nature World van.

The grounds we entered reminded me of a farmyard, with not much focus on trimming shrubs and grasses along the dirt paths, and mismatched sections of wire fencing. The enclosures, however, were large and provided with shade and amenities specific to each resident species.

Molly walked us over to the first enclosure, and in her jolly mien began very aptly to fill us in on the two large ginger-yellow dingos that stared back at us with gleaming eyes.

"This is the dominant colour of these wild dogs, but some are black and tan or all black. Dingos don't bark, they yelp or howl—though dingos kept with domestic dogs learn to bark. Unlike domestic dogs, they have long canine teeth to kill for food. Feral rabbits, feral goats, feral pigs, and kangaroo are their mainstay, with a tasty sheep if they can manage it." Molly told us that these avid carnivores (though herbivorous when in a pinch) have been roaming the Australian landscape for a long time. A study of dingo mitochondrial DNA published in 2004 placed their arrival circa 3000 BC.

I thought of a small friend back home as we approached the next enclosure. Before leaving Canada, 10-year-old Riley had said he was in "total envy" of our visit to Australia, where we would see his favourite marsupial— the kangaroo. The kangaroo and the cuddly koala were the only two animals I knew for sure to be marsupials. I was flabbergasted to find out that there are 150 varieties in Australia, with a dozen of them living in the zoo's enclosures. Most surprising were the teensy marsupial mice, bounding about like miniature kangaroos.

"Hopping, as opposed to running, saves energy and reduces the amount of water needed to survive," said Molly.

Next, a bunch of bilbys twitched their noses at us, looking like rabbits with their long ears until they stood on their hind legs, revealing the common denominator of the Marsupialia order of mammals—the tummy pouch for carrying and suckling their young. What a long and perilous journey for the minuscule fetuses of marsupials, to climb immediately from the birth canal up into the pouch for nourishment and completion of their development!

On we went to a super-sized enclosure. Dirt sprayed three feet into the air as a large ball of tawny fur dug with gusto. A fully grown wombat, resembling a 41-kilogram (90-lb) guinea pig, was working up a sweat. His rest breaks didn't last long enough to let the dust settle. A new burrow was his objective. He must have been behind schedule, as it's rare to see a wombat that active in the daytime.

"What's different in marsupials that dig?" our guide asked in her strong Aussie accent, eyeing me directly.

"I dunno." I hate quizzes, I thought.

"Their pouches are backwards, so's when digging they don't fill with dirt."

Now why didn't I think of that?

We moved on to the gum leaf gourmet compound.

"Get closer," Rick said, aiming the camera at us (the "us" being a koala and me).

"I can't. Ow! I think this mama (whap) is trying to tell me (whap) she doesn't want her picture taken." I was being thrashed with a eucalyptus branch. The koala caregiver had placed a mother koala in the branches of a small gum tree and invited spectators to stand beside her for a photo. In my peripheral vision I saw her round fuzzy ears, black patch of nose, and shiny orbs lean my way, with a paw stretched out toward me. I scrunched my shoulders, expecting another swat, only to find her pushing the branch gently toward my mouth. I had to refuse this kind gesture. As the old Irish proverb says, "One man's meat is another man's poison." The koala is the only species to find eucalyptus leaves yummy. The koalas have micro-organisms in their bodies that render the toxins in the leaves harmless. Not born with this capability, the babies lap up the "pap," a watery diarrhea passed by the mother when her baby is ready to go off her milk, which then enables the baby to produce the micro-organisms on his or her own—an amazing adaptation technique, but probably too much information for a weak stomach.

With dishevelled hair and a reddening cheek from the walloping, but some great photos, I waved goodbye to the koalas and to Nature World, feeling it had been very worthwhile.

* * *

Darkness descended as we bumped down the narrow, isolated road back to the resort. Suddenly Molly squealed to a dead stop in the centre of the roadway. A loud whooshing sound filled the air. Swarms of flapping, dark bodies emitting a deafening gurgling chatter, beady eyes glowing in the headlights, encompassed the van; some smacked against the sides.

"What are they? Bats?" I shouted above the racket from my front-seat vantage point.

"Flying foxes," Molly shouted back. They vanished as quickly as they had appeared.

When Molly could see where she was going again, she pulled the van to the side of the road.

"Look over there."

What a spectacle! Thousands of the nocturnal creatures were flitting from tree to tree. Once more Molly dazzled us with her expertise: "They don't have hollow bones like birds, yet they can fly over great bodies of water. Their lightness is due to the special way they process food. They squeeze the juice out of fruit through perforations on the roofs of their mouths and spit out all the pulp, and also eliminate within 10 minutes after eating. Neat, eh?" We all agreed as Molly steered the van toward home.

It was now week two of our travels, and we had our second set of postcards ready to send home. Our grandchildren had been presented with a world map before we left, with our promise to update our whereabouts by travelogue e-mails followed with postcards from along our route. On our first visit to an internet café, we were delighted to be inundated with e-mails from our offspring. We hoped this would continue so we wouldn't start to worry about how things were back home. It was also time for the first of our five sons and their families to receive a phone call. Every two weeks, on a Sunday evening between 7:00 and 8:00 p.m. (their time), we were to call the family according to the pre-scheduled roster; subsequently, we would talk to each family member every 10 weeks. The system was off to a good start: following the instructions on a phone card resulted in the thrill of hearing familiar voices from half a world away.

Here's the Beef

Our next stop was Rockhampton, the beef capital of the world. Of course, a steak was a must right off the hop. We found a small restaurant with an outdoor barbie and were soon sinking our teeth into a succulent, perfectly spiced, masterfully braised slab of Rockhampton's finest. This was just the beginning of the ruthless battering of our usual diet, which was composed of mostly veggies, some fish, and chicken.

Two million cows are said to live within a 250-kilometre (155-mi) radius of this city, but thankfully no telltale odours filtered into town (at least not while we were there). Rockhampton's old storefronts are relics from the past. Absorbing the bucolic atmosphere under a beachwear-calibre sun was splendid.

Finding our way to Kershaw Gardens, we were in for an expansive display of Australia's flora. As we walked down the paths, I stopped to read the common and Latin names printed on the placards at the base of each tree and patch of shrubbery. They were all varieties of eucalyptus, from the hard-leafed bushes in different hues of green to the many medium-size trees with narrow leathery leaves (some glossy, some waxy grey-green), right up to the lofty Australian mountain ash, which—growing up to 100 metres (330 ft)—is the tallest flowering plant in the world. I fished around in my purse for my pen and pad to write: The genus *Eucalyptus* is derived from the Greek *eu* (well) and *kalypto* (cover), referring to the cap that covers the flower bud. Most eucalyptus are evergreens belonging to the *Myrtaceae* family.

At about the 16th variety Rick started to fidget, sigh, and shuffle. Parks, to him, should be breezed through with a brisk arm-swinging rhythm. I reminded him we were here to "smell the roses" (or in this case, eucalyptus), but picked up my speed.

Rick had to tolerate one more stop when I recognized *Melaleuca Alternifolia* as the source of the therapeutic essential oil commonly known as tea tree oil. The study of essential oil therapy has been an avocation of mine for decades. The leaves of this variety of melaleuca tree have been used for centuries by the Aborigines to heal cuts, wounds, and skin infections. It is now known that one of its chemical constituents, monoterpenes, has analgesic, anti-bacterial, anti-fungal, anti-infectious, and anti-inflammatory properties. One of nature's remedies is reaching universal popularity.

Although I lost count partway through the gardens, there was an impressive sampling of the nearly 500 varieties of eucalyptus that grow in three-quarters of the country's bushlands.

* * *

As we travelled farther up the coast we found that the great benefit of hostelling is the kitchen set-up. By now Rick had figured we were averaging a bit over his "high financier's" budget goal of $115.00 per day for Australia. We started buying groceries; particularly at an Aussie chain called Crazy Prices, which is found in most communities. I had no objection to doing our own cooking, finding it more leisurely to eat at the hostel rather than hunt first thing in the morning for a breakfast restaurant, and often after a day's outing I just wanted to put together a simple meal and crash with a good book. The interaction with fellow backpackers was a lot of fun for us, but we also felt on occasion that our presence intimidated the younger people, such as when the noise level dropped upon our entry to a common-area room. Was it the calming effect of a grandma and grandpa?

It was in Rockhampton that Rick and I hit our first real impasse. I saw some perfect souvenirs for the folks back home: Aboriginal-design coasters and Australian jade pendants. Rick felt we should not buy any souvenirs because of the added weight to our backpacks. His ulterior motive (the budget) was not voiced, but we are at a point in our relationship where words are often superfluous. He tallies every penny.

Hmm—might his calculator go missing one day soon? I wondered.

We compromised. I chose lightweight boomerangs and less expensive emu leather key-chains. I still felt guilty about the 3 x 4 metre (10 x 13 ft) living-room carpet I just had to have while in Turkey many years ago, which Rick had hauled around for the duration of our vacation through Greece. He had never complained. Oh, for the revival of the newlywed's delight in satisfying a lover's every whim!

The Dreamtime Cultural Centre, our next excursion, was where we hoped to glean the history of the country's indigenous peoples. The site sat on land originally inhabited by the Darambal people. Their traditional culture was replicated with a burial site, rock art, and *gunyahs* (bark huts). We milled through the small building full of artifacts and crafts. One wall was dedicated to write-ups and pictures of Cathy Freeman, the Aboriginal sprinter who won a gold medal in the 1990 Commonwealth Games, a gold medal in the Olympics in Barcelona in 1992, and gold in the 200- and 400-metre dashes in the 1994 Commonwealth Games in Canada.

We hastened over to a cave-like enclosure to hear the Aboriginal didgeridoo players. Low guttural thrumming imitating a dingo's growl sent shivers down my spine; it was followed by the mirthful gurgling screech of the kookaburra (a member of the kingfisher family of birds) and other wildlife sounds. Then the drone of a hunting song and a ritualistic burial song that had been passed down from their forefathers. Based on carbon dating of paintings on cave walls in the Northern Territory, didgeridoos go back approximately 1,500 years.

Out on the grounds, we sat in the front row for a boomerang demonstration. The instructor explained the two types of boomerangs: returning and non-returning. The returning ones are used for practice, and the non-returning ones were traditionally used by the Aboriginals to kill animals for food (and probably still are in the outback) or as combat weapons.

The skilled demonstrator tossed, chucked, spun, hurled, and flung boomerangs in all directions like a juggler, always knowing when to turn and catch the incoming ones while continually launching others. After this amazing feat, he called for participants from the audience. Rick decided to try his luck. His first attempt just plopped. His second flew a great distance, but failed to make a U-turn. He was not alone. Of the dozen spectators who were briefly coached on the modus operandi of this projectile, not one boomerang came back to the thrower, but invariably veered off in unpredictable directions. We, the people sitting in the bleachers, now knew why a net 6 metres (20 ft) high divided us from the field.

On to Airlie Beach

Airlie Beach is a beautiful little resort town nestled in a quiet bay. From our patch of fine white sand we were lulled into a dreamy state by the rhythmic waves of brilliant blue. The sea breeze wafted with briny freshness and slightly cooled the halogen rays. Off in the distance we were dazzled by the lush greenery of the soft rolling hills. Puffs of white cloud dotted the canopy of robin's-egg blue. We vowed to spend many an afternoon in this bit of heaven.

As in the dynamic interplay of yin and yang, this paradise was tainted with a little hellish aggravation. We were definitely noticing a difference in how hostels treat customers compared to even the cheapest hotels we had ever stayed in. Silly rules created for the odd unruly client but applied instead to everyone, or "rulishness" as we called it, made us feel like kids in need of constant rebuking. But the price was right, as Rick kept reminding me.

Breakfast was included in the price of a room at Club 13. After handing over a hefty deposit, we were given a grubby cloth bag containing a dish, bowl, cup, and cutlery. The deposit would be reimbursed when these items were returned prior to checking out of the hostel. Fair enough.

After two fried eggs and cold toast the first morning, Rick took charge of the wash-up. When I placed my cup beside him on the edge of the sink it slipped off amid the suds and smashed to smithereens on the floor.

"You have to pay $4.30 for that," a cheeky 16-year-old on duty hollered across the room. What? I thought. For an old, chipped, mismatched cup? A glaring look back at her was my only response, and a spiteful resolve to never hand over the cash—I would replace the vessel instead. The afternoon was spent cup-hunting along the endless main street of shops that sold everything except cheap cups.

About five kilometres out I came across a better cup than the one I had broken for $2.00. Eureka! It was a vivid yellow-and-orange daisy-covered coffee mug and would be Club 13's best piece of china.

We stopped at a neat little restaurant for supper. The sun was setting before we started back to the hostel.

A section of road with heavy woods on both sides that we had barely noticed when we walked past it the first time now brought us to a standstill. We looked for the source of a deafening, cacophonous racket above. A scene from Alfred Hitchcock's *The Birds* appeared ... but in Technicolor. Crimson heads and chests and turquoise and navy wing feathers flashed by as these beauties screeched and flapped from tree to tree.

"Macaws!" a lady who stopped beside us shouted over the ruckus. And to think—we owed this serendipitous display to the broken cup.

A muscular Aussie bloke who strode by was not in the least impressed. "Hey mates, these birds carry on like this every dusk and dawn." About 20 minutes later the din diminished as most of the birds found their spot for the night. Only a few diehards flitted around still unsettled.

* * *

Next morning, as I was about to put the shiny new mug in my sack, I screamed and nearly dropped the entire contents. A multitude of teeny-tiny ants had infested the very soiled dish-sack. We had shooed away the same type of minuscule insects from the bathroom counter and noticed some along the baseboards before turning in the previous evening. Through the night every ant in the vicinity must have headed for my dish-sack on top of the dresser. I quickly pulled the drawstring shut, trapping in a hoard of the little critters, and then marched upstairs to the breakfast room.

I was elated to see that the saucy girl who had bellowed at me yesterday was on duty.

"I have a cup in here to replace the one that accidentally broke yesterday," I said pointing to the sack. "By the way, I hear there is a reduced rate for sharing a room. Is that correct?"

"Of course," she said with a taut elastic smile. "The dorm holds 20, and the rate is a third of a private room."

"In that case, you owe us for spending the night with your establishment's regulars." I undid the string. The counter turned black with the escaping hostages. A dozen ran over her hand, which to my delight elicited a gasp from Gestapo Gal.

"You know, if you washed these filthy sacks once in a while they wouldn't attract every crawly thing in the place," I said in my best lecture mode. "To comply with health regulations they must be washed between customers. I am going to report this."

The smallest apology would have been nice. Instead, I got a snotty glance and nasally nonchalant, "Yeah, ants are an ongoing problem here."

As the French saying goes: C'est la vie.

The Greatest Reef in the World

It was the day for our much-anticipated trip to the Great Barrier Reef, the eighth natural wonder of the world. Though usually not tour aficionados, due to our inexperience with anything nautical, we succumbed to a package deal that included transportation to and from the reef, snorkelling or scuba diving, and a barbeque lunch.

From a designated port in Airlie Bay, a small craft that sped along at 25 knots whisked us to the resort island of South Molle. At South Molle we transferred to a large catamaran with some reef-goers already aboard, bringing the total number of passengers to 62; then it was out onto the high seas for two hours.

Our captain announced that conditions were "moderate," with waves at 2 metres (6.5 ft); nevertheless, it was like riding a roller coaster. The attendants passed out anti-nausea tablets. Barf-bags soon followed. Rick and I refused the pills and held out just fine, although we had to keep our eyes on the horizon to ward off the impending nausea.

The waters calmed as we approached the reef. I, however, was anything but calm: I was having an anxiety attack. My snorkelling history was limited to a one-shot deal in Mexico years before. I blame growing up in the middle of the Saskatchewan prairies for this absence of experience of the life aquatic. I set my jaw in determination; today, the only cold feet brooked would be from the Coral Sea. We shimmied into our wetsuits and sat on the boat edge affixing our flippers, masks, and snorkels. A tsunami of apprehension washed over me again. I fought to regain my composure; I would never forgive myself if I did not try. I stared out to sea, deeply absorbed in my attempt to recall how this was done. Without saying a word, Rick tucked my nose in under the mask.

"But Rick, now I can't breathe."

I turned toward him to see why he was not responding. Oh my God ... Rick's face was blood red and he wasn't breathing at all! Then his puffed-out cheeks erupted into a spew of spittle as he burst out in uncontrollable crazed laughter. Perplexed, I stared at him. Tears ran down his face as he gasped and choked out: "The idea is to breathe through the snorkel."

Of course, silly me. My own laughter was just as irrepressible. Eventually able to contain myself, I sheepishly assured him: "Just nerves, I'll be fine in the water." But it was too late to backtrack, or to escape a lengthy instructional session by my concerned hubby.

Finally we jumped into the scintillating sea of blue. Once I was assured of breathing with ease, we manoeuvred away from the boat.

A silent wonderland enveloped me—a kaleidoscope of colour, shape, and movement. The coral, flaunting pale lavender, primrose, peach, and ivory colours, appeared deceptively lifeless. I have always found it amazing that these limestone formations are the outer skeletons of living animals from the same family as jellyfish, and that the fleshy core of these small creatures protrudes out of their bony frame at night to feed and is pulled back in during the day. Schools of small fish synchronously darted to and fro: glittering jewel fish, patterned butterfly fish in black and pale yellow, minnow-sized electric blue fish.

Rick motioned to the right. A lone grouper was almost within our reach. Being aware that when fully grown a grouper may reach almost 3 metres (10 ft) in length and weigh 360 kilograms (800 lb), we put this fellow in the granddaddy category. A giant sea turtle paddled by. Exhilarating! A hundred orange-and-white striped clownfish playfully weaved toward us, came to an abrupt stop, and then darted off in another direction. I wondered why these little Nemos were so far from the anemone tentacles they nestle in for safety. We watched scuba divers drifting along the ocean floor about 9 metres (30 ft) below.

Not wanting to give up this sensual water world, we stayed in until we were shivering, blue-lipped with cold, and limp with exhaustion. Reluctantly climbing back on board, we struggled out of our gear.

We flopped into seats facing the glassed-in front of the boat (called the Fantasia Pad) and gobbled down much-needed snacks while our eyes devoured the reef from a different perspective. White light, of the kind used in underwater filming, was being shone into the deep from outside the pad, bringing out the true brilliance of the marvellous rainbow of colours.

When we regained a bit of energy we got in line for a 20-minute ride in a mini glass-bottomed sub, which followed a ridge of reef at a greater depth than we had seen thus far. From the viewing chamber the coral took on mostly brown and green hues, as when light filters down through the water to this depth the reds and oranges are absorbed first. Spectacular nonetheless! While our eyes scanned the expanse of glass on all sides, an audio recording filled us in on fascinating facts: some of the coral is 2,000 years old, and in a year some types grow 14 centimetres (5 in) while others grow only 0.4 centimetres (0.16 in). This fragile environment is sensitive to climate changes and water movement, making both natural factors (like El Niño and global warming) and direct human interference (such as pollution and the constructing of breakwaters) destructive. Extending 2,300 kilometres (1,430 mi) along the northeast coast of Australia, the Reef can be spotted from outer space.

Though we had just eaten, when the dinner bell rang we knew we could easily handle the tasty and nourishing buffet lunch provided. Then it was back to the mainland, with the captain announcing: "Expect higher seas." More anti-nausea pills and little bags appeared. Unlike many around us who had more offerings for the little bags after the large lunch, we found the food seemed to calm our stomachs, and they were even more stable than on the trip out.

"Beluga whales on the starboard side," blared the loudspeaker. As everyone rushed over, the catamaran took a harrowing dip to the right. Nine great white silhouettes were cutting through the steel-blue roiling seas. The pod followed alongside for about a quarter mile before veering off and fading into the horizon. How fortunate to have been in the right place at the right time to see those beautiful, grandiose cetaceans.

When our feet touched land our mood was in the stratosphere at having experienced none other than the Great Barrier Reef.

* * *

Our bus was to leave Airlie Beach for Townsville at 2:00 a.m. Checking out of Club 13 before making our way to the reef tour had seemed sensible this morning, but now, with seven hours to fill between boat and bus times, we had second thoughts. We dragged our feet up and down the main street to stay awake, keep warm, and to find something to do besides snacking. Watching bar patrons at outdoor tables become drunker and drunker as the evening wore on became our diversion.

"From arsehole to breakfast, blow-ins join local sheilas and blokes in a piss-turn causing wobbly with clobbering, chundering and rooting until sparrow's fart." No one actually said this, but someone could have. Translated from Aussie slang it means, "All over the place strangers join local women and men in a booze party causing unpredictable behaviour with fighting, vomiting, and sexual intercourse until dawn."

1:00 a.m. found us sitting in a huddled group along with about 20 other bleary-eyed people at the outdoor bus stop. The dark sky was punctuated by an impressively large and brilliant first-quarter moon. It hovered above us like a giant tea cup, the round bottom tilted to the left; back home I knew the bottom would be tilted to the right, opposite of how we were seeing it from the southern hemisphere. I could not remember being so captivated by the positional difference due to latitude before this moment.

When the bus finally rounded the corner, we shuffled like zombies to the boarding platform. I don't even remember the bus pulling back onto the highway. Both of us were dead to the world until the driver called out "Townsville!" at 6:30 a.m.

Luckily, there was a hostel with rooms available right in the terminal. As we approached the counter, a no-nonsense middle-aged receptionist was barking out the rulishness to a timid Asian fellow in line in front of us. When it was our turn, I bristled and said we had already absorbed the establishment's do's and don'ts. A one-eyebrow-raised humph was her response.

Giddy and light-headed from not enough sleep, we dragged our packs up narrow stairs.

"You can take a bit of abruptness for $19.00 per person a night." I turned to see if it really was Rick speaking. I still find the metamorphosis of my husband remarkable. When I first met Rick, "roughing it" meant no room service. He has either come a long way or regressed, depending on how you look at it. Whereas I, once the epitome of frugality, was finding the need to meet the budget rather absurd. I had been reamed out the day before for not reporting $1.25 for an orange juice. Did I mention before that calculators can go missing?

At the end of a dingy hallway we entered a shabby but passable double room.

A Small Stop in a Medium-Sized Town

For a couple of days we did nothing but laze around Townsville. Many of the old hotels are still standing from when the town was the main port for the burgeoning cattle industry inland and for the gold rush in the 1800s. The current population is over 150,000 people. Our mood dictated many leisurely walks along the Strand, a beautiful garden park running along the river. We once came across a novel activity centre for kids. The focal point was a huge raised bucket in the centre of a water-park with several slides and climbing apparatuses. Sitting under a tree, we munched our picnic lunch and watched the giant bucket continually filling with H_2O. The children never knew when the water would reach the brim and dump the works on their little heads, begetting shrieks of glee—something to tell our grandchildren about.

The Red Centre

A restless, all-night bus ride to Mount Isa brought us into the great outback. Leaving as we had at 7:00 p.m., it was not long before dusk turned to darkness. About an hour after drifting off to sleep we were jarred awake by a thud, followed by another, and another—we soon learned that it was the bus hitting ill-fated kangaroos, which darted onto the road with lightning speed and were blinded by the headlights. Our insides jolted with each thump. From the sounds of their distressed utterances, so did the insides of the bus driver and many of the passengers. The driver attempted proceeding without headlights, but this being a particularly black night, the road instantly disappeared, so he had to turn them on again. Almost all the vehicles we saw in the outback were equipped with a big metal "roo bumper" at the front, confirming how commonplace roadkill is along these wilderness routes, mainly at night when the animals are on the move scouting out grazing spots. We spent the rest of the night sporadically napping and straining to see the increasingly more rugged terrain.

Early dawn found us glued to the windows, totally bug-eyed, surveying mile after mile of red earth dotted with shrubs and bush. We were overpowered by the immensity of raw desolation taking up the whole interior of this, the world's third-largest continent. At 5:00 a.m. the sun began rising lazily across the wide horizon, creating a panorama of changing earthy hues and mysterious shadows. We were glad to see the light of day.

Mega Mining Town

The appearance of two large smokestacks marked our entry into Mount Isa at 7:00 a.m. This mining town of about 22,000 people has an area of 41,000 square kilometres (15,800 square miles, equivalent to the size of Switzerland), making it one of the most spread-out cities in the world. The mines here are the single largest producers of silver and lead in the world, and are in the top ten for copper and zinc. It is not common for these four metallic elements to be found in close proximity. On average, 11 million tons of ore are mined each year. Having spent 27 years in the northern Canadian mining town of Thompson, Manitoba, I found the mining particulars engrossing. Thompson is where I married at 19, raised three sons, divorced one husband, and met my second husband, soul mate, and travel partner, Rick. It had now been eight years, three different addresses across Canada, and 15 countries visited since we left Thompson.

Eager to get out and experience the outback, we tossed our gear at yet another hostel and climbed the lofty hill just outside of town that is known for its great view of the surrounding area. The day was a scorcher, so we wore shorts. Mistake! Even though there were rudimentary trails in all directions, the grass was so coarse and spiny our legs were soon riddled with minute puncture marks. At least we had the sense to wear our hiking boots and were quick to adopt foot placement strategies to avoid being skinned alive. It was a prickly introduction to *Spinifex* grass, of which there are 30 varieties unique to Australia. The spikes of grass are tightly rolled leaves which shelter its sweat glands from the sun—just one more evolutionary survival technique for life in this difficult environment.

Upon cresting the hill, we saw that, other than a solitary ramshackle house, only sunburnt grasslands stretched out to the distant horizon. Since the path up to the hill had taken a big loop to the right of the town, if our calculations were correct, the town would be directly below us now. We started a downward trek and picked our way through the waist-high bush that had not looked nearly as tall from the trail.

I heard a rustling sound and cracking branches. It was coming from the foliage ahead. Rick grabbed my arm. We both froze in our tracks. More rustling. My heart boomed against my chest cavity. My eyes darted toward swaying bushes 6 metres (20 ft) from where we stood. Three tawny kangaroos sprang into the air and bounded away from us. Appearing to be a larger-sized male and two females, they astounded us with their lightning speed as they leapt between and over the thick shrubbery. I cringed with thoughts of their footpads making contact with the needles of *Spinifex* at each landing: those pads must be mighty tough! Almost instantaneously, the first group's dispersal set off a second volley of another four about 15 metres (50 ft) away.

"Wow!" I exclaimed. "What a gift, to see these beauties in the wild!"

As we started down once again, I suddenly felt edgy.

"Hey Rick, what if we inadvertently give the next bunch of roos reason to use their fight instead of flight instinct?" I recalled stories of attacks on humans who came too close to mothers of newly pouch-evicted joeys, and of males courting a female being indiscriminately aggressive. An old movie with kangaroos in a ring with boxing gloves on, pummelling each other, flashed through my mind. Of course, I kept sharing these tidbits with Rick, and soon had him spooked as well. Knowing we would be no match for their powerful hind legs—nor their short front ones for that matter—we decided to give ample notice of our whereabouts by singing, but only saw one more lone macropod head bobbing up to take a gander at the source of such discord.

"Ahh, there's Mount Isa," Rick said, pointing beyond a long line of 2-metre (6.5-ft) fences of various designs. After about 20 minutes of not finding a break in the fencing, we scaled one that was conveniently constructed with horizontal logs, passed through a private backyard, and stepped safely onto one of the town's streets. It was then that we saw the Guard Dog – No Trespassing sign posted on the front lawn of the house – fortuitously without canine interference. After all our exertion, like bears after hibernation we zeroed in on the nearest spot for sustenance a few blocks up the road.

In the Northern Territory

We hopped on a day bus for our next leg to Tennant Creek. Giant red mounds rose in copious numbers out of the flatlands along this stretch of outback, some up to 2 metres (6.5 ft) high and 1 metre (3 ft) in circumference. At one point we saw 50 in close proximity. Cattle wandered nonchalantly between, convincing us that the inhabitants of these mounds were vegetarians. Half the locals on the bus called the builders ants, while the other half said termites. Understandable, as termites are also known as white ants; it's a misnomer based on superficial similarities in appearance and habits of the two insect groups.

The underground colonies of the (real) ants are no doubt splendid. Conversely, being able to see the grand termite edifices rising from the flat topography like the New York City skyline was spectacular. It is hard to believe that these towers are the product of only soil and saliva, baked by the sun. A colony may hold between 100 and 1,000,000 of these voracious bugs, which grind plants and trees for their cellulose content. Both the termite and ant populations in Australia are the largest in the world.

* * *

Upon arriving at Tennant Creek, "no room at the inn" was the gist of the message at every hostel—our first-encountered drawback of not booking ahead. Just when we thought our lot would be bunking under a canopy of stars, we came across the very last bed in town, in a 3 x 4 metre (10 x 13 ft) dorm room. We shared it with four others: two Japanese girls who each knew two English words—"heyyo" and "bye"—but babbled incessantly in their native tongue; one dude wearing earphones who was either passed out or dead as we could hear the hard-rock screech and see his forehead vibrate; and one bed scattered with junk whose owner came thrashing in at about 3:00 a.m. We hoped never to find ourselves in this predicament again. We didn't mind sharing a loo down the hall in hostels where we had a private room, but we now knew for sure we were too old to do the dorm thing.

Alice Springs—We Are On Our Way!

"If you find a fly in your soup, you should complain to your waiter. By rights, you should get more than one," said Tom, our bus driver on this run. "Gone walkabout, for the isolated residents of the outback, is their annual vacation of walking in the bush." Tom felt it was his duty to enlighten us on the ways of the outback with his tongue-in-cheek humour. By the time we were half an hour into our trip he had dissolved every frown from the faces of his passengers.

A road-train driver occupying the seat in front of us started rambling about the high-powered semi-trucks hauling several trailers that periodically barrelled past us. This trip was definitely going to be entertaining.

"Yer average road train pulls 'tween three to six trailers, each trailer being 18 metres long. Many of the trailers have drive axles and can haul up to 133 metric tons," he proudly stated, as yet another of these bruisers roared past and left us quaking in its wake. Needless to say, they command the respect of all other vehicles on the road. When one of these titans approached, our driver slowed almost to a stop and hugged the road edge, allowing the road train to keep a steady speed so as not to lose momentum. I wished desperately I was not sitting by the window on the road centre side, but it probably would not matter where one was sitting in an unintentional tête-à-tête with one of these road warriors versus our puny bus.

A police roadblock brought us to a halt near the small community of Ti Tree. Our bus was searched by a rifle-toting Northern Territory Police Officer. A manhunt was underway for a man who a few days previous had faked a truck problem along this stretch of road and flagged down a young British couple—Peter Falconio and his fiancée, Joanne Lees—who were travelling in an old orange camper van. The man shot Peter in the head and tied up Joanne. While the perpetrator was disposing of Peter's body, Joanne escaped, staying hidden in bushes all night. In the morning she jumped out in front of a road-train and was taken to the nearest police station. She said she remembered seeing this man at some of the stops along their travel route, so it was surmised he singled them out and pursued them. As well as using helicopters in this nationwide manhunt, the police had now called in the Aboriginal trackers, who could locate a person hiding in the outback if anyone could.

The murderer was not caught by the time we left Australia at the end of July. Since then, I have followed the case from media reports.

Lees' escape story and her description of the killer and even the colour of his dog changed from her first police statement. This, coupled with her incongruous coldness and composure while reporting the details of the murder, were suspicious. In each interview she looked more glamorous. It was revealed this "devoted" girlfriend had had an illicit affair while engaged to Peter. Several suspects were initially questioned and released.

Three years later, Bradley John Murdoch was convicted for the murder of Peter Falconio and deprivation of liberty and unlawful assault of Joanne Lees. Since he was 47 years old at the time, the 28-year sentence without parole will probably take up the remainder of his life. Mr. Murdoch had a history of violence and was a drug runner. In fact, he was turned in by a fellow drug runner, James Hepi, who when caught with 5 kilograms (11 lb) of marijuana, agreed to identify Falconio's murderer in exchange for a lighter sentence for himself. Though this lesser sentence was all he came away with, he admitted later he had had his eye on the $250,000 reward being offered for such information. Murdoch denied killing Falconio. The key to prosecution was a smudge of blood on Joanne's T-shirt. The forensic expert said it was "one hundred and fifty million billion times more likely to have come from Murdoch than anyone else." Two of the key witnesses reported seeing Falconio after he went missing. Falconio's body has not been found to this day.

This case has become known as Australia's most mysterious murder since Lindy Chamberlain claimed her nine-week-old baby was stolen by a dingo from a campground near Ayers Rock in 1980.

* * *

We did a double take when the bus pulled into the next fuel stop and we recognized a trio of young travellers we had met at one of the hostels along the way. They had journeyed for seven months in a 1984 Ford Falcon station wagon purchased in Sydney for $1,900.00 (camping gear thrown in) upon arrival, and that they planned to sell before leaving. We thought this a great idea ... until we talked to them beside their clunker, which was belching steam from its radiator. They were waiting for a tow to the only garage around. We never found out how they fared, as our 15-minute break was soon over. We boarded the bus with renewed enthusiasm for the pluses of bus travel.

Resigned to only seeing a fleeting glimpse from the windows of the Devils Marbles located 90 kilometres (56 mi) south of Tennant Creek, passengers raised the roof with cheers when Tom, now definitely our favourite driver, announced he was ahead of schedule and could give us a half-hour to mill among these unique rock formations.

Piles of huge iron-oxide-red boulders were seemingly dropped from above onto the flat desert here, some on the top of a heap so precariously balanced they appear about to roll off. Even standing beside one of the smaller mounds, the marbles extended 4 metres (13 ft) above Rick's head, reducing him to toddler size in comparison. Geologists say these rocks were a part of a solid mass of granite less than two billion years ago, and over the eons have been shaped by erosion. But gazing at these giant spheres, many almost detached from the rocks below, their origin as told by the Aborigines, of the rainbow serpent laying these eggs during the Dreamtime, is more believable.

The Alice

Road-weary by the time we pulled into Alice Springs, we decided to stay awhile. We easily slipped into the unhurried way of life of the 20,000 inhabitants who call this home.

Originally called Stuart after explorer John Stuart, the town was renamed in 1933 when the most important asset to the survival of the community—a permanent spring—was combined with Alice, the name of the much-loved wife of the superintendent of the telegraph station: hence Alice Springs. (The telegraph superintendent, Charles Todd, only had the usually dry Todd River alongside the telegraph office named after him.) The small office building, constructed in 1871, still stands today. We could only imagine the significance it once held, being a crucial—and often the only—link to the outside world.

The Alice, as it is known by locals, is a long-time service centre for neighbouring pastoral communities and a major radio base for the vital Royal Flying Doctor Service (RFDS), whereby physicians using aircraft make house calls to settlements and homes scattered hundreds of kilometres apart. Last but not least, it is a neat stop for folks exploring the outback.

Feeling spunky the second day after arriving, we undertook a 4-kilometre (2.5-mi) trek to Alice Springs Desert Park, nestled in the MacDonnell Ranges. At the park entrance we got an up-close look at a small native plant we kept seeing stretched like a carpet over parts of the desert terrain from the bus window. These strange little flowering plants appeared to stare back at us from a cluster of black bulbous eye-like nodules at the centre of each fiery red-petal face. They are commonly called Sturt's desert peas, in honour of Charles Sturt, who recorded seeing voluminous quantities while exploring the country in 1844. The genus name Swainsona formosa honours Isaac Swainson, who maintained a botanic garden in London around 1789; formosa is Latin for "beautiful." These hardy little sentinels that raise their heads after a rain are birthed from seeds able to survive long periods of extreme dryness. In 1961 they were chosen to be the floral emblem of South Australia.

The sprawling gardens and grasslands of the park trails lead to sizable animal enclosures. While focusing on a mama roo and her joey, we almost stepped on the papa of the red kangaroo family (the largest of the marsupials) lying under some bushes. This particular big daddy would have stood as tall as a man had he been of a mind to stand up. Including his tail we figured his length to be about 4 metres (13 ft) and estimated his weight to be 84 kilograms (185 lb). Other than the odd tail flip and the occasional lifting of his head to peek at his lady busy with the young'un (and us silly humans out in the sweltering midday sun), he reclined motionless in the shade.

"Well, looky here—these are the walnut-like things I've been seeing stuck on trees," I exclaimed as we walked into the park info centre. My curiosity had been roused for weeks. These growths were especially conspicuous on trees now bare of foliage, but we also saw them peeking through the branches of fine-leafed trees.

A display panel in the Park Information Centre explained. Known as bush coconuts, these sap suckers are grubs that attach themselves to the tree bark and build hard crusty homes around themselves, never to come out again during their lifetime. The home continues to grow with the grub, supplied with water and nourishment by the host tree. Only one small window, usually plugged with the grub's tail, opens when it is time to mate.

First the grub lays male eggs, which hatch with wings. The same grub immediately lays female eggs, which attach to the flying male mites whizzing around outside the little window. The male then flies with the attached female egg to a vacant spot on the same tree or to another tree, whereupon the female egg hatches and affixes to the tree. The male hangs around long enough to mate with the female, then dies (sorry, guys), and the process starts over again. The Aborigines crack them open and eat the juicy grubs, which are pure water and protein.

I had never before thought of rodents as being cute, but when I came across another cage of marsupial Spinifex mice hopping around like pocket-sized kangaroos, I was swayed. They were even smaller than the kind we'd seen at Hervey Bay. An evolutionary miracle, they actually live their life without ever requiring water, getting the minimal amount they need from the seeds they eat. Also factored into this oddity is their micro-output of urine, which is the most concentrated of any animal's in the world. I was finding the adaptations to this harsh environment more and more extraordinary as our repertoire of facts expanded.

When my feet began to throb, I estimated the walk around the park had been at least 3 kilometres (2 mi). This amazing park was well worth a visit, but our bright idea of walking to get here lost its lustre as we left the gate for the trek back to our hotel. Sensible people take the bus tour.

Ayers Rock and Kings Canyon

As we were finding it increasingly difficult to obtain lodgings when we just showed up on a hostel doorstep, before leaving Alice Springs we decided to phone ahead to Ayers Rock and Kings Canyon, only to find there were no vacancies for the next two weeks.

Time to come up with plan B. We rented a Britz camper-van, loaded her up with groceries, and sped away. Well, sort of sped away. At first I had my doubts about ever getting out of the Alice. Rick ran over a few curbs attempting to master the new spatial logistics. Never having driven on the left side of the road before, to guide him he had put sticky tab reminders on the dashboard: TIGHT LEFT — WIDE RIGHT — LOOK RIGHT. I heard him mumbling these terms, my eyes shut until we made it to the freedom of the open highway. A successful adaptation of a human kind.

The landscape was rife with dry riverbeds, hollows of hard crusty mud waiting for the rainy season during December to March, or for a flash flood at any time. The desert roadways can be totally washed out, cutting off the main access to the outback communities. Coming across several billabongs, we tipped our baseball caps to the swagman's haunt and dutifully burst out in strains of "Waltzing Matilda."

As we neared Ayers Rock, we were awed by its anomalous nature. Out of a plain so flat a giant carpenter's level would hardly register variations, the world's largest natural monolith rises in solemn majesty to a height of 348 metres (1,142 ft). Geologists estimated another 600 metres (1,970 ft) or two-thirds of the rock is buried underground. It is called Uluru by the indigenous peoples, and we could easily see why this colossal red rock is a sacred site. The Aborigines—who now own Uluru-Kata Tjuta National Park—prefer that visitors not climb the rock, though it is not prohibited unless the weather is inclement. Many visitors feel cheated if they haven't met the challenge of climbing to the top of this behemoth. Choosing not to climb, we are not able to comment on the view from the top, but can assure you that the walk around the 9-kilometre (6-mi) circumference is amazing. Many of the caves in the base contain Aboriginal carvings and drawings. We scanned upward, looking for the changing configurations formed by crevices and bulges in the weathered rock. Aided by the play of light and shadow, we saw an old man's face, a bird on the wing, and an amusing mega-monkey head appearing to be talking down to an imploring human head.

At Uluru-Kata Tjuta Cultural Centre, a guide approached us and led us to a panoramic window. He pointed to two giant slashes tearing jaggedly down the face of the rock on the south side of Uluru. Then he solemnly told us the ancient story of a sword duel between Kuniya and Liru, two of the most important ancestral beings. Kuniya (a python woman) had not been treated with the respect due her by Liru (a poisonous male snake), so she performed a ritualistic dance to tell others of her right to punish the offender. But her dance brought about a righteous rage so fierce, she slashed Liru superficially once, then followed it with a fatal strike; the slashes eternally etched in the rock. He went on to say that although Kuniya had avenged her honour, her anger has to this day poisoned the plants near the battle, namely the *untjanpa* (spearwood bush) growing around the base of Uluru.

*　*　*

After leaving the Cultural Centre for a hardy late lunch in our Britz, it was time to pull out the lawn chairs from the van's storage area and settle ourselves at the base of Uluru to wait for Mother Nature's Sunset Spectacular.

Around 6:00 p.m. the parking lot filled, crowds rallied, cameras began clicking and camcorders whirring. Over the next half-hour many oohs and aahs greeted the impressive show: shades of red morphing into brilliant orange, pumpkin, peach, caramel, and burnt sienna, culminating in sombre browns with the fading last rays.

Heading back to the trailer park, we agreed to make our way back before sunrise to see this magical phenomenon again. But when the alarm jangled at 5:30 a.m., not even Uluru could move us. Any stirring before 8:00 a.m. for us feels like the middle of the night. Around 11:00, we finally pulled out on the road, headed for Kata Tjuta (also known as The Olgas), 44 kilometres (27 mi) away.

The aboriginal name Kata Tjuta—meaning "many heads"—is well suited to the 36 domes rising to about 550 metres (1,815 ft) above the surrounding flatlands. We parked for a few snapshots at several of the lookout spots, but we did not find this jumble of huge rocks with gorges between quite as impressive as Uluru, possibly because after the long walk around Uluru the day before, we were not inclined to take one of the many walks through the clefts or to stay for the sunset ...

We aimed our vehicle toward Kings Canyon. En route, a motorist in an old beater of a truck coming from the canyon waved at us to stop. He rolled down his window and called out, "If you'd come this way a few days ago, you would've had to turn back. A flash flood down a'ways is just receding, but you should be okay to get through now."

As we approached the stream flowing briskly across the roadway, we were not sure if the water depth would result in a soaked engine, or if invisible ruts or dips would swallow our Britz. Pulling over to the side we waited and watched. A couple of four-wheel-drives ploughed through. One had a high, extended air-breather coming up the passenger side of the windshield. We had often seen these extensions on outback vehicles, which now made perfect sense, as the air-breather on the engine for oxygen intake would be cut off in a flood situation. Not until we saw a beast of a 1980s low-suspension station wagon skid through did we dare to attempt it ourselves.

I saw Rick's knuckles bulge from his mega-grip on the steering wheel. I felt a wave of dizziness from my rapid breathing. Neither of us said a word. Rick tramped down on the gas pedal and we moved steadily forward. The water splashed up against our side windows. We started to slip sideways ... we were done for! Suddenly, the tires gripped something solid beneath the churning pewter liquid and the old camper van thrust forward with renewed momentum. "Yeah, we made it!" we cheered like deranged revellers.

As we drove off with mud still spattering off our tires, I got to thinking, What if another flash flood occurs while we are at Kings Canyon? Oh well, it's not as if we have a schedule to keep.

A Canyon Truly Fit for Kings

Kings Canyon is in the George Gill Range, part of Watarrka National Park. We looked forward to the 6-kilometre (4-mi) trek to the summit from the canyon floor.

The climb spanned a full range of trails, from easy to moderate to steep inclines. Every so often we came across a sizable gnarled old tree protruding out of the rock. At first glance these trees looked dead with their trunks split open; the bark and lower branches appearing as old as Methuselah. Upon closer inspection, we saw that each had one or two leafed branches with bright yellow blossoms sprouting out of the twisted grey limbs. Green blades poked through straw-like grass patches and wildflowers danced in the breeze. What splendour the desert offers after a reviving rain (which in this case had fallen a few days previous and had also caused the flash flood)!

A breathtaking vista awaited us at the rim: jagged cliffs dropped 300 metres (1,000 ft) to the commingling of red rock and greenery below, the sun using the clouds to cover the land with a variegated patchwork quilt of shadows and brightness.

When we left Kings Canyon, we encountered only dried ruts on the roadway where the floodwaters had been.

* * *

Back in Alice Springs, we bid adieu to the camper van and hopped on a bus back to Tennant Creek. As we were pulling out of the terminal, a big, old kangaroo sluggishly hopped from between two buildings and proceeded to sit with his back against the bus office wall and his hind legs splayed. His mien conveyed that it was about time we left so he could have his favourite spot back.

We stopped at the same hostel in Tennant Creek as on the way inland. Luck was with us, as we nabbed a private room. Tennant Creek has a large indigenous population. Conversation with several Aborigines who were doing laundry at the same laundromat that evening was both enjoyable and insightful. One fellow in particular shared the struggles of his people—their old way of life was destroyed, yet they found it difficult to fit into the white man's world and were therefore largely unsuccessful in obtaining new livelihoods. The isolation of the outback was an added hindrance to education and job opportunities.

The next day, en route from Tennant Creek to Mount Isa, we gleaned more about this rich traditional culture from books a social worker on the bus let us read. The culture abides by the Kinship Family System. There are taboos regarding who you can talk to and in what manner. The most serious interdiction is for a man to talk to his mother-in-law. (I saw Rick furtively grin at that one.) The aboriginals marry by "skin name." Depending on their birth parents, they are given a skin name and are only allowed to marry a person with a different skin name. Rules of society are implemented by shame (not guilt like ours).

The most difficult concept in their ideology for us to comprehend was the Dreamtime. In one of the books it was explained as "instinct from ancestors shedding enlightenment on how creation occurred and what is the right way to live with all living things in the environment." This secret knowledge is only revealed to men during initiation. Women have their own rituals and revelations. The closest word in the English language to describe the revered sites where these ancestors roam is "sacred," but it falls short of the depth of meaning and all-encompassing significance involved in their value system. These sites are where ancestors manifest the physical and psychological maps by which people are governed in all matters, including relations with other tribes, one's own tribe, one's family, and self-identity.

In most other cultures, land is considered property; however, the Aborigines believe they are only custodians of these ancestral pockets of land, and it makes no sense to them for anyone to claim ownership. It was not until the privacy of their ceremonial sites was interrupted that they were forced to claim back the land by our method: through the legal system. The very act of proving the sacred association to reclaim the sacred site, though, defiled the secrets revealed in the Dreamtime, destroying its fundamental principles.

Here is yet another rich and beautiful culture devalued by the European culture that became dominant in former colonies such as Australia; it is not unlike the fate of indigenous peoples in many countries around the world, including Canada. In fact, delegations of the Australian Aboriginal Council have been sent to Canada to gather information from our First Nations People for insight into meeting these challenges for positive change.

Second Time Around

Mount Isa provided a new experience this time around. We picked up the name and phone number of a hostel on the bus-station peg board. Penny, a real estate lady, owned a small hostel and had a room available.

She picked us up at the bus depot and drove us to a small three-bedroom house. She led us through the kitchen, living room, and into a bedroom that she designated as "ours," while at the same time proceeding to push someone else's belongings to the side. "Charlie knows if I have another chance to rent this room that I won't hold it for him," she said. After briskly changing the sheets, she collected our money, gave us instructions to place the key in the mailbox when we left the following day, and raced off.

The home was fully equipped with a television, good furniture, pots, pans, dishes, appliances, towels, ornaments, a barbeque, and lawn furniture. What a trusting soul, to just hand people keys, with no supervision as to what goes on during their stay—an open invitation for theft, vandalism, or a fire caused by carelessness.

While we were in the process of making supper, two twentyish fellows came in, saying they had the other two rooms rented. We hoped this was right, as somehow Penny had omitted mentioning this. After chatting awhile to Klaas and Barent (who hailed from Holland), we toddled off to bed. It was not until I went to lock the door that I realized that there was no lock. There would be no way I would have a peaceful sleep unsecured. I executed the old chair-under-the-door-handle routine, with the added measure of pushing a dresser up against the chair. Nothing against our house mates, except that they were strangers, and what if we woke up with Charlie between us? And how would we know for sure it was Charlie, with the number of outer door keys we imagined floating around town? The night passed without a hitch, but we resolved to stay away from such strange lodging arrangements in the future.

Cowpoke Country

We took a different route back to Brisbane. After leaving Mount Isa, an eight-and-a-half-hour bus ride brought us to Longreach, a rancher's town, with one main street lined with buildings out of the old Wild West. All that was missing was hitching rails. It was Friday afternoon and the jillaroos and jackaroos (the Aussie equivalent of cowgirls and cowboys) were so fresh off the ranches that manure was still caked to their boots as they milled around the town. These boisterous cowpokes were ripe and ready for a reprieve from their sheep-shearing, fence-building, cattle-driving, calf-wrestling existence. Tagging along with a cluster of jills and jacks aimed at the hotel bar, we noted a large arrow, also pointing to the bar, which read Room Bookings.

The multi-functional bartender got out the registry log, and spying my fully stuffed backpack said "My, you have a heavy load on your back." A beefy, ruddy-faced patron with a piss (beer) in hand, stared right at my breasts and slurred, "Hey, lady, you gots a heavy load on your front too ..." The last few words died on his lips as my super-sized husband rounded the bar corner.

"Pardon me, what'd you say?" I shouted back as if a little on the deaf side. He sheepishly turned away and his buddies roared with laughter, while Rick scanned faces for a clue as to what was so funny.

The Central Hotel was one of the first hotels built in Longreach. The original skeleton key locks had never been removed, but we were happy to see barrel bolt locks had been installed as well. The second floor had access to a deck overlooking the main street activity ... or lack thereof. Surprisingly, by the time we got back from our walk around town, the Friday night din was done. The next day, even the early Saturday morning bustle faded as the day wore on, since almost every business establishment closed Saturday noon until Monday morning. We headed out to the hot spot for the evening, the Legion, for the Saturday Night Special.

Every last man, woman, and child in Longreach must have been present, the place was rock'in with some folks in the food line, others bellied up to the bar, kids playing tag or yowling, and lots of laughter and catching up on a week's worth of gossip. Joining the festivities, we fell into the food line with its 20-person wait. Mouth-watering aromas wafted our way. A superb homestyle feast of rissole was heaped on our plates. This local dish is composed of breaded minced beef patty flooded with gravy and topped with vegetables, sided by slabs of bread. Including two drinks, the two meals cost us 12 Aussie dollars.

A corner was cleared for a suave gentleman with a shock of grey hair and a resounding tenor voice for a night of old favourites; his specialty was blasting out Tom Jones lyrics. We giggled our way home, having a hard time deciding if our not being sure of the way was due to there only being the odd dim streetlight to guide us, or one too many 'pisses' ...

Even the breeze was stilled on the Sabbath; nary a soul did we see stirring from our balcony vantage point, and it was almost noon. It's a good thing we had stocked up on snacks at Crazy Prices on Friday evening, since the restaurants were closed up tighter than a jar of grandma's preserves. Even the stray dogs usually sniffing around the garbage cans were taking the day off. Oh Lordy, what to do with the seven-hour time span between check-out at the hotel and bus departure? We left our gear in a storage area of the hotel and trekked out to the Qantas Aviation Museum and the Australian Stockman's Hall of Fame to kill several hours. We then parked ourselves in the canopied sitting area in the middle of Main Street, read and munched the day away, watching the odd straggler (both human and canine) materialize, then recede from view onto a side street. The last few hours seemed endless.

Time to Say G'bye, Mates

Safely back in Brisbane, thoroughly bushed from our 17-hour bus ride, we settled once again in the City Backpackers' Hostel. Gathering up our salient purchases (such as the aforementioned boomerangs and key chains) and CDs containing our photos taken thus far, we posted the parcel to one of our sons in Canada. Upon hearing by e-mail of its safe arrival, we could then safely delete these photos from our camera and thus use fewer memory cards with this rotation.

Mulling over our Australian experience, we realized it was no wonder we felt at home here. There are many similarities to Canada: wage structure, retail prices, the large middle class, mining and cattle ranching as major industries, and lots of wide-open spaces with populations not matching the breadth of land.

Another comparable factor is our social system. Like Canada, Australia has a highly ranked health care system, pension benefits for seniors, and a safety net for the unemployed. The plight of the Aborigines is even similar, but headway is being made. Overall, Australians feel good about their lot in life.

Our first month was drawing to a close. We were not at all homesick, but then again our time away so far was not out of the ordinary, as previous travels had always been three weeks in duration. As well, there were no worries from the bean-counter yet. Rick cheerily related that with the cheaper hostel prices outback and with us often preparing our own meals, our spending came in at an acceptable $120.00 per day, including the bus pass. He figured the cost for a couple travelling and staying in dorms would be under $100.00 a day.

One lesson we drew from our Australian adventure was to slow down our pace. Our bodies were telling us it would be gruelling to keep up the distances we had covered in this past month for a whole year—just short of 11,000 kilometres (6,835 mi) by bus, plus the kilometres we racked up in the camper van in the outback. From now on, especially in large countries, we planned to choose several destinations and stay a while longer in each.

As our plane lifted off from the Brisbane airstrip, we added Australia to a list of countries we hoped to return to someday.

It seemed surreal that we would be travelling for another 11 months.

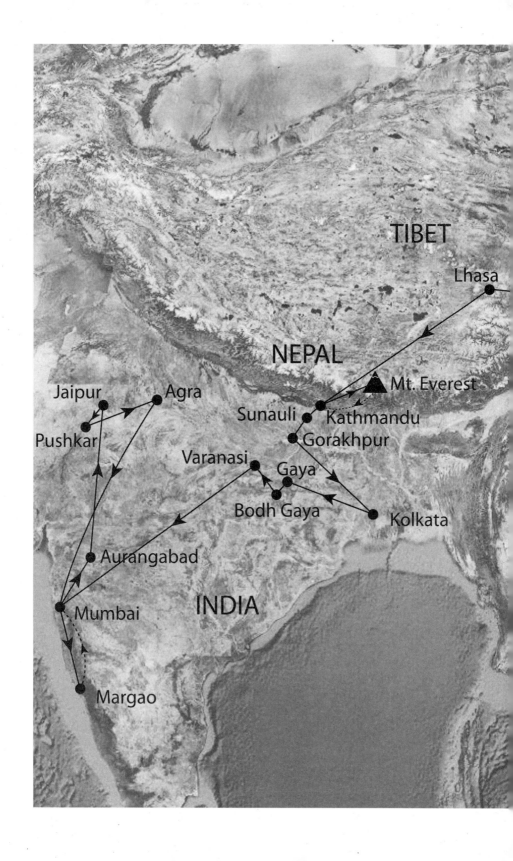

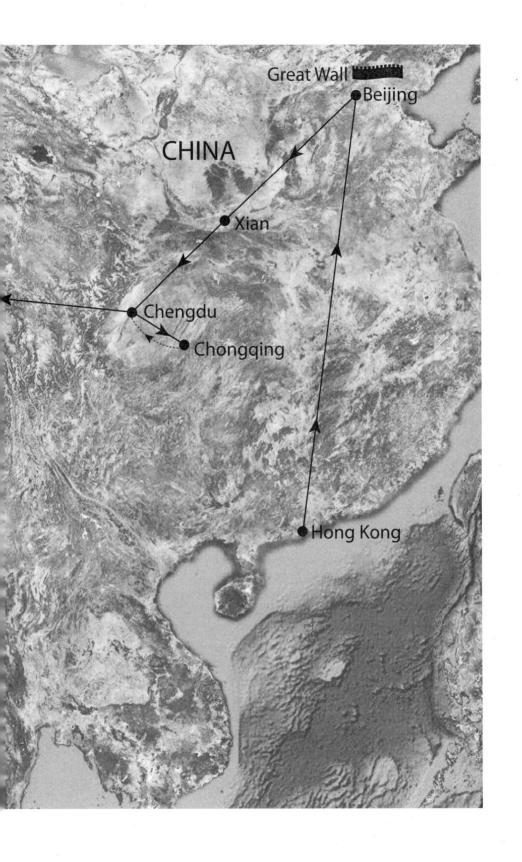

Chapter Three
China

Confounding and exhilarating is how we pegged Hong Kong. A cacophony of movement, flashing lights, insane traffic, bodies jostling for space on the sidewalks: a jumble of Western and multi-Asian influences. Kowloon, where we spent the majority of our time, was the part of this massive city we envisioned as being truly Chinese in flavour. The high-amp milieu was intensified by the 33°C (91°F) sultry weather we encountered; we swirled and sweated to the sights and sounds.

Hong Kong is made up of four regions: Hong Kong Island, Kowloon (a peninsula on the mainland across from Hong Kong Island), the New Territory (sharing a border with China proper), and 234 outlying islands, for a total of 1,076 square kilometres (or 415 sq mi). The greatest concentrations of Hong Kong's approximately 7 million people live on Hong Kong Island and in Kowloon. The difference between these two regions could not be starker: Kowloon's well-worn lower high-rises contrast with Hong Kong Island's skyline of huge financial edifices and ultra-modern hotels.

I remember Hong Kong being a hot news item in the mid-90s with the 1997 handover from British rule and its new status as a Special Administrative Region (SAR) within the vast Chinese state. Prior to the handover, the uncertainty of how this monumental change in government would affect their lives prompted many Hong Kongers to emigrate to other countries, including Canada. In fact, our keen interest in all matters relating to China stemmed from the high influx of these immigrants to Canada's west coast. After the dust settled and the post-transition laws did not result in drastic changes, many went back to Hong Kong, while others now saw Canada as their permanent home.

In central Richmond (part of Vancouver), where Rick and I now reside, 70 percent of the population is ethnically Asian. Glancing around in a restaurant or a mall brings out a chuckle at seeing just how much we Caucasians are in the minority.

Owing to the lengthy British influence in Hong Kong, we found that most employees of businesses frequented by travellers and tourists spoke some English. Although Mandarin is the official language of China, Cantonese is more prevalent in the south. In fact, Cantonese and English are the official languages of Hong Kong. We would have to wait until Beijing to test out the six months of Mandarin (Putonghua) that we crammed in before leaving Canada, which had proven to be a convivial diversion from the mundane chores of packing up our household and the taxing travails of finalizing the sale of our business.

We arrived in Hong Kong on August 2. Thinking we had to go into the city to find a China Travel Service (CTS) office to obtain our 90-day visas, we were pleasantly surprised to see a booth at the airport.

After parting with Hong Kong dollars equivalent to $275.00 Canadian, the clerk said, "Now you must take papers to CTS office in city to pick up visas."

"But the sign says we get our visas here."

"We take applications. Go tomorrow to CTS office to pick up visas."

"Then give us our money back and we will just go to the CTS office tomorrow to get our visas."

"No, you just go tomorrow with this paper and visas will be ready."

The following day at a downtown office we discovered—much to our chagrin—that had we waited to obtain our visas from this office, the cost would only have been $147.00 Canadian. The clerks were unsympathetic to our plight, and just shrugged their shoulders when we asked how we could be charged almost double the cost by the CTS airport outlet. Judging by past travels, our "buyer beware" warning signals are blurred when first in a new country, and we almost always fall into what we have dubbed the "first day rip-off" while acquiring street-smarts for a particular country. I quickly adopted our normal response—"Oh, well!"—and carried on. Not Rick; he had his calculator a'whizzin' and I knew we would be making up the difference elsewhere. If his calculator ever wore out from the daily poundings, I was not sure I'd resurrect the extra one buried in my backpack.

Our first hotel cost us $96.00 Canadian per night. Rick stewed. On the second day we managed to find a hostel for $44.00 Canadian. Not as commodious: in fact, there was hardly room for the door to swing open before the remaining space was filled with a double bed. With not even enough floor space left for our backpacks, we resorted to shoving them under the bed with the dust bunnies. But who stays in their room anyway when there is so much to see and do? What had really sold us on this hostel, compared to a few others in the same price range, was the rickety window air conditioner laboriously emitting puffs of cool air over our slumbering bodies. The temperature had now climbed to a whopping 38°C (100°F) with drenching humidity.

After late breakfasts, our daily routine was to wander the teeming streets absorbing the local colour. When we needed a reprieve from the blasting heat and noise, we stopped at a well-treed park in the middle of Kowloon. Several small lakes dotted the grounds with benches around the edges. One day a sinewy old man with a thin white goatee that ended almost at his waist approached us. He flapped his arms, then motioned for us to follow. His smile reached his gleaming eyes as he brought us to the small aviary in one corner of the park, which no doubt was special to him. We didn't have the heart to not go in. It's a good thing we did, as he was waiting at the exit to gauge our avian appreciation and to bid us farewell.

Each evening after dark we made our way to the bustling Temple Street Night Market. Rows of brightly lit stalls were filled with every imaginable sort of knick-knack (things you never need but buy anyway). Mouth-watering aromas flooded the air. Deep-fried tidbits of unknown substances sizzled in vats of oil, and unrecognizable greens in jumbo woks were stirred with large wooden utensils, all peculiarly delicious. Around 11:30 p.m. vendors began shutting down and the crowds, on cue, began to disperse.

* * *

The first cool day (only 29°C, or 84°F) seemed like a fine time to explore Hong Kong Island. The ferry over was packed. Noticing that approximately 85 percent of the passengers were women toting shopping bags, I figured Sunday must be a heavy market day on the island. The women scattered like mice from the ferry ramp, leaving us standing alone, trying to figure out the best route to the Peak Tram. In a convoluted way, we eventually found ourselves at the base of the vehicle that would whisk us up to Victoria Peak, the highest point on the island.

Feeling a sensation of vertigo, with my head bent back as far as it would go, I watched the tram we just missed disappear up the side of the lush mountain at a 27-degree incline. Soon, the counter-balancing tram of this funicular railway descended, and we lucked out with a seat near the front and on the right side for the best view. A short jerk started us upward. The soft clacking sound levelled out as our car ascended. The breeze was deliciously pine-scented from hillside trees. At the top we left the tram and walked to the viewing platform. Victoria Harbour glistened far below, draped with the skylines of both Hong Kong Island and Kowloon. Far off in the distance, a backdrop of grey-blue mountains was silhouetted against the sky. Since 1871, the Peak Tram has been transporting people to 552 metres (1,811 ft) above sea level for this breathtaking vista.

After our descent, we spent several hours perusing the shops along the streets below the tramline, and finally decided on a restaurant for lunch.

Taking a different route back to the ferry, we happened upon a four-foot metal bulletin board with glass panels. Extremely disturbing pictures of badly beaten and tortured practitioners of Falun Gong were displayed. In 1999, President Jiang Zemin outlawed Falun Gong (also called Falun Dafa). He proclaimed it "an evil cult that jeopardizes the Chinese society and the Chinese people" and declared that it was imbued with "malicious fallacies and superstitions resulting in suicides and members refusing medical treatment." Li Hongzhi, the founder of this movement (which was introduced to the Chinese public in 1992) claims Falun Gong is apolitical; an organization based on meditation, breathing exercises, and mysticism drawn from traditional Chinese philosophies, fostering truthfulness and benevolence in its followers. They felt it was Jiang's jealousy of the popularity of Falun Gong that prompted the ban and persecution of its followers, forcing Li Hongzhi to flee the country. He now lives in Manhattan.

Reports of mass arrests, torture, labour camps, and abuse in psychiatric hospitals began leaking out of China, spurring an international outcry. China simply shrugged off the litany of serious human rights complaints by the United States and European countries, not changing its stance on Falun Gong one iota. President Hu Jintao has continued Jiang's position on the practice of Falun Gong.

In TV news clips we saw before leaving Canada, Falun Gong participants were shown doing their distinctive form of tai chi exercises. Being neophytes to tai chi ourselves, we thought about how wonderful it would be to practise our routine on the soil where this soft martial art originated. Our untrained eye could not differentiate between the many forms, which all resemble a cross between shadowboxing and slow-moving ballet. Seeing these graphic pictures of torture changed our mind against any public display of our moves; we feared being mistaken for Falun Gong followers. These posters gave testimony to China's stand on Falun Gong practitioners: a freedom axed with the termination of 156 years of British rule.

As we neared the ferry dock, there was hardly a square foot of unoccupied space for blocks around. Women sat on blankets, newspaper, mats, and bare concrete. They were sharing food and beverages while cheerfully chattering and showing off their purchases. An English-speaking lady told us the majority of these women were Filipino housekeepers and nannies who were employed by executives who almost unanimously gave these domestics Sundays off. She said it was an expectation that executives employ domestic help, especially expatriates. Of the 240,000 domestics in Hong Kong, 150,000 were Filipino. The remainder were from Indonesia, Thailand, Nepal, and India. The minimum wage set by the government for domestics was $3,670HKD per month ($611CAD, based on exchange rate of $6HKD = $1CAD) making it the lowest wage in Hong Kong.

With the cost of living here ranked as one of the five highest on a global scale, we could not imagine how they managed to live and also send money to families back home.

All in all, the historic dichotomy of Western and Asian characteristics made Hong Kong a good stepping stone into the country. We were primed to make our move into mainland China.

North to the Capital

We purchased soft sleeper train tickets to Beijing. We learned there were "hard seats" and "hard sleepers," which were just that: a very thin pad over wood. There were also "soft seats" and "soft sleepers" which were softer, thicker pads over wood.

Our soft sleeper on the 27-hour trip to Beijing was in a deluxe private room with two parallel bunks and a small table between. As we snuggled down in the pile of foam pillows and serviceable grey blankets for the long haul, the enormous red disc suspended in the evening sky spilled its rosy glow through our tiny compartment window. The next thing we both remembered was the morning attendant chanting "Cha, cha." Still groggy, we sipped the sweet, milky tea and watched the varied landscapes pass by: emerald rice paddies, terraced crops with rich brown soil visible between the levels, and vast cornfields. Lush jungle interspersed the farmed land. The smog would periodically thicken, signalling the appearance of a smorgasbord of buildings in the distance with belching smokestacks: yet another industrial city.

We pulled out our Mandarin books for a quick review, and paid particular attention to vital phrases such as "toilet," "how many yuan," "please," and "no, thanks."

Before leaving Hong Kong, we had gone to great lengths to find out if and where we could easily exchange Hong Kong dollars and/or American dollars for Chinese yuan in Beijing. We arrived in the capital at 7:30 p.m. and hurried to find the money exchange we had been told was conveniently located in the train station. After an hour's hunt in the multiple-storey edifice, we established that yes, a money exchange did exist, but no, we could not exchange our money because it closed at 5:30 p.m. Of course, the banks were now also closed, so there was no sense in testing out the manageable phrase "Nar you yinhang? (Where is the bank?)"

Not a single idea came to us while sitting on our packs: no yuan, no map to hotels in the area, no English speakers, not one Caucasian in the sea of faces (not that finding one would guarantee conversing in one of Canada's two official languages). It was now growing dusky. At least there were benches in the train station.

An accommodation hustler (no doubt working on commission) whom we had brushed off when we first arrived reappeared with her book of hotel room pictures. Now, like putty in her hands, we allowed the lady to show us on a map where the hotel she suggested was located in relation to the train station.

Rick asked, "Duo yuan? (How far away?)"

"Yi gongli (1 kilometre)," she answered.

It appeared to us, from her map, to be about eight city blocks away. She pointed to a price in American dollars; we consented with the universally understood "Okay." She made a quick call on her cellphone and led us to a van with a poker-faced driver who gave us a terse nod. She jabbered to him in Chinese, paid him some coinage, and bid us farewell.

The driver took a series of rights and lefts, then sped onto a major highway taking us farther and farther out of town. At about 5 kilometres (3 mi), Rick and I exchanged worried glances.

"Where are you taking us?" Rick called out. "Irene, how do you say that in Chinese?"

"I can't remember. My God, what have we gotten ourselves into?" At 10 kilometres (6 mi), my panic rose to unprecedented terror.

"Ting! Ting! (Stop! Stop!)," I shouted.

Rick grabbed my shoulders. "Irene, calm down."

I couldn't. The radio was cranked and the driver either did not hear me or chose not to acknowledge my shouts.

"Jiuming! Jiuming! (Help! Help!)," I screamed, the only other Chinese word I could think of in my frenzy. My banshee shrieks only merited a brief glance back at us through the rear-view mirror. Just as I was ready to open the side door and bail, he pulled off the highway. The vehicle bounced down an embankment and screeched to a stop in front of a small hotel. He pointed, but stayed glued to the steering wheel (he probably didn't want to chance a close encounter). We flung ourselves and our backpacks out of the van.

Knowing a little about the salient feature of *mianzi* (face) in the Chinese culture buffered the need for any parting verbal exchange or explanation. *Mianzi* includes "saving face," "losing face," and "giving face," but there is a division as to when it is appropriate or even necessary.

In *wai* (or "outside" relationships, such as with bus or taxi drivers, store clerks, people on the street) there is no need to do any "face work," which reduced the significance of my crazed outburst, as it did not affect either the driver's or my face. Politeness is not an issue in wai dealings. In stores we often saw shoppers shove money at a clerk and the clerk throw back the change without our accustomed "thanks" and "you're welcome." Rick's pet wai-related peeve was in grocery store lineups, where he would complain in exasperation "Look at the little folk, they keep squeezing in the queue from all directions."

On the other hand, the Chinese have a very strict set of rules for *nei* (or "inside" relationships, which includes family, friends, schoolmates, and co-workers, based on a hierarchy of status). For example: when a subordinate shows proper respect (face-giving) to a superior, this is "face-saving" for both, as the superior is shown the deference due, and in turn the subordinate gains the trust and protection of the superior.

With my "face" intact but no immediate options, we warily plodded into the hotel reception area. What a relief it was to find a lady with a hand outstretched in welcome, and who spoke a little English. Ms. Li Lin was the epitome of graciousness, and even agreed to take Hong Kong dollars for the room, and exchanged additional Hong Kong dollars for yuan so we would have some to start off with the next day.

The room was stark: a bed without a headboard and one small, battered table. Faded greyish paint splotched with the accidental leavings of a million previous occupants covered the walls. One lonely light bulb dangled from the ceiling. Rick performed his usual ritual of pulling down the bedspread to inspect the sheets.

"I can't sleep here," Rick proclaimed matter-of-factly, pointing to the pillows.

"Not everything comes out in the wash," I said while inspecting them, "but I do think they were laundered."

The pillowcases were mottled with dark brownish stains, conjuring up visions of past homicides. Rick left it to me to point this out to Ms. Li, who brought us a relatively unstained pair. Seeing Rick was still wrinkling his nose in disgust, I gave him my best "stifle it" glare. It was almost midnight and we were thirsty, hungry, and tired. Our gal Li led us to a hole-in-the-wall store next door to buy bottled water, and after we were settled back in our room, she appeared with two big, steaming bowls of delicious noodles. There was a solid lock on the door; all's well that ends well.

Our mouths gaped in shock when we stared out the window the next morning. It was a good thing it had been pitch-black when we pulled off the highway the night before, because if the cabbie had pulled into this area in broad daylight, we would have been sure his motive was to rob us or worse. I have never seen such an eerie desolate place: low shanties were slapped together with odd boards, crates, and scrap metal sheets leaned against them, garbage heaps and piles of wrecked vehicles were everywhere, and everything was covered with a thick layer of black soot coughed up from nearby chimneys. The whole area was stuffed under a string of major highway overpasses.

When we were ready to leave, Li led us up a steep dirt path to a highway and flagged down a taxi for us. After asking the driver repeatedly how much it would cost to go back to the Huoche Zhan (train station), we finally got the tones correct and his puzzled expression morphed into a beaming response of "15 yuan." We found that we remembered words, but forgot which tone to use, there being four tones in Mandarin, each changing the meaning of the syllable. For example: mā in a high level pitch means mother, má in a rising pitch means flax, mà with an abrupt falling pitch means to scold, and mǎ in a low dipping pitch means horse. Some niceties are best avoided, such as, "Is she your mother?"

When we arrived in front of the familiar massive structure of grey stone, Rick handed the driver 15 yuan. He said it only came to 13 yuan and insisted Rick take back the change. It's uncanny how right after we feel we've been duped, a very honest or helpful person always comes along to restore our faith in humanity.

Don't Bank on a Bank

The money exchange was what we were after in the train station, but it was still closed. I didn't bother to ask anyone why, as I probably would not have understood their response if it was more than two simple words.

A two-block walk to the bank nearest the train station—an ICBC (Insurance Commercial Bank of China)—was not fruitful: they didn't do exchanges, but they did direct us to the Bank of China about 10 blocks away. With fully loaded backpacks in the 31°C (88°F) weather, it was easy to decide that Rick should venture out alone while I parked myself with our packs outside the train station among the thousand Chinese people sitting on mounds of baggage.

I found a place in the shade of a large pillar. When I took out my journal and began to write in it, I noticed a few men looking over my shoulder. I switched the journal for my colourful Chinese in 10 Minutes a Day textbook and pointed to pictures, saying the word in English. Soon I was surrounded by a dozen people, young and old, pointing to pictures as I turned the pages and with much laughter saying the words in Chinese as I continued to respond with the English words.

Periodically, I checked my watch. After three hours I figured Rick must be in the clutches of a four-clawed, demon-eyed, snake-necked flying dragon or have some other such fantastical reason for not returning, as Rick never gets lost ... at least, not when he's on foot.

I tucked the book away and thanked the people around me for the fun Chinese lesson. As the group dispersed, one young fellow stayed, introducing himself as Wang Xiaoling. He told me it was his first time hearing English. We hilariously attempted conversation, with much gesticulating. After about 10 minutes, he held up his index finger—the universal sign for "just wait"—and tore into the train station, reappearing moments later with a big brown bag of tiny buns. He popped two or three in his mouth, as if to reassure me they were not poisoned, then offered me some. The rich doughnut-like balls filled with a delectable sweet paste titillated my taste buds. I suddenly realized how famished I was. Then lo and behold, Rick materialized around the corner ... and just in the nick of time, as Wang and I were down to the one-quarter mark on the bun bag. After introductions, Rick partook of the scrumptious treat, saying between chews we were now rich in yuan, followed by his protracted tale.

"I found the Bank of China we were originally directed to with no problem; but the clerk said 'no exchange' and gave me directions to another Bank of China," Rick fumed. "I felt I somehow missed this next bank, so I walked into a big post office and asked the guard if he knew where the Bank of China was." Rick described how the guard left his post and walked him around the corner to a large ICBC. Since the guard had gone out of his way to assist him, and Rick was not able to explain properly in Mandarin that he wanted a Bank of China, he tried not to look as frustrated as he felt. "I bowed a few times with a few thank-yous and went through the doors to wait until the guard was out of sight before I left." Serendipitously, an older lady in the lineup asked him if he needed help ... in perfect English!

"Most banks will exchange American dollars but very few will exchange Hong Kong dollars," she explained.

"What?" Rick said. "Hong Kong is China. Why the aversion to Hong Kong dollars here? Do you mean to tell me if I had held out the American dollars instead of the Hong Kong dollars, any bank would have exchanged them?"

"Yes, that's correct," she said.

"I should have known from all the countries we have travelled to that the American dollar is recognized as a world currency."

After Rick traded some U.S. dollars at that very bank, the rescuing lady took the time to walk him up a block and around a series of jogs and corners to yet another Bank of China, where they did exchange our remaining unpopular Hong Kong dollars. His mission was finally accomplished.

* * *

Next, we had to find accommodations that qualified under our "We're not here to suffer" motto. We checked our Lonely Planet and picked out a centrally located hotel. Wang, who was still with us, wrote the name and address of the hotel down in Chinese characters. We bade this fine fellow a warm goodbye and wished him *liu liu da shun* (double lucky six) in life, six being the Chinese equivalent to our lucky seven.

We hoisted up our packs and headed out toward the taxi stands. A bunch of men were leaning up against a fence about half a block from a row of taxi cabs. As we passed we were intercepted by a clean-cut fellow in a crisp white shirt, with a military crease in his black pants.

"Rou wan taxi?" he said. "Where go?"

After showing him the hotel name in Chinese characters, he motioned to the other men who huddled around him. Though they were chattering in their mother tongue, we knew they were disputing the exact location of the hotel. It seemed an agreeable consensus was reached when Mr. Clean-cut turned to us with a price, to which we agreed. He waved at us to follow him to his taxi ... or so we presumed. He walked past the row of taxis and opened the door with a flourish to his private car—a clunker, its faded brown paint mottled by rust and the whole vehicle tilted slightly to the left. Rick and I exchanged an "oh, no, not again" look.

"No, no, we want taxi," Rick said as we turned to escape.

He bounded in front of us, hands clasped in prayer-like fashion, desperately pleading in broken English, "Sir, I take rou. Sir, I take rou good. Prease, sir." My next eye contact with Rick conveyed "ah, what the hell," and we arranged ourselves and our packs in the backseat.

After about an hour of bumper-to-bumper sluggishness—peppered with pedal-to-the-metal spurts in open areas, plus several stops for our driver to quickly jump out of the car and ask people standing on the sidewalks which way to go next—he got us there. Wouldn't you know it: the hotel was full. Down the street, however, we found the Dong Hua, which suited us perfectly in price and amenities ($29 Canadian per night).

Now, it may seem this day was a total hassle or waste: yes and no. As we sat that evening in the hotel's restaurant Rick succinctly summed it up with "Now, if a limo had picked us up at the train station and chauffeured us to a five-star hotel, think of the adventure we would have missed."

"Not to mention more than two stars would blow your budget to smithereens," I could not resist adding.

The beauty of having no set schedule and lots of time made a day such as ours a minor blip. We found humour in how travelling simplified our needs, and how reaching the most elementary of goals filled us with such a sense of accomplishment.

Even with a guidebook on China, we found our old motto "Have guidebook, will travel" did not live up to its promises, with English speakers almost nonexistent and alien Chinese characters on all the signage. We dwelled in jest on the potential for future floundering in the countries for which we did not even have a guidebook. But not for long; the server came with our order. Our full attention was given to our quart-sized bowls of steaming rice piled high with braised chicken and greens in a sumptuous sauce.

* * *

Our gusto for Beijing began with our first walk of many down Wangfujing Dajie, the city's prestigious pedestrian shopping street. While we were swept into the explosion of neon and glitz, we knew these young women with fashionably scant outfits, men in expensive business suits, and families carrying loads of purchase were not true representatives of typical Chinese living standards.

Midway down the street we noticed an exceptionally lengthy line-up and wondered what the attraction might be. To our surprise, it was a McDonald's, complete with a clowning Ronald entertaining the crowd. Inside the mega-proportioned eating area, people were seated elbow-to-elbow munching Big Macs, while others patiently inched forward waiting to get in. Along the side of the building was an equally busy take-out window. As McDonald's applies their American pricing worldwide, the cheap meal deals we associated with the outlets in North America were expensive fare in the Chinese economy.

As for ourselves, it was the swirls of tantalizing aromas coming from a side street that lassoed us off of Wangfujing every time we passed by. Once pulled into the sardine-can alleyway, there was no turning back. We were propelled by like-minded people into a square lined with kiosks. Vendors were furiously serving up noodles from steam-billowing vats, spicy meat from sizzling grills, and numerous other delectable combinations.

Once, on our quest for Snack Street tidbits, a friendly thirtyish Chinese man put his arm around Rick and said, "Watch stealing. Put day pack to front." Rick thanked him and they exchanged a few more pleasantries. We lined up and made a purchase of two heaping orders of skewered beef. While I held the plates, Rick reached into his pocket to figure out the Canadian equivalent of the yuan we had just parted with. His precious calculator was gone! Missing! Vanished! The chummy fellow who had warned Rick about theft was indubitably the culprit. It was as if he had lost his best friend. I had a hard time keeping a straight face as he stewed and continued to do the conversion from yuan to dollars in longhand.

The longhand calculations continued for every purchase. I began to soften about never revealing the one I was hoarding in my backpack, but figured what's the rush? Tomorrow, or the day after, or maybe next week. I finally did unveil it when he started looking in earnest for a replacement. I also had to admit keeping a running calculation of our expenses was rather interesting.

Hutong Hopping

Physically near but seemingly a world away from the flamboyant Wangfujing Dajie, we roamed the *hutongs*. The translation for *hutong* is "narrow alley," expanded to mean "traditional neighbourhood" for foreign visitors. Most date back to the Yuan, Ming, and Qing dynasties, which (all combined) spanned the years from 1279 to 1911.

The alleys, some only the width of two people, led to *siheyuans* (courtyards with a dwelling on each of their four sides). Influenced by feng shui, most of the doors face to the inside of the rigid quadrangular layout. The courtyards are arranged in concentric circles around the Imperial Palace (the Forbidden City). The aristocrats once lived in the *hutongs* closest to the Emperor on the east and west, and the common people—such as merchants, labourers, and artisans—lived farther from the Palace to the north and south. Of course, under Chairman Mao's class-levelling, all the *hutongs* were filled with loyal communist cadres.

Today, ordinary citizens fill the approximately 1,000 remaining *hutongs*—reduced from the 3,600 that existed at the beginning of the century. They have their own culture, and some families have resided here for generations. The *hutongs* farthest away from the Forbidden City were the most memorable; the smaller, poorer mud-and-timber dwellings buzzed with everyday activity. Vendors sold traditional foods from carts and small stalls. I was drawn like a magnet to the skewers of baked tart crab apples doused in sugar. Jovial old men sat around crate tables furiously clacking mah-jong tiles. Many still wore Mao suits (four-pocketed grey tunics buttoning up the front to a small collar, with matching pants). An elderly lady with tiny bound feet stood near us, a testimony to the ancient custom, which was officially banned in 1911.

Our *ni hao* (hello, pronounced nee-how) was always met with a smiling response. Some people called out "Meiguo? (United States?)" Our Mandarin lessons paid off as we replied "Jianada (Canada)."

One day, a half-dozen children ranging in age from about four to eight ran up and handed us some kind of plant branches. Our gestures, showing we did not know what to do with them, brought on a giggly demonstration. Pulling the little green balls off the branches, they first peeled them before popping them in their mouths. It was then our turn to sample the tasty nut-like treats; not knowing to this day what they were. None of the children seemed to understand a word of English. Several women soon surrounded us also. We attempted to converse in Mandarin, and the odd time were rewarded with a nod and the women repeating a word we said.

We never once felt unsafe or threatened in our extensive wanderings through the *hutongs*.

Even though we knew China is the most populated country in the world with 1.3 billion people (the 2007 estimate), it still did not prepare us for the mass of humanity everywhere; and yet less than half of this gigantic population lives in urban areas. Even with the one-child-per-family rule, official statistics from 2004 indicate that with a 12 percent birth rate (approximately) and 6 percent death rate, the national growth rate is almost 6 percent.

Often we would just come to a complete stop, astounded by the hum of voices and people scurrying in all directions, the dizzying traffic, and the hundreds of bikes. Perhaps the impact was even more pronounced for us, being from sparsely populated Canada, our population being only 33 million spread out over the second-largest landmass in the world.

* * *

Our next venture took us to Tiananmen Square, which was constructed in the 15th century and restored in the 17th. This, the world's largest square, is where Mao Zedong proclaimed the People's Republic on October 1, 1949. Gazing at the expansive sweep of concrete, we envisioned Chairman Mao's periodic review of a million soldiers marching through the square during the Cultural Revolution (1966–1970). We also pictured the shocking events of 1989, when army tanks rolled into the square and massacred thousands of pro-democracy demonstrators, mostly university students.

As we stood in the middle of the square, Rick's camera clicked in all directions. To the north was the Forbidden City. Above the Gate of Heavenly Peace entrance and facing the square was a gigantic picture of Mao with a slogan on a red background on either side. To the right of the portrait, the Chinese characters proclaimed, "Long Live the Unity of the Peoples of the World," and to the left, "Long Live the People's Republic of China."

To the west was the Great Hall of the People, where China's legislature meets. All 10,000 representatives can be seated in the auditorium simultaneously. A galaxy of lights circles the great red star on the ceiling.

To the east was the People's Revolution Military Museum, with displays of antiquated weapons and military equipment from the history of the People's Liberation Army up to and including modern-day machinery.

To the south was the Mao Mausoleum.

As we absorbed the atmosphere, we knew we'd have to make more than one trip to the square to do these national monuments justice.

During the late afternoon, the sky above the square filled with a profusion of dancing kites and bobbing helium-filled balloons. When it was almost time for the sunset flag-lowering ceremony, the flying objects were towed in, and crowds swarmed the designated area. At least 10,000 people were all vying for the best view. Rick had an advantage with his six-foot height. Luckily for me and my shorter stature, we were only three rows back from the People's Liberation Army (PLA) marching at precisely 108 paces per minute, 75 centimetres (29.5 in) per pace. The same ceremony takes place at sunrise.

* * *

On our second trip to Tiananmen, we planned to see the Forbidden City and Mao's mausoleum. The Mausoleum was closed, and we were unable to find out why. Judging from the many individuals and large tour groups that continued to gather and then disperse after being approached by the guards, it must have been an unannounced closing.

We turned our sights to the Forbidden City (Zijincheng). First built between 1406 and 1420, the Imperial Palace complex containing 800 halls and palaces had burned and been rebuilt many times. Most of the structures seen now in the 74-hectare (183-acre) area were constructed or restored after the 18th century. Off limits to any unauthorized person for over 500 years (with a penalty of death for those who disobeyed this law), the Imperial grounds became known as "the Forbidden City."

The 10-metre (33-ft) wall surrounding the Forbidden City was skilfully angled wider at the base than at the top to thwart attempts to scale it. Even the lowly chicken played a part in its construction: the structure's great strength was due to a combination of egg whites and glutinous rice for the cement that held together the lime and glutinous rice bricks. Four sentinel towers loom ominously at each of the four corners. A 6 x 52 metre (20 x 171 ft) moat outside the wall was once an additional deterrent.

As we passed through the Heavenly Gate entrance, the yellow roof tiles of the palaces gleamed brilliantly in the bright sunlight. During dynasty days, only members of the royal family could don frocks of yellow. My eyes moved down to the bold red outer walls, the colour denoting power. The use of red ink is still unsanctioned for use by common folk, as we had witnessed first-hand a few weeks earlier. While passing through customs between Hong Kong and China, the lady in the lineup in front of us had her form abruptly thrown back at her: "Do over. Red ink only for Emperor." It's hard to imagine what the Communist leaders would think of that!

A prominent feature of the Forbidden City is the wide, central pathway extending in a straight line from the Meridian Gate and through the middle of each of the long chain of halls and palaces that once were most frequented by the emperor. This pathway, now beneath my sandals, could once only be touched by the soles of the emperor's shoes. Even if the emperor was being carried in his sedan chair, the carriers were careful not to step on this Imperial Way. There were narrower paths for all others between the secondary halls and palaces that flanked both sides of this royal path.

The first seven halls, considered the outer court, were where the emperor met with his governing representatives from each state and with visiting dignitaries. Other buildings served different functions: the Hall of Ancestor Worship, the Hall of Mental Cultivation, the Hall of Protective Harmony, the Hall of Literary Glory, and so on. There was even a hall to hold the 25 jade seals of the Imperial Court. The inner court behind them was where the emperor resided with his family.

Between two of the palaces, nine dragons sculpted onto a 200-ton marble ramp is considered a perfect art piece by the Chinese. Massive incense burners once permeated the air with the sweetness of jasmine or the pungent scent of sandalwood. Lion sentinels still gush water from their mouths when it rains.

It was easy to understand why the emperors from the Ming and Qing dynasties who ruled from the Forbidden City never left this hedonistic haven of obsequious eunuchs, wives, and concubines (and the empress, of course) unless absolutely necessary.

While sitting on a bench under a shade tree in a Palace garden, a novel occurrence took place, one we would soon find commonplace: Chinese families asked that we be included in their family photos. Other foreigners were also being photographed. It was amusing to think that we would forever be a part of their travel albums, so we agreed.

It turned out to be a good thing that we had found Mao's final resting place closed that day. After several hours in the stifling heat, we were as withered as unwatered seedlings. It was Confucius' wisdom in China to use an umbrella to ward off the sun's rays. Almost everyone wields one. It was good not to feel out of place like I had in Australia when I popped open my umbrella on long walks. I recalled how previously, in Greece, both Rick and I had burned so badly we had to just lie naked on our hotel bed for days, slathered in aloe vera, only donning our loosest garments when we had to venture out to find food. I had vowed "Never again," and was sticking to it, as there were still 10 months of "following the sun" ahead. Rick, who tans more easily, was by this time flaunting a bronze exterior, or more correctly a "farmer's tan": a brown face, neck, and exposed sections of arms and legs, and a lily-white body.

* * *

The following day, we made an exception to the rule of no early risings. We dragged ourselves out of bed at 5:30 a.m. and hustled to catch a bus at Xuanwumen Station, making it there by 6:15. The bus that was supposed to leave at 6:45 a.m. finally got rolling at 8:10, but nothing could sour my mood. I was about to spend my 57th birthday on the Great Wall (Changcheng)!

Our choice section of Wall was Simatai (chosen over the restored Badaling and Mutianyu sections, which are where the majority of Great Wall viewers go). The 19-kilometre (12-mi) section open to tourists at Simatai was left in its natural crumbling magnificence, and its high elevation grants rewarding views of the surrounding mountains.

While investigating Simatai, we reviewed other accesses that had not been restored. One in particular, Huanghua, is said to offer a wild Wall experience, being very remote and unspoiled, with none of the usual tourist trappings. A ticket was not even needed to walk the wall at Huanghua, but it was difficult to get there because there were no direct bus routes. We ended up rationalizing that this would be a goal to pursue if we were ever lucky enough to return to Beijing in the future.

It was novel to be travelling on the highway. Train travel in China is better for long trips, but the action of the highway was missed. There was a steady stream of oncoming cars and rickety trucks. A few daredevils chanced darting out from behind to pass our bus only a hair's-breadth away from a head-on collision. Donkey carts competed with bicycles and motorcycles for space on the roadsides. Every so many miles, crews with hefty brooms swept the shoulders with only surgical masks to protect them from the whirling clouds of dust. Sheep and cattle grazed in the fields. We passed village after village where old men sat on benches smoking, peasants transported wares in yoke baskets, and cyclists stirred up fine powder from arid paths. Roadside fruit stalls displayed big slabs of deep red watermelon.

The bus unexpectedly pulled into a park for *yi xiaoshi* (one hour). Oy! We thought the bus was to go straight to Simatai. Only a few people paid the entry fee to go into the park, and after about 10 minutes they were back and reported it was not worth the 20 yuan. We got off the bus during the wait for a breath of fresh air, and were serenaded by a dynamic cricket orchestration. The bus driver waded in the thick grass to catch a few "good luck" crickets. He brought them back onto the bus and built little homes for them out of paper, stuffing grass on top to keep them in. When the bus was en route again, one escaped. More than half the passengers were on all fours searching, and eventually retrieved it.

At last we arrived at Simatai. Passing by the T-shirt stands, we headed straight for the cable car that would take us halfway up the mountain. Out of the busload of people, two ladies laying-in-wait pounced on us (because we were the whitest and tallest, according to Rick). They flailed a large, heavy, exorbitantly priced Great Wall book at us; just what a budgeting backpacker needs. They were hardworking peasants by the look of their rough hands and feet, short-bobbed hair, plain and well-worn loose shirts, and capri-style pants; they were indistinguishably aged somewhere between 30 and 40. I said "Bu yao (don't want)," and smiled to be polite.

"Aren't those the same two women?" Rick said as our cable car rose up the mountain.

Sure enough, there they were, charging up the winding path below us.

"See, I told you not to talk to them. You should have just walked past them." When the cable car unloaded, the ladies were already there to badger us as we climbed a series of stone steps that would take us onto the Wall.

"No. No. Bu yao!" I said squeezing past them. They aggressively followed us onto the wall. We almost toppled over the edge as they waved the book in our faces. This left me no other option but to raise my voice to the "never in a million years" calibre. They looked downcast and turned to start down. Then I felt bad. I ran up behind them and passed them some yuan so their efforts at making a living would not go totally unrewarded.

Now that I was free to gaze about, my breath caught at the sight of the ancient stone path wending its way across mountain ridges. The greens of forests and grasses and the brown rocky patches melded into shades of shadowy blue where the distant peaks met the sky. I inhaled and exhaled slowly to still my racing heart. It seemed surreal that a lifelong dream was now in the present moment: we were standing on the Great Wall of China! I bent down and ran my hand over the stones, rounded smooth from the elements and from guards treading over the centuries. My mind swirled with the immensity of it. Extending over 6,530 km (4,058 mi) from the East China Sea to the Gobi Desert in Central Asia, the building of this massive monument surmounted all difficulties caused by mountains, valleys, rivers, and deserts. Its length is equivalent to the breadth of Canada from the Pacific coast to the Atlantic coast, which we knew from experience to be a ten-hour-per-day eight-day drive on the Trans-Canada Highway, which added a stark reality to the Wall's awesome length.

In attempts to keep out marauding nomads from the north, the first defensive walls had been unconnected mounds of earth, which dated back over 2,500 years. The First Emperor of China, Qin Shi Huang (259–210 BC), after unifying the warring states in 221 BC, took on the major feat of joining these sections. Huge masses of earth were moved to fill in the dips between the mountains, making this a continuous stronghold snaking across the miles. It took 10 years to complete, mostly with prison labour. This Great Wall, however, did not prove to be a deterrent to Genghis Khan in 1215 when he overtook Beijing, or to his grandson Kublai Khan who established the Yuan Dynasty (1271–1368).

When the Mongol rule collapsed at the hands of the Ming rulers (1368–1644), major reconstruction of the wall was undertaken. Lengthening and restoring this mega-structure took 60 million cubic metres (79 million cubic yards) of stone and brick and the manual labour of hundreds of thousands of workers over a span of 272 years. The costs in resources and human life were staggering. It gained the gruesome nickname "longest graveyard on earth." Many believe thousands of bodies were actually buried within the wall, but others say this would not have been sanctioned, because decomposing bodies would have weakened the structure.

The wall was mostly forgotten during the Cultural Revolution, with the exception of neighbouring peasants pilfering the stones to build their homes and other structures.

As we proceeded along the top of the wall, which was only a little more than a metre wide, without guardrails or handholds, the precipitous drop on either side was a bit unnerving, especially when groups—which tend to move in clumps—passed by. Pausing at each of the five turreted watchtowers along the way, our eyes scanned the horizon, keeping watch like the soldiers of yesteryear. The levelness of the path was sporadically interrupted by dips and inclines; the most challenging was an 8-metre (26-ft) drop followed by a 60-degree incline, which brought us down on all fours to negotiate our way along.

Just when I thought the panorama could not get any more spectacular, we reached a peak from which the view of the convoluting path was not obstructed by other peaks. The magnitude of the structure reached a new level of intensity. It was one of those times when logic registers something as being impossible, yet there it exists to boggle the mind. With the breeze fanning the sun's torrid rays, I stood wrapped in a cloud of euphoria, not wanting the moment to end.

In the cable car on the way down, we opened our bag of small birthday cakes.

"Being on-the-wall takes the lead as my most off-the-wall birthday," I declared between mouthfuls.

Rick did not mention the budget when we finished the day splurging at a white-tablecloth restaurant.

* * *

We decided to give Mao one more chance when we arrived back at Tiananmen Square the following day. The line was about seven blocks long, in front of and down the side of the mausoleum: a good indicator that it was open again. Rick only brought a Nalgene water bottle and I only brought my umbrella, aware that it was a standard practice to check in day-packs and any sort of carry-case before entering any public exhibition. When a young couple asked if we knew where the bag-check for the mausoleum was, we couldn't find it anywhere, which proved to us that not bringing a pack had been ultimate wisdom. While moving up slowly in line, we watched guards go down the line and pull people aside who were carrying various prohibited items. A bit of excitement erupted when a man left his place in the queue and tried to cut in closer to the mausoleum entrance. Not just one but three guards jumped him and escorted him right out of the area.

A guard came up beside us and pointed to Rick's water bottle. He shouted something in Mandarin, shaking his head from side to side.

"What? Can't take it in?" Rick said.

The guard knocked on Rick's bottle, and again shook his head.

"What do they think I'll do? Baptize old Mao?"

"Just leave it," I said.

"This is a Nalgene. I can't replace it." Rick scowled, incredulous that I would even suggest giving it up.

"You go," Rick said.

"No, you go."

"No, I'll stay, you go."

After we ping-ponged this matter back and forth half a dozen times, we decided that I would see Mao. Rick went to sit on the museum steps.

Slowly but surely, the line shortened in front of me. There was a stand where you could purchase a bouquet of plastic flowers to place near Mao's remains (a lucrative business, since the flowers were gathered up each night and sold again day after day).

An hour had passed since Rick had left me. I was only one of three Westerners in the crowd of sombre and unusually quiet Chinese. Though it was half an hour to closing time, the line behind me kept growing ... there were far too many people to get in today. I crossed my fingers, hoping I'd be one of the lucky ones. The guards signalled the cut-off about 20 people behind me.

We shuffled along one behind another, through a small entry where pictures of Mao were displayed. A turn took us to the foot of the sarcophagus with the Great Helmsman lying under a glass dome, his head resting on a red cushion. Guards watched our every move, prodded people to place their flowers at the feet of Mao, then split the line, one person to the left and one to the right of the body. We walked slowly, and were not allowed to stop. Perhaps they didn't want his face scrutinized too closely. I had read that every so often the mausoleum closes for long periods of time while Mao's face undergoes repair. Since he died in 1976, I figured his pasty white features must by now be composed mostly of plastic.

It was compelling to actually be seeing the remains of this infamous dictator and to gauge the emotion and veneration he was commanding. No matter what he did in his life of tyrannical rule, he is revered by his countrymen in death. He is looked upon as a great revolutionary leader who "made some mistakes."

Exiting from the back of the mausoleum, I ran the gamut of sellers with every imaginable type of Mao memorabilia and found Rick snuggled up against a pillar with his Nalgene bottle. I bought him an ice-cream bar for so generously being the one to forgo the Mao-sighting. What did we walk by on our way out of the square? The bag-check booth, stuck in a corner across from the mausoleum.

* * *

We stopped at a little restaurant almost across the street from our hotel that evening and put away a good portion of delicious steaming hot veggies on rice. The fact that the rice was only lukewarm should have triggered our common sense to leave it no matter how hungry we were. On the way to our room, we berated ourselves for not following the rule of only eating piping hot food and hoped for the best, but within a few hours we knew we were doomed.

The night from hell began: sweats, chills, and desperate wrangling over whose turn it was to use the squat toilet (we had not seen a Western toilet since Hong Kong). This one in our mid-priced hotel at least had a recessed porcelain basin with a flush mechanism. I could not have handled a fetid hole-in-the-ground toilet right then. But even the most deluxe squatter did diddly-squat to alleviate my quivering Western thighs and disastrous loss of equilibrium. I have since gained a new admiration for cultures where squatting is a natural stance from early childhood, not only for toileting, but for eating, relaxing, and even child-birthing.

Why did our first intestinal upheaval have to happen the night before our gala evening at the Beijing Opera, for which we had already purchased our tickets? By morning we were as weak as newborn kittens. We didn't budge from our room all day, still afflicted with bouts of cramping innards. By late afternoon we felt the worst was over. Not daring to consume anything more than water, we risked leaving for the opera.

Our first priority upon arriving at the theatre was to locate the *cesuo* (toilet) just in case. Then we settled down in our front row seats. With no English on the brochure, we had to guess what the play was about. Act I seemed to portray a lost princess and a fisherman who came to her rescue in his boat. The performers glided across the stage of fluttering blue paper water, seemingly without moving a muscle, as the story unravelled in song, dialogue, and mime to the clangs and screeches of traditional Chinese instruments. In Act II, the princess was abducted by scoundrels, and soldiers performed amazing acrobatic feats in the ensuing battle for her freedom. Luckily, our constitutions were stable enough that we did not have to miss a moment of the performance, which I truly enjoyed. Rick liked the cost: $11.65 Canadian for two.

* * *

Since our hotel was located only a block away from the pedestrian street Wangfujiang Dajie, we walked it daily en route to various sites, and almost daily we were gently accosted by university students promoting art shows. We figured they earned a commission if they managed to drag customers into the art shop they were representing, or maybe only if purchases were made. We did not succumb, but each youth was fairly fluent in English and seemed thrilled by the opportunity to converse with English-speaking foreigners. They were as keen to find out about our country as we were to find out more about the Chinese system.

They were amazed university students in Canada could live outside of strictly regulated university dorms, which they said were mandatory in China. They were also surprised that students could enter the field of their choice. One young lady related her story: "I was placed in Russian Language Studies because the country now needs Russian translators. I wanted biology, but if there is an overabundance of biologists it would not be good for the country to produce more."

* * *

There is a good-sized upper class in China, though the bulk of the population is working class and farmers. Though still very small in comparison, the middle class has been growing steadily during the past 20 years. We were told that many of the big stores in the cities are owned by wealthy families and are run by managers. The government still runs services such as the buses, trains, air transportation, and postal services. The Chinese government says the country is practising socialism with Chinese characteristics of capitalism. A friend of ours who conducts much business in China, including many visits to all parts of the country, views it as rampant capitalism.

Though people are allowed new freedoms nowadays, they are definitely still controlled. On the internet, Rick could get into Canadian national business news websites—such as the *Globe and Mail* and the *National Post*—but could not access a single article. We could get into our bank sites, but could not access any of our bank accounts. Our later travels to Nepal and India revealed China was the only country from which we could not access this information, leading us to believe there were blockers in place.

Almost every hotel room we had stayed in so far had a television that usually had one English channel. After a time it sunk in that all the news about China was positive. Happy faces were shown of people being relocated to the outskirts of the city ... while the *hutongs* where their families had lived for generations were being demolished. Most programs were accolades to China's progress in industry and technology. The only negatives we saw about anything having to do with China were occurrences considered detrimental to the good of the motherland, such as repeated coverage of Falun Gong followers self-immolating in Tiananmen Square (in protest of not having the freedom to practise their beliefs). Several were shown burning to death. Others, who were stopped before they managed to set themselves on fire or were found to be involved in Falun Gong in any way, were shown being sentenced to death; a warning to others not to be involved in this banned practice. The only news clips of anything outside of China were of meetings with various country leaders and the Chinese President.

* * *

In between taking in the sights, we were working on obtaining train tickets from Beijing to Xi'an. (Anyone out there who has travelled China by rail, we know we have your empathy.)

It was Thursday. We wanted to leave for Xi'an on Saturday. Our ticket quest commenced with a trip out to the train station where we were told that the earliest we could buy tickets for Saturday evening was on Friday morning. Er, okay?

We next took a cab from the train station to the CTS (China Travel Service) office, where we were told yes we could book our tickets on Thursday for Saturday, but we would have to come back the next day to "pick up" the tickets. We were back to square one. If we had to go back for tickets anywhere, it might as well be to the train station, which by taxi was an hour from our hotel (as opposed to two hours to the CTS office).

Checking our guidebook, we decided to check out a CITS office (China International Travel Service). They were like the train station, and couldn't book seats for Saturday until Friday morning.

"Well, can we book today for Friday?"

"No soft seats Fly-day," said the clerk.

"Can you believe this?" I looked over at Rick.

Back at the hotel, I phoned the Foreign Tourist Hotline and relayed our dilemma to a Ms. Wong, who said it was her job to help tourists with such problems. She was also restricted from purchasing tickets for Saturday before Friday morning, and she would not be able to aid us with ticket purchases tomorrow as Friday was her day off.

"How about soft-seat tickets for Friday?" I had to sit down before I fainted when this fabulous lady guaranteed us these tickets ... if we could come back to the train station before 5:00 p.m. that day. Alrighty-righty-then! There was no way we were losing Ms. Wong.

Back at the train station, as per instructions from Ms. Wong, we went up to the Inquiry Desk to ask for her.

"Call Ms. Wong please," did not get a response in either English or our version of Mandarin. The man at the desk summoned someone from somewhere that spoke a little English. This fellow led me to a phone in a dingy back room where I called Ms. Wong's number. She would be down from her upper-floor office directly.

Raven-black tresses levitated around the divinely radiant face of Ms. Wong as she gracefully descended the mountain of stairs. Moses-like, she led us to the very same counter we had first come to early that morning. Raising her pencil-staff, and with the slightest nod at the lowly ticket agent, she parted the crowd to allow herself immediate access. She brought us to the promised land of two heavenly soft-seat tickets for Friday. Amen.

* * *

While on the subject of tickets: there is a dual system in China for pricing, one for locals and one for foreigners. This duality is not only for train and bus tickets, but also for admissions, as well as most hotels. We came to expect it, and the cost was still very reasonable even with the tourist price. For example, our train from Beijing to Xi'an cost $37.73 Canadian. We could eat all day for $5.00 Canadian—both of us. Rick relaxed, feeling we might be able to meet our financial goal for the year.

Xi'an

Xi'an city, with a population of 7 million, is in the province of Shaanxi. Most of the province's 36 million people live in the central and southern regions, as the northern territories are geographically uninhabitable, with vertical cliffs and ravines leading up to the Great Wall.

The May First was a gem of a hotel: large, bright, comfortable rooms, with the most sensational dancehall-size restaurant on the ground floor crammed with dozens of 6-metre (20-ft) wooden tables and benches. From the open stainless-steel kitchens along one side wall, wiry cooks at a running pace churned out every conceivable dish one could wish for, all (vitally) steaming hot and oh-so-delicious. I would wager half the city frequented this restaurant at least once a week, as there was never a time from early morning until late in the evening that it was not hopping. Added to these amenities was its prime location in the centre of the main street, just down from the Bell Tower.

Consequently, the Bell Tower (Zhong Lou) was a good place to start our sightseeing. Originally built in the 14th century, then rebuilt by the Qing in 1739, this sizable structure dominates the centre of Xi'an. The large gong bell was once used to indicate the time of day. It was comical to see tourists pull back the big pendulum, releasing it to contact the sphere for a resounding gong, which in turn triggered attendants to dart out from behind a booth and point to a sign. The nondescript sign—indicating "one jiao (one-tenth of a yuan) per gong"—was usually missed. When pointed out, most tourists dug in their pockets to pay up.

On the lower floor, musicians performed on ancient instruments. Climbing to the top of the tower, we saw a shocking layer of smog suspended over the city. Since our arrival a few days earlier, we had already started feeling its effects. My contact lenses developed a thick film. I had to resort to wearing my glasses. Though the onset was in Beijing, by Xi'an we were both manifesting symptoms of the "Chinese hack"; mine worse than Rick's. Our son and his partner had warned us about being plagued by a deep, phlegm-ridden cough, such as the one that had consumed them for the three months they travelled through the interior of China. They had not been able to shake it until they left the country. Mornings were the worst, reminding me of a few old chain smokers I knew.

The new Kaiyuan (which appropriately translates to "bring money") Mall was in the final stages of construction across from the Bell Tower. Workers in front of the mall were in the process of erecting a sign between two metal posts 9 metres (30 ft) in the air. We watched as they first had to build scaffolding out of bamboo poles to get up to the sign's level. With no safety harness, work boots or hard hats, one fellow stood 3 metres (10 ft) off the ground on a horizontal pole, which was tied to several vertical poles. As he wavered precariously in the air, he was passed another pole by his assistant on the ground, which he proceeded to hoist over his head and tie to the vertical poles, thus adding a new horizontal level. This exercise was repeated until the desired height was reached. I held my breath each time he balanced like a tightrope walker on the wavy bamboo, keeping his hands free for knotting the ropes. It had the highest accident potential we ever remembered seeing, with no disability settlements to fall back on (pardon the pun) if he should lose his footing.

Noting lights on top of the Bell Tower, we also saw workmen up there doing repairs. There were no guardrails or any other safety equipment on the metal roof with its 45-degree slant. There is a workers' compensation program in China, but companies are extremely proficient at getting around paying out monies. Recently, advocates for seriously injured workers ("serious" meaning they have lost limbs) had gone to court for them, but if adherence to safety standards was any indicator, companies were still not too worried about the ramifications of work-related accidents.

Another construction-related modus operandi that shocked our Western sentiments were the worksites paved with cots. A big new McDonald's Restaurant was going up at the Kaiyuan Mall. Dozens of narrow canvas beds with collapsible frames were lined up against the building, with men sleeping amid the bright lights, noise, dust, and debris until shift change, when the off-shift workers took their turn on the cots. Again, safety regulations and workers' rights were unheard of; the workers felt lucky to have jobs.

The Immortalized Army of Qin

Our senses were juddered by the stunning magnitude of this memorial to one man: 6,000 life-sized soldiers, many were standing upright and in battle formation facing the entrance of the enormous earthen vault. The terracotta warriors, created to guard the tomb of Qin Shi Huang (259–210

BC), were proclaimed a UNESCO World Heritage Site in 1987, and are one of the most important archaeological finds of the 20th century.

Intrigued by the rare artistry we'd first seen in a documentary several years before, we could hardly believe we were now standing before this awe-inspiring display. The ancient army fills three consecutive vaults (unromantically called Pits 1, 2, and 3) covering an area of 16,300 square metres (172,224 sq ft), located 35 kilometres (22 mi) east of Xi'an. The excavation of this national treasure began in 1974, after pieces of terracotta were fortuitously discovered by peasants digging a well. The site was opened to the public in 1979.

The power wielded by Qin Shi Huang, albeit mostly by oppression and brutality, was of titanic proportions. Born Ying Zheng, after uniting the six warring states for the first time in history he proclaimed himself Qin Shi Huang (First Emperor of China—yes, this is the same ferocious ruler who built the original Great Wall). He made positive advancements in the standardizing of currency, measurements, and the written script; contrarily, he ordered any books that challenged his beliefs be burned. His passion, however, was executing plans for his splendid necropolis, which he started building soon after succeeding his father at the age of 13. An estimated 720,000 labourers and artisans toiled during his 38-year rule, many of them dying during construction.

We proceeded slowly to view the legion in the first and largest pit, marvelling at the unique countenance of each warrior. Some are proud or fierce; others are contemplative or have a sliver of a smile. They are also different ages, and have a variety of builds. Some have beards, and many have locks swept up into ornate topknots. Speculation is that they were modelled after Qin Shi Huang's own fighting men. Bulky, belted knee-high tunics over short trousers, puttees winding from ankle to knee, and creases worn across the toes of curved shoes complete the clay-carved uniforms. The once flesh-tinted skin and brightly coloured garb have succumbed to the ravishment of time.

Moving on to Pit 2, we noted the specialization of the 1,000 soldiers. A total of 334 are archers. The front half are in a kneeling position and clad with heavy armour; the remainder stand behind, poised to shoot over their heads. I became captivated by the numerous horses that followed, some beside charioteers primed to drive the 64 chariots or with cavalrymen to the left of their bridles. The bulging muscular flanks of these steeds strained forward; their flaring nostrils belched streams of vapour that evaporated as I blinked away the trickery of the sculptor's genius.

In the last pit, along with a lone chariot drawn by another four equine beauties, 68 special commanders are, interestingly, positioned randomly, rather than in military formation.

Many of the warriors originally held weapons of the day. Placards describe the crossbows, long bows, spears, and dagger axes that were among the 10,000 pieces removed and sorted to date. Arrowheads contained a poisonous lead alloy. Bronze swords were found in the hands of generals and senior officers. Surface treatment made these swords resistant to rust and corrosion; they are said to be still sharp today.

The lengths of the pits are partitioned with thick brick walls, with corridors left between, upon which the soldiers stand. Cresting the support walls, there were once wooden roofs of stout timbers and crossbeams topped with woven matting and clay to prevent water seepage—all hidden from sight by a deep covering of earth. Though plundering rebel troops, grave robbers, and collapsed roof sections took their toll, this skilful construction made it possible for the fairly intact pieces of this venerable legion to be reassembled and to once again stand on the 2,000-year-old floor of black brick.

The Emperor's army is believed to comprise only one-fifth of the subterranean mortuary complex. In 1980, a pair of half-scale bronze chariots and horses was unearthed 20 metres (66 ft) east of the mausoleum. Eager archaeologists are hankering for the green light to be given by the Chinese government to excavate the 47-metre (154-ft) grass-covered mound 1.5 kilometres (1 mi) from where Rick and I now stood. According to theories based on preliminary exploration, historical records, and conjecture, a replica of the imperial palace still remains entombed with rivers of mercury to create the image of flowing water; satellite tombs for dignitaries, princes and princesses; pits of buried horses and rare birds; and the burial chamber of the Emperor himself.

The daylight dwindled. The tour groups took their leave. We had time before the last public bus would arrive. In solitude we lingered at the entrance, the figures becoming draped in an eerie twilight. Eventually, in response to a waving attendant signalling closing time, we bid farewell to the warriors, yearning to know the story behind each pair of silent eyes.

* * *

Waiting for bus #306 to get back to Xi'an, we mistakenly boarded a "hawker's bus" with the number 306 on the dashboard. These alternate buses whip around the city bus routes, hollering their destinations at each public transit stop and anyplace they see a bunch of people that might be enticed onto the bus, packing them in until way over capacity. The 33°C (91°F) temperature outside spiked to 40°C (104°F) in the bus and we were in for a tour of the winding narrow back streets. Nearing what we recognized to be the city centre and not knowing where the bus might head from there, we bailed and took a taxi back to the May First.

It was great to be home. We glanced around for the little ragamuffins who always greeted us. Every country has its beggars and street people, but we found it very difficult to witness the small children with mangled legs begging. Unable to walk with their atrophied and twisted limbs, they dragged themselves up and down the sidewalk with a donation can. We had read that some children (orphans, or children sold or given away by a starving family), were controlled by a "boss" and were maimed intentionally so they could go into the begging business. Others were cases of a legitimate deformity, where the child was bringing money into the family. The first scenario was clearly more horrific, as at least if the child had a family, there was some hope the treatment of the child would be better.

Two little boys in particular—approximately seven or eight years old—frequented the sidewalks for a block in front of the May First. We always tossed coins in their cans, and since a contribution was hit and miss with the locals, whenever we appeared they scuttled over, the little leather patches on the cheeks of their split pants making pitiful scraping sounds as they pulled themselves along. These commonly used split pants, eliminating the need for diapers, are fine if the child is young enough to be carried or able to walk, but for these children the open backsides resulted in weeping sores from dragging on the cement.

Only one approached us today with his eyelash-batting plea. Having noticed these children look up longingly at the food sold from the take-out windows in front of the May First, this day we thought of getting this little fellow a treat. I pointed to the drink machine. His head bobbed up and down. I pointed to the orange drink. He shook his head and pointed further to the right. I pointed to Coke. His head bobbed up and down. Rick and I relished every minute. Rick pointed to some meat on skewers. The boy once again nodded furiously as he sipped on the straw protruding from his paper cup. We purchased a chicken and a beef skewer. When I turned to hand them to him, something was amiss. His face showed unadulterated fear. He turned to flee. Then as if acutely torn, he reached up for the skewers, stashed his loot in his can, and scuttled off.

I became cognizant of the small crowd that had gathered around us. Scanning the faces, I tried to discern if it was one of these people who had caused this child's extreme distress.

"Does anyone speak English?" brought no response. We walked a little way down the sidewalk, but the boy was no longer in sight. Still feeling flummoxed and uncomfortable with the situation, we went inside the hotel. We never saw these little boys again. We watched for them all week and tried to inquire, to no avail.

Were they removed from the area? Was the little one who accepted food punished? Or—worse yet—did someone deem him more trouble than the worth of the coins he collected? A sinking feeling flooded us. *Where are you? Where are you?* Feeling somehow responsible for the fate of these children, we thought if we could have relived that moment in our lives, we would have just dropped the usual few coins in his can. We guessed that our gift of food had been detrimental to these children. Possibly, the authorities banned these child beggars from this central district since it would be shameful for visitors to the country to see them. Acting from our North American ideology, we had forgotten we were in a country where individual rights were almost nonexistent. Our heavy footprints will forever haunt us.

As China becomes increasingly more open to the eyes of the world, we wonder what changes in human rights this will precipitate.

* * *

To start the process to get train tickets to Chengdu, based on info in Lonely Planet, we went to the Bell Tower Hotel to purchase them.

The gentleman manning the ticket office said, "No tickets!" before we had even finished our request.

"Are you sold out today?" I inquired.

"No, never train tickets," he snapped.

Oh, no, not again! It appeared he was about to lock up the office and didn't want to be bothered.

Off we went to the CITS office (China International Travel Service). I was right about the Bell Tower employee, as this agent told us we should have been able to get tickets there. We were also informed that there were only hard seats available for the next few days. Shucks. We weren't really keen on coming back day after day trying to get soft seats, so we made a snap decision to take the hard seats.

* * *

Tuesday, August 28 was a rainy day. Check-out time at our hotel was noon. The train did not leave until 10:00 p.m. Luckily, we were able to store our backpacks at the May First. We had a great day frequenting malls and indulging in snacks at cafés. In the late afternoon we both spotted a movie theatre. It was still sprinkling and our feet were crying for mercy. Our "let's do it" nod led us to the ticket wicket.

The only movie I recognized by the posters was an oldie, Jurassic Park III. Pointing to the poster with the word "subtitled" at the bottom, the lady took our yuan. It came to less than five bucks (Canadian) for two. Armed with a big bag of popcorn, we proceeded inside to where the bellowing and screeching of dinosaurs was already underway. We groped our way through the dark to a vacant spot along the very uncomfortable wooden church-pew seating.

The movie was dubbed in Cantonese, and there were subtitles all right ... in Japanese. It was silly of us to have assumed the subtitles would be in English. But the theatre was dry and toasty warm, and by the time the show ended it was time to pick up our backpacks and head for the train.

Xi'an to Chengdu

The station was as jam-packed as a stadium for an NHL Stanley Cup playoff game. The loudspeaker blaring intermittently added to the bedlam of noisy, sweaty, rushing crowds jostling their way in all directions. We found the platform indicated on our tickets. The benches were taken, so we found a vacant spot and sat on our packs until departure time.

Everyone should do the hard seat thing once. Pushed and squeezed along by bodies charging into the coach, we didn't understand the rush when the seating was assigned, but it soon became clear that there was limited space for luggage. By the time we found our seats, it took three men plus Rick to squash our packs on top of the mountain of baggage already precariously spilling from the racks above the seats.

On either side of the aisle, the seating consisted of wooden bench seats facing each other a few feet apart; the high, straight backs were bare wood, and the seat portion had a mere sliver of padding. There were three numbers on the back of each bench section. Two ladies took up the whole of our bench. I pointed to the numbers on our tickets, and we wedged ourselves in the middle and window seats, displacing one of the two women, who disappeared down the aisle. It was still mighty tight. These seats were made for three Chinese, or two and a half Caucasians. A family of five was sitting across from us. After all the seats were filled, more people piled in and perched on their stuffed red-checkered plastic luggage in the aisles.

We ni hao'd everyone around us. Shy nods were returned. Not long after getting underway, some children aged 11 or 12 came by to practise their English on us. We, of course, tried out our Mandarin on them. The grown-ups around us instantly warmed up and attempted to converse with us through the young interpreters. Several four- or five-year-olds used every excuse to race past so they could holler "Herro!" The din of people talking above each other and laughing boisterously as well as eating, hacking, smoking, spitting on the floor, and throwing garbage out the windows threw us into sensory overload. I have yet to glean the secret of these slight-statured people who put away half their weight in food at one sitting. Besides emptying big baskets brought on with them, passengers were keen to get the attention of vendors stepping over bodies to sell their fare. The most popular item seemed to be noodles in Styrofoam containers, drenched in boiling water drawn from the spout of a large, dinted metal container. We subsisted on crackers to ward off vertigo and nausea. Besides the insane degree of activity, alas, our hard seats were opposite to the forward motion of the train, and through the mountains the train simulated a roller coaster, gaining speed on the downward slope, then jerking before the next climb.

Being a 19-hour trip, it was inevitable that we would at some point succumb to the call of nature, but nothing could have prepared us for the gag-inducing hole-in-the-floor train toilets. The novelty of hard-seat travel was fading fast. The lights were blindingly bright all night. At about 3:00 a.m., I wished my camera was not in my backpack: every last person in the coach was asleep except for us, and every position and inch of space was being utilized. Snoring bodies covered the floor, or were draped with legs and arms askew on the seats. We kept glancing at an old-timer to see how long he could sleep standing, supported only by stacked-up luggage. It was impossible for us to get comfortable. Once I woke up as the lady across from us threw up, just missing Rick's shoe. We collapsed into a sporadic pattern of fitful sleep and being jarred awake by some racket, or by our own circulation-distressed limbs twitching out of control. It made for a beastly night.

After what seemed like forever, the fields outside the train window became suffused with the pale light of dawn, but there were still another 11 hours to go ... the slowest 11 hours of my life! I have never seen anything more celestial than the Chengdu Station still swathed in welcoming rays at 5:00 p.m. We hobbled off the train with elephant-sized ankles.

"Hey, remember our motto, we are not here to suffer? Let's not ever do this again."

"Ditto," Rick replied.

What is the norm for people in one part of the world is no longer even a remote reality in other countries today, so scrap my previous comment that everyone should go hard seat once.

Chatting Our Way Through Chengdu

We settled into Chengdu's backpacker favourite, the Traffic Hotel (Jiao Tong): clean, spacious rooms, satellite television, and located next to the bus depot and lots of good restaurants. Dorms were 40 yuan, doubles with shared baths were 100 yuan ($18.86), and doubles with private baths were 210 yuan ($39.62). I asked for a double with a shared bath. They only had high-end rooms available, with private baths, they said. Really? Or did they look at our age and figure we could pay the extra? Even bean-counter Rick did not want to try somewhere else after the hard-seat night we had endured. Besides, once settled in our expensive room, I could keep checking back to see if a mid-range room came available.

It really was rather sweet not to have to trek down the hall to the loo, especially through the night ... and hallelujah, there was a bathtub instead of a shower. I foresaw many luxuriously steamy, bubbly soaks, not to mention an ample laundry tub.

Breakfast was included in all the room prices. The first morning we thought we had ascended into heaven. There was a choice of a Chinese breakfast with the usual fish or egg drop soup with doughy buns—which to us was the height of foreignness—or (are you ready?) an English breakfast! We could have either oatmeal with toast and jam or eggs with toast and jam, and either selection came with a banana and coffee. What more could one ask for?

Well, I'm not normally a whiner or complainer, but the kitchen staff did not know the meaning of toast—it is not warm bread—and it had been forever since I had sunk my teeth into a nicely browned crunchy piece of toast. The next day I pointed to the word toast on the chalkboard and said "kafeise (brown)." Still got warm bread. The following morning I tried "hei (black)." No luck. Someone suggested "huang (yellow)" or "ying (hard)." Ying worked the best. Delightfully crisp, not-quite-brown pieces of toast began to arrive with my order. The server was always apologetic when leaving this outré daily bread, so I overemphasized my "xie-xie (thank you)" while pointing to the toast to let her know this was a good thing (well, as good as it was going to get).

* * *

Each Chinese city has a flavour all its own. Chengdu (meaning Perfect Metropolis) has a population of almost 11 million and is the capital of Sichuan, one of the largest and most heavily populated provinces. We found the coexistence of traditional and modern ways of life vividly pronounced here: local basket vendors walked alongside business-types toting cellphones, while traditional architecture was left standing next to high-rises in the same neighbourhood. Outside of the central area there were refreshing tree-lined boulevards. More shopkeepers knew some English, leastwise "Hello." Chengdu even boasted an English Corner, where those wishing to speak English congregated every Wednesday and Friday evening to hear speakers vying with one another to draw the largest crowd with their rhetoric.

Though it rained during our first week in Chengdu, we were finding once more that all that grey in the sky was not cloud cover but a canopy of smog, to which my worsening cough was attestation.

Influenced by our previous (excruciatingly painful) booking experiences, we decided to put sightseeing on hold in favour of commencing our travel plans for Tibet. First we investigated the possibility of bus travel, and found out that foreigners have trouble getting on the buses which locals travel on. No matter: they were not for us in any case after our hard-seat ordeal.

Foreigners can go by sleeper bus, paying double what a Chinese citizen would pay for a three-day, four-night marathon over rough roads in decrepit buses. I was worn out just thinking about it.

The only sane thing to do—especially at our age—was to fly. Proceeding to a travel agency for an airline ticket, we were told that the only way foreigners can fly into Tibet (legally) was to take a tour package, which includes airfare, round trip, three days' accommodation in a dorm, and a few guided sightseeing tours.

"Must take tour" (which cost 2,700Y each) did not sit well with us. Direct to the airline office we marched. There were five flights to Lhasa per day and tickets cost 1,270Y each (the foreigner's price). The airlines would sell us a ticket, but told us we must have a permit to enter Lhasa. No one knew of a place to get this elusive permit, except at a travel agency as part of a tour package.

We did not want to miss Tibet, so an air package tour it would have to be. With this sorted out, but not ready to commit to a date yet, we geared up for a few weeks more in Chengdu.

Note: There are now direct trains from Chengdu, Beijing, and other major cities. Also, the highway options have been beefed up with tours that stop each night at hotels along the way and vary from between 9 and 18 days in duration.

* * *

The Giant Panda Research Base was first on both our lists ... or so I thought.

"What? Get up at 5:30 a.m. just to see some furballs?" Rick lamented.

"If we don't get there between eight and ten we'll miss the pandas feeding, and only see them at their other favourite pastime: sleeping."

Rick caved, as he really did not want to miss these unique mammals, who are (surprisingly) related to the raccoon as well as to the bear.

The Base was started in 1990 in an attempt to breed this endangered species in a natural environment, opening to the public in 1995. It is believed there are only about 1,000 pandas left in the wilds of northern Sichuan, Gansu, and Shaanxi provinces. Other near-extinct species in these mountainous regions include the snow leopard and the golden monkey.

Pandas were mentioned in Chinese writings 3,000 years ago, and even more startling, the earliest panda remains date back 600,000 years. It was not until the mid-1800s that Westerners found out about them, and though short-lived, the demand for panda furs became a vogue.

A decreasing food supply is now seen as the greatest detriment to the panda's survival. Each adult panda consumes up to 20 kilograms (44 lb) of bamboo per day, to compensate for a digestive tract that absorbs very little nutritional value from the bamboo. They are—surprisingly—also carnivorous; but post–cub stage, their slow movements do not result in many catches.

* * *

Our early rising was rewarded. Two full-grown pandas lay on their backs, their white furry stomachs spread out to form a banquet-sized table; thick black hind legs splayed out from the bottom. Glossy eyes embedded in black fur circles casually looked us over. Black ear-spheres twitched above their white fuzzy faces. Soft huffs of contentment accompanied the leisurely swipe of a bamboo branch from one side of their mouths to the other, leaving them with a mouthful of leaves to munch. They next nibbled the tender twig bark from the branch. Often they nonchalantly stretched over to collect a branch or two from the other's stash, with no objections from the other party. It was easy to see why miniature replicas of these loveable creatures are cuddly favourites with children.

The Base proudly boasted four new babies, bred by artificial insemination. One was being cared for by its mother. The other three were in incubators. It is hoped that a future expansion of the Base to 204 hectares (504 acres), which would be five times its current size, will inspire the giant panda to procreate naturally, with the greater similarity to wilderness terrain.

Outside the nursery, there was none of the adult indolence in five young pandas at play. Through an enclosure we watched them climb spindly trees, stopping to tug at each other with the hand not clinging to a branch. This roughhousing often left a youngster momentarily airborne but always able to catch another limb. Another game was to scramble up and down as fast as they could. At one point, three ended up on the same slender trunk, causing it to bend almost in half. Just when it looked about to snap, the chubbiest lost his grip, fell, and bounced several times when he hit the dirt.

One trail led to the Red Panda or Lesser Panda area. These are so different from their white-and-black relatives that the majority of us wouldn't recognize them as pandas. This type of panda is reddish-brown in colour with a long tail and a narrow fox-like face; it is also much smaller in size. The adults spend much of their time in the upper branches of trees, making it difficult to view them through thick foliage.

I could have watched these enthralling creatures forever, or at least for the rest of the day. Rick reminded me that there was no public bus service to and from the Base. We thought we were so clever taking an early morning taxi and beating the tour buses, which gave us almost an hour before the bulk of visitors filled the grounds. By 1:00 p.m., we thought we had better check the parking lot to see if any taxis were lying in wait for a fare. If not, we could eat humble pie and beg a ride back to Chengdu on one of the tour buses that would soon be departing.

Finding no taxi waiting, we chanced a walk out to the highway.

"Hey, Rick, is that a mirage I'm seeing?" I squinted against the sun at a gaudy yellow vehicle approaching from the distance. Rick was already galloping down the side of the road, flagging to beat the band.

"Can you believe it?" Rick called back as he charged for the taxi, which was pulling off onto the shoulder and stopping 6 metres (20 ft) away. *Wu fu lin men* (the arrival of five happinesses), in the form of one beautiful taxicab.

* * *

The next day we had an engagement at the South Ocean School on the outskirts of Chengdu. Dressed in our finest duds (albeit faded and a bit frayed around the edges), we waited outside the front entrance of our hotel for our pickup, which had been arranged by the school. A black Mercedes— no less—pulled up, and a uniformed chauffeur got out. Spotting us, he said "Butroor?" Close enough. He opened the rear door with a flourish.

We were on our way to meet the principal and visit with the students. On our second-last day in Beijing, we had found an ad in a brochure at Starbucks for English-teaching jobs in China. We had called the number, and a Ms. Teng had wanted us to meet with her in Beijing. As this was not feasible with our departure tickets purchased for the next day, she said she would call ahead to Chengdu and give us a contact number for when we arrived there.

A warm welcome and a tour of the facilities were given us by Gena Wang, the Assistant Principal and Director of South Ocean International School, which left us impressed with the grounds and buildings. South Ocean was a private boarding school with an enrolment of approximately 2,800 students from kindergarten through to grade 12; obviously for the very rich.

In an office area, eight students 15 or 16 years of age sat on chairs in a semicircle, waiting for the two empty chairs facing them to be filled ... by us. Members of the school staff—including Ms. Wang—were within listening distance of the sitting area.

Introductions out of the way, we had a delightful exchange with the students, who were keen to hear about our travels and what it was like in Canada. Their English was very good, and all had decisive career goals and very positive outlooks on future opportunities. A couple of the boys were fixated on the subject of workload. They felt they were under too much pressure to always focus on school assignments. They would have liked more time to do what they wanted: to listen to music, or travel, or read books other than those on the school curriculum. A version of my old standby regarding the importance of education spilled forth—the one our grandchildren are no doubt tired of hearing.

"Who knows what an analogy is?"

"When something disagrees with your body and you get a rash," a young man named Bai offered.

"Well, that's an 'allergy.' It sounds very similar."

A resourceful person thought to bring in a marker and a sheet of paper to print both words and to illustrate my following comparison. "An analogy is when one compares a likeness between things that are otherwise different. Life is in stages, and this is the stage in your lives for learning. I will use an analogy between 'constructing a building' and 'your education.' The first stage of constructing a building is to prepare the land, to level and pack it—this is like your time as a baby and toddler. Next comes the building foundation—your education. This is the stage in your life for laying a foundation for your future. The stronger and bigger the foundation, the better it can support the many storeys, which are the remaining years and stages of your life. Aim to have a foundation able to hold up a skyscraper."

The two hours at the school flew by. We left far richer from the encounter. The exuberance of these young people was contagious. Caught up in the moment, we were ready to take up a totally unexpected offer from Ms. Wang to teach English at the school ... almost. There was an immediate opening for kindergarten. Knowing our nerves would be frayed beyond repair with 30 ankle-sized munchkins with no concept of the vital phrases "sit down" or "be quiet," we declined, but exchanged e-mails for future position openings in the higher grades.

After a month of not encountering many English speakers, we found Chengdu an oasis for discourse in our mother tongue. A favourite spot to frequent was Paul's Restaurant, which was always filled with travellers, each with a great story. We also latched onto the Highfly Eatery, which had a Chinese version of pizza (a doughy crust slathered with tomato soup and cheese). The restaurant was full of striking photos of Tibetan people. Winna, the restaurant owner, was a font of information on the Tibetan villages in the northern regions of Sichuan province. She had visited these villages many times and felt they portrayed the most authentic Tibetan culture, saying they were "not yet influenced by tourism, like Lhasa."

The second time we dined at the Highfly, the next table resounded with English chatter. Soon we were rearranging the furniture to join our tables. Pol, a handsome and suave bloke from England in his late 20s, taught English at the American English Institute. His two attractive, similarly aged Chinese lady friends were Elaine and Juliet. Elaine was an executive secretary at a large computer hardware company. She spoke excellent English, and had found Pol a few months before to tutor Juliet. Juliet was doing quite well in Chinglish, as she facetiously dubbed it, but mostly sat silent as the pace of conversation kept accelerating from the learning mode. Juliet and her husband Li (who was not there that day) had relocated from Beijing a year ago, when Li was promoted to a top executive position with the same computer company Elaine worked for.

Pol suddenly glanced at his watch, and in a panic announced he had a class at the institute in 45 minutes. He invited us all to come along and asked Rick and me to take part in the conversation class where students practised their English with questions on any topic. Why not?

We paid our portion of the bill. Pol fumbled for his wallet long enough for Elaine to say their lunch was on her. Then we all squeezed into a cab and headed to the other side of town. Pol rode shotgun up front and hassled the driver to speed up, knowing he had not left sufficient time to get from the restaurant to the institute. The four of us, crammed in the back, became increasingly antsy with the need to unfold our contorted bodies. Almost before the car came to a complete stop in front of the institute, Pol bolted out of the car and into the building, leaving Elaine to settle the fare with the cab driver.

The mostly adult students had been waiting for 25 minutes. Everyone introduced themselves, and Rick and I, as guests, gave them a bit of our background. The students seemed shy to ask questions until we broke into three groups, with Pol, Rick, and me each heading a group, while Juliet and Elaine opted to sit together and chat. The pleasurable non-stop interaction went on for two hours, and even the students with minimal English ventured comments.

After class, the owner of the institute and a few of his colleagues invited us all downstairs to the first-floor restaurant for a feast of assorted dishes. Taxiing back to the hotel, we got out with Pol (who coincidentally also called the Traffic Hotel home, paying a monthly rate), while Elaine and Juliet went on to their homes.

Such rich experiences with people that you chance to meet while travelling are what hook people into this mode of life. I have heard travel compared to an adulterous affair: excitement charged with unpredictable twists and turns.

* * *

It still rained for the greater part of every day for another week. Donning our Gore-Tex jackets and opening our umbrellas, we trekked out in a different direction each morning, sometimes to a particular site, but mostly with no destination in mind. We can honestly say we got to know our way around Chengdu.

School entrances were decorated lavishly in red and yellow dragons, balloons, and messages painted on large air-filled plastic archways. Teachers stood along the pathways to the entrance each morning calling out welcoming greetings to arriving students, turning the first week back to school into a grand celebration.

Now bikes are ubiquitous throughout the country, but as we moved farther away from the east coast, the number of bikers seemed to increase exponentially. It was engaging to behold a solid band of a hundred bicycles moving synchronously, zigging and zagging like a school of fish, flowing as melodiously as notes in a well-orchestrated symphony. The harmony was occasionally interrupted by the clash of tires or fenders. The parties involved inspected the damage to their bikes (and sometimes bodies), then carried on, seemingly undaunted.

As we walked the streets it became apparent that Chengdu had not escaped the destruction of its traditional neighbourhoods. Wooden barricades with bright painted lettering in both Chinese and English were outside of demolition areas. One such sign read: Realistic Progression for the Future Appearance of Chengdu.

The high-rises replacing the old structures were too expensive for the displaced residents. We wondered where these multitudes would live. Open opposition to such government decisions rarely occurs here. In North America the protest would have been thunderous.

* * *

The Tomb of Wang Jian (an emperor from the Kingdom of Shu) was our destination on the first sunny day. We totally miscalculated the distance (even with a map). Finally reaching the gates to the site, we figured it had been 10 to 12 kilometres (6–7 mi). The write-up in the guidebook sounded better than what we found: a few ancient sarcophagi with smallish stone musicians around the bottom playing instruments.

By then we were out of water and famished. Back on the street, it didn't take long to gauge the futility of finding a taxi in such a remote area. We started marching. Halfway back, we were completely enervated. Hunting for sustenance became critical. A restaurant nearby looked promising. There were no other customers inside, but being around three in the afternoon, we ignored our "The busier the restaurant, the fresher the food" rule. Besides, the moment we walked in chairs were pulled out for us, cups of tea were poured; we were fussed over to the nth degree. How could we leave?

Deciding vegetables and plain rice to be our safest bet, we said "Shucai" and "Bai fan" and were met with understanding nods ... or so we thought. We got noodles and meat in a sauce.

I asked, "Na shi shenme? Ji?" and hoped their agreeable nods were a confirmation to my question as to whether the chunks were chicken. Whatever it was, it was tasty and steaming hot.

With renewed energy, we were off. I turned back and took a picture of the restaurant's sign. I figured if we were to meet our end with ptomaine poisoning, the photo found in our camera would serve as evidence to link our deaths with this establishment. I was gripped by pangs of queasiness as we passed the windows of nearby restaurants and saw slithering snakes doing their utmost to escape their large glass jar prisons. We would never know. No ill effects came of the meal, but we adamantly agreed to always carry extra water and snacks in the future.

Most of our evening meals were partaken at our own convenient Traffic Hotel Restaurant. Though the supper menu was not extensive, the toothsome fare made up for it, along with English descriptions of the selections. As for other eating establishments in our hood, the one and only time we came across English under the Chinese characters was at a hot pot place around the corner from our hotel. After being seated and reading the menu, we got up and politely said we would be back later, but never did. The restaurant bragged of such delicacies as cow belly, goose lips, and loach soup; the only one we may have considered was the loach soup, knowing it was a type of fish and thereby fitting into our definition of edibles.

The Sichuan chicken at the Traffic Hotel Restaurant was wonderfully volcanic. My palate is sensitive to spicy food, so I would pick out the chicken pieces, and eat a lot of rice. Rick could not get enough, he devoured the succulent chunks of chicken dripping with the peppery sauce; when the chicken was finished he would put down his chopsticks and use a soup spoon to scoop up the remaining sauce. The next evening the restaurant was out of Sichuan chicken, so Rick ordered the Sichuan beef (every bit as zesty).

Rick said between mouthfuls, "This is going to be my standard order." By the next morning, he had changed his mind. The fire-breathing sauce had worked its way through to other orifices. There is no delicate way to put this: he blew his guts out. Hemorrhoids, for the first time in his life. Walking was out of the question for a few days. Trying to explain wanting medication for this malady was hilarious, but we did walk away from the small pharmacy with a tube of something. Beware all who partake in Sichuan cuisine.

Once he recovered, we hopped a bus to Chongqing, which is on the Yangtze—the longest river in China and third-longest in the world. We had debated whether to take the economy three-day, four-night boat cruise down the Yangtze (Chang Jiang) to see the Three Gorges Dam Project. First class would have given us a private room. The second through fifth classes were shared rooms and baths (the higher the class number the more beds per room). Several younger adventurers, having just returned, told us of the cramped conditions, which prompted a realization that we were not in the mood for discomfort right then.

Some of the dam facts: this mega project, which has been underway since 1994, was completely operational a year ahead of schedule in 2008, with 26 generators churning out hydroelectric power. Six additional generators, currently being installed in the underground power plant, are expected to be functional in 2011. Yet to be completed is the ship lift (or lift lock) to transfer boats between levels. The total cost is in the range of $27 billion US. It has been called the biggest construction project since the Great Wall, and it is now the world's largest water reservoir. When the last six generators are up and running, it will generate as much electricity as 18 nuclear power plants, and will supply one-fifth of the electrical power used in the country. Another pro is said to be flood control; the natural catastrophic floods that have plagued the area over the years have been reduced by the provision of flood storage space. On the downside, 1–2 million people have been displaced, archaeological sites have been flooded, and major ecological changes have occurred, making the building of this dam controversial both in China and abroad.

Our four and a half hours by bus from Chengdu brought us to a different world. Chongqing is built on a steep hill. Because of that, the numerous bikes seen in other locales dwindled to a scant few here. Heavy industrial development and total lack of pollution control made Chengdu look pristine in comparison. Each morning the low-lying grey smog was so thick it totally blocked out the river across the road from our room at the Fu Yuan Hotel. When the sun finally broke through the haze around noon, the rays were thick with particles spinning and dancing to the movement of citizens milling about. I fit right in with the hacking crowd. It was hard to tell the age of most buildings. All were covered by a sooty residue; only the design differentiated traditional architecture from more modern structures.

The main means of transporting goods throughout the city was by carriers: men and women on foot with baskets suspended from wooden neck-yokes, the weight forcing their heads into humble bows under the strain.

The uptown area is literally at the top of a series of wide, well-worn steps (228, to be exact). Every few steps, on both sides from bottom to top, vendors display every conceivable item for sale.

Our favourite walk was along the Yangtze. Concrete embankments run along the river. People sat dangling fishing lines affixed to bamboo poles; others enjoyed a vigorous swim in the murky water. Further out, Chinese junks floated by. Sometimes we took the high road and sometimes the low road—the lower walkways being right along the river, and the higher paths 3 metres (10 ft) or more above the riverbank. The latter, dotted with small stores and living accommodations, teemed with life. People waved and greeted us constantly. We loved the attention. Ninety-nine percent of foreign visitors to Chongqing are only seen between the bus station and the boat dock when departing for or returning from a Three Gorges Tour.

After three days of absorbing the local flavour, we made our way to the building where the bus had dropped us off when arriving in Chongqing.

There was not anything remotely like a counter to purchase tickets for the return trip. A man nodded and grinned in response to our saying "Gonggongqiche shoupiao (bus ticket)," then waved us on to follow him.

He led us through a low door, through a dingy warehouse area, then through another door and into a tunnel. Soon we emerged into a room 2 metres (6.5 ft) square stacked with boxes, then headed into another tunnel, this one so narrow our packs snagged the sides. The concrete floor ended. Water dripped off the ceiling beams forming little mud puddles on the earthen floor. I gasped in the stale, dank air.

"Rick, I don't like this. Everything we own is on our backs, our passports, credit cards, money."

"I don't like this either. I don't think I could even find my way back," Rick said looking over his shoulder.

The tunnel ended. We entered an arena-sized area where workmen were digging up the dirt floor, illuminated by two lonely light bulbs dangling from the rafters. They stopped what they were doing and stared.

"Ohhh ... doesn't look good," I managed to squeak, my gut churning out danger alerts. The man leading us noticed we had stopped and were huddled talking. His lips curled into a fiendish smirk as he waved us forward through a hole-in-the-wall door.

We entered a small office. The man pointed vigorously to a ticket counter. The light from a window washed away his diabolical mien. Phew! Was that supposed to be a shortcut? My rattled state calmed with a few deep breaths. A smile crinkled our escort's whole face as he waved and headed back into the abyss.

* * *

Realizing one morning that time was flying by with not so much as a thought of furthering our plans for Tibet, we were jarred into action. The travel agency conveniently located in the Traffic Hotel made the arrangements: we were to leave in a week.

Rick kept mumbling, "Ouch!" I knew he was referring to the $1,060.00 x 2. Next time we walked by the reservation desk at the Traffic Hotel, I decided to check on a cheaper room, and yes, there was one available. For our last week, I was willing to give up our $39.62 room with a private bathroom for one with a shared bathroom that cost $18.86, in sympathy for Rick's burst budget.

Tossing our stuff into our backpacks, we trotted to the end of the hall on the same floor and entered the human-sized equivalent of a cracker box. We unpacked a few things, plopped them on the small table at the foot of our beds, used the down-the-hall biffy, and decided that since it was already 10 p.m. to just stay put for the evening. I tried to read, but couldn't concentrate because Rick had the television on. Time for a little negotiating. I agreed to watch the program, but when it ended, we would both read. As we stared at the tube, our peripheral vision picked up a brown, furry thing scurrying across the two feet of floor space between our beds.

"What the hell was that?" Rick shouted.

"Ahaha, a mouse in the house! That's a pretty bold mouse, coming out when the lights are on and with the noise from the TV," I related from what little I knew about murine habits. Rattling a stick under the bed did not bring it out again, so we figured it had exited through some crevice.

Around 11:30, we turned the lights out and settled down. At about 2 a.m., Rick, hearing a noise, flicked on the light and stared straight into the beady eyes of a whopper-sized rodent perched on the foot of my bed. He let out a yelp, which of course brought me thrashing to a sitting position and sent the critter leaping for safety back under the bed. The shampoo bottle, my face creams, and other notions on the table were knocked over, and a bar of soap left leaning against the plastic soap dish was half-eaten. Suddenly, the rodent dashed from under the bed, making horrid little clicking sounds with its nails, then flattened and squirmed through the half-inch crack under the door.

"That's no mouse! Too large, long hairless tail ... that's a freaking rat!" I shrieked.

Rick left the lights on and watched a second rat, then a third exit under the door. We surmised that it was the location of this room (right across from the fire escape connecting to the great outdoors) that allowed these critters such ready access. After a reasonable wait, Rick stuffed towels into the crack so no more could enter the room.

I wanted to march right down to the desk and demand to be moved immediately to another room. Rick argued that we should wait until morning. I pulled the covers over my head; if Rick didn't want to deal with this now, let him be on rat patrol.

Rick's cursing jolted me awake again. He reported that another straggler had torn across the room and bumped into the towel barrier, almost knocking itself out. Dazed, it zigzagged back under the bed. Rick removed one corner of the towel and we both watched it charge out, its solid tail slapping against the floor as it reduced itself to cardboard-thickness and squeezed through the portal to freedom. Rick waited a while longer, then stuffed the towel back under the door.

* * *

Scratching sounds kept coming from somewhere within the walls; we hardly slept the rest of the night. At dawn we tramped down the stairs to the reception desk, only to find the girl on duty barely spoke any English.

Back to the room I went, and returned armed with our Mandarin dictionary. I was pointing to the word "rat" when another lady who spoke English came in for the day shift. I gave voice to the incident and insisted on being moved to another room.

"Why did you not come down last night? Why did you wait until now?" she responded, insinuating prevarication on my part. I raised my eyebrows at Rick (conveying "I told you so"), but we impressed upon her in our defence how little good it would have done, as even if the night crew had understood us, they would not have had the authority to do anything about it.

I love happy endings. We were put back in our old room for only $5.00 more than the rat room. During breakfast we wavered between exhausted slumps and bouts of irrational laughter as we rehashed the night's events. Expect the unexpected. What astounded us most was how accepting we were of outlandish occurrences. This was not typical behaviour for us; we recalled being upset and wanting restitution for much more trivial inconveniences back in Canada. Will this hardiness remain after we get back? Only time will tell. Now I must clarify that the Traffic Hotel was generally clean and well run, not over-run by the genus Rattus; though an inner room is recommended.

*   *   *

Elaine and Juliet had invited us for tea so we could meet Juliet's husband before leaving. The ladies picked us up in a taxi. Our destination was a very ritzy area that we had not known existed, even with all our peregrinating.

"Oh, my, this is totally palatial," I gushed as the teahouse attendants rushed to seat us. Sinking into clouds of velvet, with handy little cushions to further perfect our repose, we were handed tea menus an arm long from which we selected our ambrosias. A waiter for each of us arrived with our individual pots, filled our porcelain cups, then silently hovered behind us, ready to top up each dainty receptacle the precise moment our sipping brought the tea an inch below the rim. Dishes of sunflower seeds, popcorn, sweets, and nuts were placed within easy reach. The dozen or so sitting circles were well spaced for privacy, and the usual din was noticeably absent.

Li was a very engaging man with vast business experience. He wanted to hire Rick to teach company employees business-related English. Pol joined us later, adding his witty Brit humour to the gathering. I welcomed the chance to visit more intimately with Juliet. She had given up a good position in a major company when leaving Beijing, and all her family members were still there, so she was having a hard time adjusting. Li desperately wanted them to have a child. She was terrified to add such a monumental change to her life when it was already in flux. Our affinity for each other (which had been present from the first moment we met) grew, and we promised to keep in touch by e-mail.

It was dark and pouring rain when Elaine, Pol, Rick, and I hailed a taxi to take us back home. Li and Juliet left in their own vehicle. Elaine asked to be dropped off about halfway to our hotel. She told the driver to just pull over to the curb and she would hop out.

Wham! Crash! Crunch! A female cyclist went flying when Elaine opened the back door to get out. She helped the woman up, and told us she would take care of the mishap and insisted we carry on to the hotel so our taxi (illegally and dangerously stopped by the curb) would not be hit in the blinding rain.

I called her the next evening to see what had transpired. She had taken the lady to the hospital and paid the hospital bill; the injuries were some abrasions on her hands and a painful arm, though an X-ray did not show a break. The woman asked for a monetary settlement, and Elaine paid her "a generous sum" (she would not disclose the amount). The wounded cyclist first seemed satisfied, then asked for more. Elaine knew she probably looked rich to the villager, and also it is very common for an accident victim to keep coming back for more money for months and even years. She ended up giving her a false name and address, being assured by the hospital staff that the lady was not badly hurt, and feeling she had done enough to right the wrong.

It was too bad that delightful evening had to end on such a sour note.

* * *

It was our last shopping day before Tibet to stock up on vitamins, toothpaste, and items we had heard would be difficult or impossible to obtain after leaving Chengdu. While in our favourite department store, we spotted a public scale near the vitamin counter. Should we? We had not weighed ourselves for over two months. There were four people ahead of us in line for the scale; we elected to give it a go.

As soon as we entered the queue, a crowd gathered. I guess they wanted to see what giants weigh. I got on first: 63 kilos (139 lb) ... fully clothed, don't forget. Everyone around peered to see. There were a few oooh's and aaaah's. I outweighed most of the male onlookers.

Rick stepped on. Thinking he would dazzle them with his Mandarin, he loudly proclaimed his 201-pound weight in kilos: "Jiu shi yi (91)." A tiny lady crouched at his side twisted her body around his knees so that her face ended up directly over the digits on the scale. "Jiu shi er (92)," she emphatically corrected. She puffed out her chest as if she had caught a player cheating at a high-stakes poker game. You could have heard a pin drop ... until we burst out laughing, and the whole crowd joined in, with many coming over to shake our hands. Such encounters were golden.

Our six weeks in China had been mostly enjoyable, at times frustrating, but always thought-provoking.

Napoleon Bonaparte once said, "Let China sleep; for when she wakes, she will shake the world."

When I try to come up with an all-encompassing description of China, an astronomical steamroller comes to mind—one that is forever grinding and moving forward through every and any obstacle, whether it be entanglements with the forces of nature, opposition of other countries, or defiance to government edicts by its own citizens.

"People are trapped in history and history is trapped in them," said the American writer and civil rights activist James Baldwin.

The fear of opposing or objecting to what the government decrees is "best for the Motherland" still permeates the culture. This undercurrent of fear stems from occurrences exemplified by a Mao decree of the late 1950s: it was decided that sparrows were eating too much of the grain in the fields, so a government edict went into effect that for a 24-hour period, all farmers were to beat pans so the birds would not roost, causing them to drop out of the sky with heart failure. Obedience without protest ensued, as those opposed did not dare to chance being turned in by others for non-compliance and face brutal consequences from the authorities.

Being raised in democratic, multicultural Canada—where we are continually flooded with group protests and minorities claiming rights—it was difficult to conceive of the Chinese fear of retribution for speaking out. Advocacy groups within China's growing middle class are now coming forward to fight for various causes, though individual rights are still mostly superseded by what is considered best for the country. A comment made by a Chinese university professor about their system of government added a shade of grey to my black and white perspective: "Democracy would not work in China. With our long history of dynasties, the citizens have need of a Father figure to guide them."

China is throwing itself headlong into the future. The transformation is rapid and with clear intent. The 2008 Olympics, the country's coming-out party to the world, was succinctly summed up as "truly exceptional" by IOC President Jacques Rogge. The face they displayed to the world was of paramount importance to the Chinese, and will no doubt have an effect on future policy. The country had a huge impact on us; we had an intriguing journey, and came away from the experience with a glimpse into a different and very complex system.

Rick's final tally of our six weeks in China came to $81.00 a day, almost dead on our targeted goal (not including our Tibet package). As September 17 neared, our bout of gloom over leaving mainland China was only lightened by the anticipation of flying over the Himalayas to Tibet.

Chapter Four
Tibet

As the cloud cover vanished with our descent, our eyes feasted on the panorama of glistening white peaks, expanses of barren hills of earth and rock, shimmering ice-blue rivers, and patches of emerald forest below.

We were of two minds about Tibet. Excitement bubbled over as we anticipated being enveloped in the heart-stopping beauty of this land high in the Himalayas, but it was tempered by our knowledge of the suffering of the Tibetan people under the strong mechanisms of repression of the Chinese government.

Yet another feeling surfaced as we neared the landing strip. Knowing the air would be thinner than we had ever experienced, I was gripped by a fear of not being able to breathe properly upon deplaning. Stepping onto the tarmac, I was super-conscious of the cool, clear air amply filling my lungs, feeling relieved and silly about my paranoia. As we made our way to the terminal my face was drawn in an upward tilt to the bluest of skies, catching the warm rays slicing through the morning crispness.

We picked up our backpacks from the pile inside the terminal and walked about a block to our waiting tour bus (really only a van).

"Who added the rocks to my pack and lead to my boots?" I wheezed. Suddenly the notion of gasping for air didn't seem so foolish. Leaving the 508-metre (1,666-ft) altitude of Chengdu and being hoisted to the 3,800-metre (12,467-ft) elevation of Lhasa within hours was now equating to light-headedness and breathlessness with the added exertion of carrying our gear. The recommended few days of taking it easy to allow our bodies to acclimatize—that is, to produce more oxygen-carrying red blood cells— suddenly made sense. (The overland routes to Lhasa provide a slower progression to higher elevation, thereby reducing the effects of the sudden increase in altitude after deplaning.)

An hour and a half of bumpy roads brought us to the Snowland Hotel. The legendary beauty of Tibetan faces was all around us—bright skin tones with high, rosy cheeks—though intermarriage with the Han Chinese has diluted these distinctive features in some. Many men and women still wear their thick black hair in traditional-style braids interwoven with colourful cloth.

Our van was unloaded and we seven newcomers were taken up to a third-storey dorm room adorned with colourful Tibetan flags and rugs. We were to choose our niche from the seven empty beds left for us, out of the eleven projecting out from all four walls of the ample room.

On the flight over we had discussed not staying in the dorm—immediately seeking out a private room instead—but we did ... not ... have ... the ... energy. It was dizzying to even think of walking from hotel to hotel checking out room conditions and prices. We surrendered and curled up in the dorm with a good book.

The younger travellers in our group set out to wander the streets. At that moment, we were not sure we had enough spunk to take in the two excursions included in the price of our tour package during the next two days. Along with short periods of rapid heart rates and the sporadic sensation of being smothered by an invisible entity, within a few hours we both developed a dull headache.

An incident soon after our arrival left us gasping for breath for reasons other than the change in altitude. We had chosen the two beds farthest away from the entrance of the dorm; the snoring body in the bed beside us—completely covered by blankets—did not deter us from nabbing this prime location. The hubbub of the newbies getting settled in no way disturbed this vibrating, rumbling mound. After a few hours of reading, we decided to venture out to feed our lethargic bodies and to restock our water supply.

As we walked past this bed, a head poked out. To say we were flabbergasted, dumbfounded, and bowled over would be an understatement. It was Pol—the English teacher reported by Juliet and Elaine as missing before we left Chengdu, along with Juliet's English textbook, which was in Pol's keeping to make up her lessons. They had had us inquire at the front desk of the Traffic Hotel for a forwarding address, which he had not left, but one young office girl said he had mentioned Shanghai.

Pol was equally shocked.

"Tashi dalay!" we sang out, the Tibetan greeting. "Hey, Pol, when did you get here? Juliet called the school where you worked, and they said you just didn't show up one day."

"I decided on the spur of the moment to come back to Tibet. I don't know how long I'll stay or where I'll go from here," he said noncommittally.

"Juliet called the hotel trying to track you down, and they said you had gone to Shanghai. Both Juliet and Elaine could not understand why you didn't

say goodbye, and Juliet is lost without her English text, which you borrowed."
I felt driven to tell all. Who knew if he would still be there when we got back
to the room?

"Oh, I left her text with a friend. Now that I am sure I'll not be returning
to Chengdu, I'll e-mail him to get hold of her so she can pick it up from him,"
Pol prevaricated.

"Well, we are going to e-mail Juliet anyway, so we will tell her about seeing
you and pass on the name and phone number of your friend who has the text,
and then you can just let your friend know she will be picking it up," I offered.

"That's okay ... I'll let my friend know, and he'll get a hold of her," he
said, visibly relieved by the interruption of other hostellers trooping through
the door.

"Well, I'll tell her you promise to get it back to her," I said, unconvinced
it would ever happen.

We slowly descended the three flights of stairs to the Snowland's ground-
floor restaurant.

"Boy, would I ever like to search his backpack," I said. "Or maybe he has
already sold it for some quick cash."

Pol was not in the room when we got back. Though I was itching to play
detective, I managed to stifle the urge to do a little rucksack-rummaging. I
did, however, e-mail Juliet with the details of our startlingly comical meeting
with Pol, which perfectly fit the old cliché, "It's a small world."

* * *

We saw him a couple of times during the next few days. Once, down in the
Snowland foyer, he introduced us to a few new girls he was teaching English
to. Another time, he was in a restaurant with a bunch of people, including
these two new students (who were no doubt footing the bill).

Two days later, the dorm bed Pol had occupied was empty; indubitably,
he had gone on to greener pastures. Nice guy ... just don't loan him anything.
When we e-mailed Juliet to tell her that Pol had once again flown the coop,
her good nature prevailed in her responding message: "Pol must need the
book more than I do."

Juliet and I stayed in contact and, a year later, still no book. No one was
surprised.

* * *

All that first evening, the dorm tenants filtered in and out, sometimes for
a rest, to pick something up, or to change clothes. Rick didn't mind one
exhibitionist chick who pranced around in her thong panties and skimpy bra
while trying (or pretending) to find some lost item.

I asked two girls who had arrived at the same time as us (and had clothes on) how they were feeling. They both were plagued with many of the same symptoms—including headaches—and were popping Tylenol like candy. We decided against painkillers, rationalizing it would be impossible to know if we were succumbing to altitude sickness if we camouflaged the symptoms. Several times that night, Rick suffered sleep apnea. Jarred awake not breathing, he would go through a period of panicky gasps until his breathing levelled out again. My dull headache was accompanied by the creepy sensation of fluid shifting in my cranium every time I moved, which was no more conducive to peaceful sleep.

* * *

When the alarm rang at seven the next morning for the Sera Monastery tour, we somehow miraculously felt we would survive, and were more than ready to escape the confines of the dorm.

May—our tall, willowy Tibetan guide—was waiting for our group in the hotel lobby. En route to the monastery, she eloquently revealed some historical facts. "There were once over 6,000 monks in Sera Monastery, but only 550 remain today." She told us that many of the Buddhist sculptures were 600 years old and that these were spared during the Cultural Revolution because this particular monastery was used to store barley and they were hidden under the grain throughout that time. (She did not dare to add that during the Chinese takeover hundreds of the monks who were living here died and many of the structures were badly damaged.)

The entrance to the Great Assembly Hall is most spectacular. We walked through a portico of 10 columns. Suspended from the ceiling on the side walls are large thangkas, the brilliantly coloured sacred paintings on silk created by monks.

In one of the chapels we stood before a mural of the wrathful horse-headed Hayagriva, one of the many manifestations of Avalokitesvara, a Bodhisattva (enlightened being). Hayagriva is considered the protector of the monastery. Our eyebrows rose in surprise as many worshippers proceeded past us, carrying babies with blackened noses. May told us that the monks applied a powdered charcoal to each tiny nose as they entered, as part of a blessing to keep the child safe from all harm. This ritual is often carried out in Tibetan homes as well; soot from the hearth is dabbed on the baby's nose, particularly before any outdoor activity, as it is believed this will protect the child from evil spirits.

This monastery is still a university for monks. Some *chortens* or stupas (small temples) contain the ashes of lamas (monks) or the embalmed bodies of high lamas who have taught over the centuries at the university. Many old Sanskrit volumes line the ancient walls.

The mountain directly behind the Sera Monastery is where sky burials are performed. When a Tibetan dies, the family consults with an astrologer about the recommended element by which the body should be returned to the cosmos: air, fire, water, wood, or earth. Sky burials are the most common. In early morning, the flesh—which has been removed from the body—and crushed bones are mixed with barley flour and scattered on the mountaintop, where vultures, hawks, and ravens come to feast on the pieces. It is considered honourable to feed other creatures with one's remains. This, coupled with the facts that wood is sparse and the ground is rock-based and usually frozen, makes sky burials more practical in Tibet, rather than cremation or traditional burials. The bodies of children and paupers are put into the rivers. Cremation is normally reserved for lamas. In the unusual wood burial, the body is placed in a hollow tree for the cleansing elements of nature to take their course.

The tour moved on to the Norbulingka (Treasure Garden). This 40-hectare (99-acre) complex of pavilions, small palaces, and gardens has been the summer residence of Dalai Lamas since 1755.

The New Palace, which is open to the public, was completed by the current Dalai Lama (Tenzin Gyatso). It was from this palace that the Dalai Lama slipped away with some family members into exile to Dharamsala, India, in 1959 at the age of 25. From that time until the present day, he has been an active spokesman for the plight of the Tibetans, and Dharamsala is now home to many more Tibetan exiles.

The palace rooms are not ostentatious, with the exception of the main hall with its solid gold throne, gilded beams, and ruby-red walls. We were allowed access to the Dalai Lama's sitting room, audience room, bedroom, "plumbed" bathrooms, and his mother's day-room. May told us women were not allowed to stay in the palace overnight, not even his mother.

On the second floor we were awed by elaborate murals tracing Tibetan history, from the mating between the Bodhisattva of compassion in the form of a monkey and the goddess Tara, up to the current (the 14th) Dalai Lama. Another presence in the room was a large mandala—a circular mystic diagram symbolizing the universe.

May led us into what she called the Meditation Room. A soft golden light filtered through the window. The room was heavy with the musty—but not unpleasant—odour of past incense burnings. I felt a difference in the thickness of the warm air. May's voice had a deeper resonance with a curious sort of echo. My eyes were drawn to an ample red cushion on a dais, which still had an indent as if someone were sitting on it. Could it be the Dalai Lama transporting his spirit back to his favourite room in his beloved Norbulingka? If that was within the realm of anyone's capabilities, I believe it would be within his. I read Rick's "something's weird in here" expression.

We were not the only two to feel some mysterious essence. A lady asked May afterward, "Why did I feel odd vibrations in that room? I could swear it's not a part of the same building." May was silent; her eyes seemed far away.

"Yes, it is very beautiful," was May's delayed response. An arcane half-smile on her face made me believe her mind had met with Tenzin Gyatso's. I would blame this all on an overactive imagination, except I know I don't have one.

Exhausted from the day's activities, we slept much better that night. The younger set, we noticed, headed for bed at the same time we did. Any exertion still made our hearts race. "Go slowly" was the advice we heard from the locals.

* * *

Bright and early the next morning, our tour bus headed for the mountain-crest site of the 1,100-room Potala Palace. As we gazed waaaay up at the imposing structure from the parking lot, we knew why it had been scheduled for the third day. Before starting up the long winding paths and multitude of steps, we joined the Tibetans along a line of prayer wheels spinning their invocations up to the heavens. Mine included a plea for the stamina to make it to the top.

The Potala Palace has been the home of the Dalai Lamas since the seventh century. Many of the past Dalai Lamas are buried in the section with a deep ruby coat of paint known as the Red Palace. Their remains are encased in elaborate and jewel-encrusted dome-shaped stupas. Pilgrims bring *khatas* (ceremonial scarves) to place in the chapels. The flames of ghee-butter lamps cast flickering shadowy fingers against the walls and flooded the air with their strange pungent odour.

The White Palace—also named for its colour—was the administrative building and living quarters of the Dalai Lamas. When in the study room of the 14th Dalai Lama, I recalled a familiar scene from the movie *Seven Years in Tibet*: a young Tenzin Gyatso, perched on a cushion a step above Heinrich Harrer (his Austrian mountaineer-cum-teacher), absorbing the English language and Western geography lessons. The movie was not filmed in Tibet, but the movie set they built of this room was a great replica.

"Our people come to the palace to gain inner strength from the spirits of all the Dalai Lamas who once occupied this space," May said. Over a million Tibetans have died in the conflict with China since Mao first began his takeover of Tibet in 1950. All manner of atrocities have been and are still being committed against the Tibetans in their fight for freedom: *thamzing* (public torture and humiliation), prison sentences, executions for fictitious crimes, and property confiscation. The Chinese government has even created famine in Tibet by crop destruction or by transporting harvests to China.

Our guidebook and some other informative publications we read on Tibet still warn visitors not to engage in long conversations with Tibetans, as talking too long may be interpreted as plotting a conspiracy, with disastrous consequences for the Tibetan. Plainclothes police and khaki-attired PLA (People's Liberation Army) soldiers were everywhere. A few times we saw soldiers approach a group of Tibetans, instantly scattering them.

At the Potala exit we were met with large panda-shaped garbage cans, where one could dispose of unwanted items through a belly flap. These garbage cans are a ubiquitous Chinese addition throughout Lhasa—a grim reminder of who is now running the show. Ironically, it's a good thing the Chinese government is using a portion of the Potala as their Tibetan headquarters, and that the sections open to visitors bring in a fortune in entry fees. Otherwise, this palace would have long since been destroyed or fallen into disrepair like most other Buddhist temples in Tibet.

We left with a sense of sadness, knowing that the palace would never again be the spiritual centre and seat of government of a free Tibet. I had not previously realized how much additional landmass the takeover of Tibet meant to China. What we see on today's maps labelled Tibet is but a small part of the original Tibetan territory. In total, it spanned an area equal to one-quarter of the People's Republic of China. After the Chinese takeover, portions of the former Tibet were added to Qinghai, Gansu, Sichuan, and Yunnan provinces. China was after more than the traditional crop of Tibetan highland barley: though their motives were multifaceted, a large part of their desire to possess this environmentally harsh land was nuclear gold. During the 1950s—when the Cold War was in full swing—most democracies saw Tibet's uranium deposits as less lethal in China's hands (as opposed to Russia's).

*　*　*

One more night's stay in the Snowland dorm and our package deal was over. After the Potala tour we spent the remainder of the day investigating our hotel options. The Yak Hotel won out hands-down: a spacious private room on the second floor with a shared bath. Our certainty that we were now well-acclimatized fizzled. I felt like an ant carrying a whole tree as we walked the four blocks from the Snowland to the Yak with all our gear.

Or maybe we were still winded from the kerfuffle before departing the Snowland. The all-important permit—the one we could only obtain with the tour package to Tibet—had been confiscated by an authoritative fellow from everyone on our flight upon our arrival into Tibet. When we attempted to hang on to ours, the fellow said he was coming into town with us on the tour bus, and that he needed the permits to check us in. He assured us that they would be returned to us the following day. They were not.

We questioned the lady at the reception desk the next day and asked May before going to the Norbulingka as to the whereabouts of our permits, but no one knew.

"Ask at the travel agency in the hotel," was the advice we were given. The problem was that it was never open ... not until we were ready to leave the Snowland, that is. The employees at the travel agency knew nothing of our entry permits and just shrugged their shoulders when we explained that when purchasing the tour package in Chengdu, we specifically asked and were told that yes, the same permit would be valid for exiting Tibet down the Friendship Highway to Nepal.

Now we were informed that we needed to buy a new permit to travel anywhere outside of Lhasa, and this new permit could only be obtained as part of a jeep- or van-rental package, or as part of a public bus ticket. Furthermore, the four-day travel packages sold in Chengdu were technically only valid for the four days. Since the majority of travellers stay longer, there were a lot of people walking the streets sans-permit. Apparently the authorities do not concern themselves with this unless one attempts to leave Lhasa. Recognizing this as yet another Chinese-travel discombobulation, we also decided to go forth permit-less and enjoy Tibet.

* * *

The insouciance of being on our own again was wonderful. We savoured our time in the Barkhor area. The old buildings on both sides of the square in front of the focal point—Jokhang Temple—had been modernized. A small café with a top-floor balcony located on the corner of the square was the perfect perch from which to watch the activity below while sipping lassi. This fruit-flavoured, soy-based drink is positively scrumptious and super-addictive.

A lively bazaar was underway in the square selling jewellery, prayer wheels, prayer flags, rugs, and the colourful embroidered Tibetan felt hats with ear flaps. Farther along an adjacent street were the food stalls: fresh yak-cow yogurt, yak-butter tea, and *chang* (Tibetan barley beer) were just some of the specialties foreign to our taste buds. Vendors pressed for sales once one stopped by their canopied tables; understandable, considering the poverty here.

* * *

Around the periphery of Jokhang Temple was a well-worn *kora*, the sacred path of worship that circles the temple. From early in the morning until late in the evening throngs of pilgrims arrived to make the circumambulation in a clockwise direction to earn religious merit.

Inside the temple, another *kora* circuit flowed with more worshippers. In the centre of the cavernous interior, the glimmer of ghee candles pulsed in the half-light to the melodious chanting of maroon-robed monks. Devotees filled every conceivable space outside the waist-high circular partition separating the rows of monks from the laypeople. Some people were allowed into this inner sanctum by the head monk after giving donations to the temple. A few benefactors handed money to each of the monks individually.

The euphonious chords still reached our ears when we climbed the steps to the rooftop. Over the railing, we saw the pilgrims below prostrating themselves in front of the temple. Others stood spinning hand-held prayer wheels. On a rolled piece of paper on the inside of the prayer wheels—or engraved on the outside of the wheel itself—is the mantra *om mani padme hum*. This mantra in its simplest form translates to the phrase "Behold! The Jewel in the Lotus!" However, this most significant of Buddhist mantras is so complex that we were told there is not a single aspect of the 8,400 sections of the Buddhist canon that is not contained in this six-syllable mantra.

* * *

The following day found us on a bus back to the Sera Monastery for the famed monks' debate. One hundred maroon-clad monks were divided into groups of six or eight. Each group sat in a circle around a standing monk, who was a spectacle to behold—speaking non-stop, fancy footwork, arm-swinging that culminated in a loud slap as he skimmed one hand over the other as if striking cymbals. It appeared to us that the central figure was the teacher giving instruction to the monks sitting around him, with his claps signalling their correct answers.

Spotting May, our Tibetan guide, we chiselled our way through the crowd to find out the particulars. Our assumptions were a little off: the sitting junior monks were the ones firing questions at the standing senior monks about Buddhist scripture. When the lively senior monk completed an answer, he clapped his hands in said fashion, often raising one foot to strike the ground at the precise moment his hands smacked. The debate became quite raucous, with the senior monk engaging in much teasing and head-patting when the younger monks were unable to stump him with further disputation to his answers.

The couple of hours we planned to stay turned into a whole afternoon of sitting on the fringes, being royally entertained without understanding a single word.

A Scatological Saga

Rick had been in a mental fog for the past two days. "Kind of comes and goes," he said. He also developed stomach cramps when walking. Then one morning, he had a dreaded bout of diarrhea after eating breakfast. He felt fine again throughout the day and was glad to be feeling up for an evening's chomp-down of sizzling yak steak in the fantastic company of our new friends: Ana (from Mexico), Carolina (from Colombia), and Julie and Eric (from the United States).

Rick took a hasty detour to the bathroom on the way out of the restaurant. Back at the Yak, he handed me the key to the room while he took another jaunt to the loo at the end of the hall. Quite a while passed. I was about ready to hunt him down when he reappeared. He told me that even if the place had been on fire, vacating the toilet seat would have been out of the question.

A guy had come in while he was sitting and waiting for the next explosion.

"Jeez, this'd curl your hair," the fellow bellowed to his friend at the door. Both turned on their heels, deciding to forgo entry. Sick as he was, Rick said he almost rolled off the seat with laughter.

Rick trotted back and forth down the dim hall throughout the night. Imodium was ineffective. I had never seen such greenish pallor in a human, and he said he had never been so sick. Soon he had to resort to using a pan in the room, which I diligently kept running down the hall to empty and rinse. I kidded him about forever being indebted to me.

Knowing he was becoming dehydrated, I made up a batch of hydration powder from our first-aid kit. It tasted so vile he couldn't stomach it. Some powdered orange juice with added salt for his sodium loss made a more palatable concoction. He consumed great volumes of this, but the uncontrolled blasts—now from both ends—were winning out. He had terrifying spells where he gasped for air.

I felt my way in the pitch-blackness across the courtyard to the office for more purified water, which we were nearly out of. My banging on the door went unanswered—it was now four in the morning. I knew our friends Eric and Julie were in this hotel but had no idea where their room was. Distressed, alone, and exhausted, we waited for the long night to end.

By morning Rick was so weak he crumpled as he descended the stairs, almost pulling the two male hotel employees supporting him down with him. It was a disturbing sight to see my six-foot husband buckle under his own weight.

After a heroic effort, they were finally able to fold him into a waiting taxi, and we headed for the hospital. A hand-sized cylinder of oxygen with a face mask that I purchased from the hotel did nothing to alleviate his laboured breathing en route.

Praise the Lord! An English-speaking doctor was on call. After the hospital staff got Rick into bed, I was called back for questioning at the hall desk. I gave the doctor the lowdown on his symptoms, adding that he was on medication for high blood pressure. The old sphygmomanometer's reading showed his blood pressure was now in the stratosphere. After I paid on the spot for the hospital bed and for saline solutions for rehydration, the doctor prescribed medications—one bottle of pills for altitude sickness, one to stop the cramps and stomach pain, and a powder to abate the diarrhea.

I was given directions to pick them up at the dispensary. After the third attempt at clarifying the convoluted route, a young girl accompanied me through a maze of halls, across an open court, and through many more twists and turns. I was so thankful, as with no English signage and hardly a soul along the way to motion to while pointing to the prescription, I never would have found my way alone.

Rick slept soundly all day, waking only when one of the attendants (I don't believe the scruffy young man or the giggly girl were nurses) came in to replenish the intravenous solution, or when I woke him up to give him his medications.

When my head was not flung backwards or drooping forward catching a few zees in a very uncomfortable wooden chair, I had ample time to take a good look at the surroundings.

I hadn't noticed before how very old and dilapidated the whole hospital was. There were eight beds in this room. Aside from Rick's and one other fellow's, the beds saw a constant rotation of patients on the same sheets, no matter what fluid souvenirs were left behind by former occupants. Nary a doctor entered the room the whole time we were there, so it must have been standard procedure to have ailments assessed at the front desk, as when Rick was admitted.

Oh, if I could only lie down! At one point I jumped out of my chair just in time to side-step a rumbling bulldozer coming head-on (oh, wait, just a nightmare), and I must have been jolted awake by my own snoring (no, it was my stomach growling). I realized I had not eaten anything yet today and it was almost three in the afternoon. I left Rick sleeping and went out to forage for myself—Rick not being allowed solid food for the next 24 hours.

There were a few restaurants about a block from the hospital. I bypassed these as they did not have a salubrious appearance; one of us being sick was enough. Finding a small store, I purchased whatever I recognized by the pictures on the packaging: cookies, crackers, candy, pop. Salivating, I ripped open the bags and started shovelling in my stash the minute I was out of the store.

On the way back to the ward I inquired about the length of Rick's stay. The same doctor, who was just leaving for the day, said he should stay until eight that evening, but to come back if any of the symptoms reoccurred.

I took a taxi back to the hotel for a shower and a real meal. I ran into Julie and Eric, who had heard about what happened—as had everyone else at the hotel. They were most concerned and supportive and offered any help we might need.

It was then back to the hospital. Rick was awake and he wanted to use the toilet down the hall. The toilet was disgusting! Fly-infested shit-piles that had missed their hole-in-the-floor mark were numerous. Rick picked the best of the three stalls. The thought of ever having to be in this stench again was enough to bring on a preternatural cure. Later, while walking the hall to stretch my legs, I discovered an outside door that was propped open, letting in more than fresh air—construction workers from a nearby site were sneaking in and using the toilets.

The hospital was medieval, but the care was first rate. The one-day hospital stay and medications came to $38.00; a mere pittance to us, but a great expense to a Tibetan. A revived Rick and I taxied home around 8:30 p.m. and we both slept for the next 12 hours straight.

Rick was now in a weakened condition, which left us with a dilemma. It was now September 27. We had agreed to rent a jeep with Ana and Carolina for the drive over the Friendship Highway from Tibet to Nepal the first week in October. There was a standard price for a jeep, regardless of how many people were in it, so the most economical plan was to find six people wanting to leave on the same day. The booking agencies were self-service; they did not help organize groups. Customers were on their own to fill a jeep by advertising on hotel bulletin boards and by word of mouth. Ana and Carolina had put in a lot of time and effort locating two more people and our bowing out would mean they would have to start recruiting again; not to mention how much we were looking forward to the highway's sensational scenery and camaraderie of our well-travelled, highly educated, fun-loving young friends.

On the other hand, the five-day duration of the highway route meant increases in altitude over Lhasa's 3,800 metres (12,467 ft). The Himalayan terrain would reach altitudes of 4,700 metres (15,420 ft) at Shegatzi and 5,500 metres (18,045 ft) at Tingri.

Although Rick felt his illness was not altitude-related, there is a standard rule: if you have any of the symptoms of altitude sickness (Rick's dizziness, nausea, and lethargy all fit the bill), you treat the illness as if it is altitude sickness. The best remedial action was to descend to a lower altitude, which made going higher foolhardy. Common sense prevailing, we booked our flights (which included permits) to Kathmandu for September 29. Ana and Carolina totally understood.

During our last days of walking through this lofty city, our admiration swelled for the soft-spoken Tibetans, who have always lived in sympathy with nature in one of the harshest environments in the world, and whose strong Buddhist convictions continue to outshine any oppression or adversities hurled their way.

Developed countries have been stymied in attempts to aid the Tibetans in their struggle for peace and freedom. Aggression has never been the answer to peace ... and besides, the nations that have the military power to be aggressors have nothing deemed worthwhile to gain from intercession on behalf of Tibet: no oil, gold, diamonds, or the like. One thing is certain:

China will never give Tibet back to the Tibetans. All that can be hoped for is a lighter-handed presence, allowing Tibetans a good life with the right to honour their culture and religion.

So, what David will tackle Goliath to allow this to happen? I still believe that as China opens up to the eyes of the world, it will want to show an "honourable face," and that the time is right for a joining of the world's nations to be the David for Tibetan rights.

Countries must not cower under threats of economic sanctions used by China as clout to discourage discourse on Tibetan rights. Can individuals make a difference? Our dollars are certainly political. In the words of writer Pat Schneider, "We are all political. If we are silent, our silence is political. We owe our voice to those who cannot speak freely."

We left Tibet much more appreciative of Canada and all it stands for in terms of human rights and freedoms. Our usual complaints about our Canadian system seemed like a few grains of salt in life's ocean.

* * *

By our departure date, Rick was feeling about 80 percent his old self. The clear fresh air had eradicated my pollution-induced hacking. The old budget was not as healthy with Tibet's average of $234 per day, reflecting our expensive package tours to get here and our unanticipated flight to Nepal.

Departure procedures at the airport were painfully slow because everything was checked twice, including our permits. Then, at last, we were airborne and looking down at the sun's golden rays as they bounced with sweet abandon off voluptuous cumulus clouds and into the ether. Suddenly the peaks of the Himalayas jutting through the white swells commanded our full attention. We were flying at 9,449 metres (31,000 ft). The plane dipped its wing for a view of Mt. Everest at 8,850 metres (29,035 ft); it looked within reach. The immensity of the moment took hold; we would never in our lives be closer to the "top of the world." Replete with the majesty of the Creator, I became profoundly aware of the interconnectedness of all things in the universe, and my own connection to the infinite and eternal.

Chapter Five
Nepal

Efficiency met us in Nepal like a twister, which was startling after our travel-related woes in China. We were spun and swept out of the airport within minutes, obtaining our visas and changing some money into Nepalese rupees on our way out. Hopping into a decrepit cab, we rattled through the narrow, crowded, sinuous streets of Kathmandu, cows grazing around us wherever they pleased. Wheels squealed as we pulled up to the Hotel-Hostel Patala ($4.00 per night) for a private room and shared biffy.

Our hotel and most of the other hotels in Kathmandu are clustered in the exhilarating, touristy Thamel area. Compulsive shoppers—like me—should beware. Vibrant shops with congenial owners lined the streets with everything imaginable. Sewing machines whirred from canopy-entranced embroidery shops, where nimble fingers created mountains, dragons or gods right before our eyes. Catchy folk tunes bounced out of music shops. Mouth-watering aromas idled in the air from numerous eateries. Internet cafés, banks, and travel bureaus were all also in close proximity.

What a first day! After a fabulous Nepalese meal of dal, bhat, tarkari, and roti (lentils, rice, curried vegetables, and flat bread) at the Thamel House Restaurant, we were treated to a traditional floor show, where young men swirled and leapt with acrobatic finesse.

Walking out into the warm evening with throngs of people still cavorting in streets lit with multi-coloured bulbs, we fought off our exhaustion until our legs could carry us no further. Even then, we lingered for a time watching the city lights from our hotel balcony, completely enamoured with the amicable laid-back atmosphere.

After a fortifying breakfast the next morning, we headed for Durbar Square. The mood was electric. Swarms of people milled around vendors who were selling wares set out at the base of a temple, side streets gleamed with stacks of highly polished copper, cramped tool shops were heaped with an astounding inventory, and rows of gunny sacks brimming with exotic spices added to the already deliciously fragrant incensed air. A tiny lady emerged from around a corner balancing a load of recycled cardboard and plastic three times her size strapped to her back. We jumped back as a young cyclist shaved past us with a dozen squawking chickens strung by their feet to his handlebars, their heads bobbing upward attempting to peck themselves free. Crowds divided to go around a gigantic bull nonchalantly plunked in the middle of a main thoroughfare. Wild monkeys swung by one arm while watching us from the intricately carved wooden eaves of a temple.

As we worked our way to the site of the old palace, the activity around the grounds confirmed the rumours that it was once more occupied by King Gyanendra. The gossip was that he had again vacated the new palace, located a few miles away, because it was haunted ... and he was probably right. A bloody massacre had taken place there in 2001. In a drunken rage—believed to have stemmed from his parents' disapproval of his chosen marriage partner—Prince Dipendra had shot his father, King Birendra Bikram Shah. There had been no stopping the crazed scion as he gunned down his queen mother, his brother and sister, before turning the gun on himself. Since all the direct heirs to the throne were dead, the king's brother, Gyanendra Bir Bikram Shah Dev, was officially instated into the monarchy.

Gyanendra was not a step up for Nepal. In 2002 he suspended the democratically elected government. In 2004, after massive protests, he re-instated the prime minister. By 2005 he had again dismissed the government. In 2006, again after massive protest, he restored the elected government's power. Gyanendra was the last King of Nepal. Parliament abolished the monarchy in 2008, after our visit, ending 240 years of monarchy rule.

* * *

The temples in the square date back to the 1500s. The most famous was the impressive Kumari Ghar, which houses the living goddess, the royal Kumari. In the convoluted fashion of Hindu deities, she is believed to be an incarnation of the goddess Taleju Bhawani, who in turn is a manifestation of the fierce female deity Durga. A young girl—usually four or five years of age— is chosen by senior priests. The candidate has to fulfill 32 specific criteria to be declared a goddess. First and foremost, the candidate's horoscope must match the king's, to ensure compatibility. Being free of deformities is also a requisite; and such things as expressive dark eyes, lustrous hair, and white teeth without gaps are some of the prominent features looked for. Placing the child in a dark room with terrifying noises or men dancing around with horrifying masks are some of the rigorous tests to confirm her possession of the compulsory attributes of calm and fearlessness.

As we entered the Kumari Ghar's outer doors, the steps descended to the inner court, which faced a sizable three-level brick building with ornamental wood casings around the windows. Following the lines of vision of the gathering assembled, our eyes rose to a larger, more elaborately decorated window on the top level. An hour passed by. Hardly anyone moved. To glimpse the goddess in one of her random appearances through the window is said to bring good fortune.

As the tour leader of a group began to speak in a hushed voice, we squeezed in closer to hear his monologue.

"The new Kumari is brought to the Kumari Ghar with her family to live until first blood, whether by an accidental cut or first menstruation. At this time the girl loses her status, she and her family must leave the temple house, and a new Kumari is chosen. We will see her, if luck is with us, wearing an elaborate costume with facial makeup. Most prominent are the heavy black kohl triangular shapes around her eyes and a third eye painted in the middle."

All of a sudden, not the Kumari, but a gnarled old woman with wispy white hair appeared at the window, pointing and screeching something in Nepalese.

The guide swung around. "There are no cameras allowed. Now the Kumari will not appear." Everyone glared at the red-faced, paunchy middle-aged man trying unsuccessfully to conceal his Sony camcorder. He slunk out of the courtyard past the prominent sign on the back wall of a camera in a circle with a slash through it—the universally accepted symbol for No Photography.

The wait started again. We hoped the penalty period for the offence would not be too lengthy, but after another 30 minutes our rumbling bellies won out and we went off to seek sustenance.

But our wait was not all in vain; our curiosity was satisfied as to the reason many little girls poking out from behind their mother's skirts along the streets had black kohl around their eyes. Though the current Kumari was, no doubt, watched very carefully so she would not fall or play with sharp objects, one never knew when the next Kumari would have to be chosen and another family would live in luxury and prestige for a time. Apparently, when a Kumari is sent back to her old way of life, both the girl and her family often have major problems adjusting. The situation is probably analogous to that of a child star in North America, whose popularity eventually ends, resulting in an evaporation of the family's lavish lifestyle.

* * *

Near the square we roamed Freak Street, which had been a hippie haven during the 1960s and '70s. It was easy to imagine the long-haired flower children tokin' and lovin' and waiting for enlightenment. A few still milled around, their colourful bandanas now covering lengthy locks of grey, apparently unaware that the era was over.

After a few days, we decided to upgrade our hotel for one with a private bath, as the lineups for the shared facilities at the Patala were irritatingly long. The Hotel Earth, which we relocated to, did not pan out either. For both the first and second mornings there was no hot water. The desk clerk always related the same story: someone had forgotten to turn it on and he would make sure that someone would switch it on tomorrow. By the third morning we had lost faith. Down the street we went with our packs to the Downtown Hotel. Ahh, a hot shower in a private bathroom moments after we plunked down our belongings; and a good-sized, clean room to boot. We had found our niche for the duration of our Kathmandu stay at $7.50/night.

Nepal has a population of approximately 28 million (2007) and over 60 ethnic groups. With Tibet to the north and India to the south, Buddhism and Hinduism have become commingled, with most Nepalese following an inextricable blend of both beliefs. With the mostly mountainous terrain, only one percent of the land is cultivated, but even so, 80 percent of the people live in small, rural villages. It is one of the poorest countries in the world. Political corruption is endemic.

The abject poverty was increasingly apparent the further we ventured from Thamel. A two-hour walk led us to the confluence of the Vishnumati and Bagmati rivers. Both were extremely polluted, yet were the main source of water for all uses. Dead cattle carcasses rotted at the waters' edge. Children played in garbage dumps. The numerous beggars were pitifully skeletal, often with exposed parts of their bodies eaten away by disease.

In Thamel, another type of desperation was evident in the tiger balm salesmen who worked the streets. The police kept driving them away, not wanting tourists to feel hassled. We got to know a few tiger balm touts very well over the next six weeks, especially Bhimsen and Pundya. They told us that by the time they paid the supplier for the tiger balm, there was only 50 rupees (25 cents) to be made per container. Some days they luckily sold several and other days they sold none. The crackdown by the police gained momentum during the time we were there, and we gleaned that it was spurred on not by tourist complaints, but by pressure from the shop-owners along the streets who believed it was cutting into their sales.

Jobs in the city were hard to come by and there was no livelihood in the villages, so these men invested all they had in tiger balm, along with other small souvenir items, and walked the streets from early morning until midnight. Out of their meagre earnings, they had to pay rent for a room in Kathmandu, feed themselves, and send support home to their families. There was no safety net in Nepal; no welfare system to aid a starving family, no government-funded medical system in case of accidents or illness.

One unusually cold and windy evening as we were walking to supper, we saw a number of tiger balm touts huddled in their thin jackets, no gloves or hats, some with just flip-flops on their feet. We gave them some rupees, as we already had a stockpile of balm purchased from them. Their lifelong struggle for survival was tearing at our hearts. We felt so helpless, and kept trying to come up with some things we could do in our small way.

* * *

It was a 20-kilometre (12-mi) round trip to and from Patan Durbar Square, south of Kathmandu. Could we walk it? The few cold, rainy days were over and the sun was shining. Armed with a map of the main thoroughfares, we meandered along the winding streets. Nepal has practically no middle class; and the poor are the overwhelming majority. Coming across an area of opulent villas with impeccably manicured grounds, we saw samplings of the extreme wealth at the other end of the scale. After getting lost and backtracking several times, a feminine trait won out—I asked for directions—and we made it to the square.

This square was smaller than the one in Kathmandu, but the temples were much more ornate and in better condition. Lots of photo-ops here, like capturing an interesting local with a temple backdrop. We walked home by a different route, through yet another abysmally impoverished area, and were bombarded by merchants, taxi and rickshaw drivers calling out for business every step of the way.

The next day we ventured out to Pashupatinath Temple on the Bagmati River, which is the holiest Hindu site in Nepal. Shrines to the god Shiva lined the hillside. Sadhus (Hindu holy men) walked with staves in hand, dressed in scarlet or mustard-yellow cloths tied over one shoulder, faces painted in polychromatic designs. They vie to plant a *tika* on tourists' foreheads from small pots of red colour they carry, or to have their pictures taken for a small donation. Their dreadlocks were awesome. One fellow had matted strands trailing along the ground as he walked.

Beyond the shrines and surrounded by *gompas* (Buddhist monasteries) is Nepal's largest stupa, called Boudha or Bodhnath among many other names. Its massive whitewashed hemispherical dome, rising 36 metres (118 ft) above the terraced platforms, is symbolic of the Buddha's enlightened mind. Atop the dome is the *harmika*, a cubed section with two striking bow-shaped eyes painted on each side of the cube, personifying the omnipresence and all-seeing eyes of the primordial Buddha. In between these eyes is a third eye that represents the wisdom of looking within. Below this third eye (in place of a nose and looking like a stylized question mark) is the Nepali number one, signifying that the single way to enlightenment is the Buddhist path and unity of all living things. Extending from the *harmika*, a 13-step gilded spire represents the stages of enlightenment. Prayer flags on streamers are draped from the pinnacle to the outer edges of the bottom platform, sending mantras heavenward with each flutter.

Across the river, two funeral pyres crackled and billowed great volumes of smoke. It is a great privilege to be cremated at Pashupatinath. The area directly in front of the temples, reserved for cremating royal bodies, was not in use. In another section, for wealthy citizens, two bodies burned on cement slabs jutting out above the water. We sat on stairs across the river to watch. Male family members stood or sat in the background throughout the three-hour process. (It is customary for the women to mourn at home.) Near the end, an attendant sifted through the ashes with a pole and with swipes of his bare feet. When he was sure the body had been satisfactorily consumed, he pushed the ash and still burning embers into the sacred river. A short distance downstream, life went on as usual, with people bathing or washing clothes. From behind us, monkeys swooped down to the river for a drink. One sailed over so closely, his tail parted my hair.

Up past the temples, we climbed to a belt of lush jungle to check out the monkey-business, as that was where they were leaping down from. We found the trees were charged with an abundance of swinging, screeching primates. Many more sat in circles preening each other in the thick grass. Having heard stories of monkeys in the wild attacking humans carrying food (though we had none ourselves), we backed off when a bunch came over to investigate us.

On the way out of the Pashupatinath area we visited the Biddha Ashram, a home operated by Mother Teresa's Missionaries of Charity. The most wretched and destitute are welcomed there with open arms. Many come to die in peace. Seeking out and financially assisting these shelters for the poor was one way we found to deal with our frustration and powerlessness over the overwhelming poverty we saw around us.

* * *

It was time to investigate our options for organizing our base camp trek in earnest. After several meetings with various companies, we settled on the Mother-Land Nepal Trekking & Expedition Company. We were told to expect the trek duration to be approximately 20 days, with elevations of up to 5,545 metres (18,187 ft). Before we handed over our money, we requested a meeting with the guide-slash-porter who would accompany us. Coming back the next day, we were introduced to Milan, a jovial young fellow with a fair command of English, who left us confident we had made the perfect choice.

We decided to fly to Lukla, which is an airstrip at an altitude of 2,800 metres (9,186 ft). Another option would have been to trek from Kathmandu to Lukla, which would have meant a more gradual ascent, but would also have added five days each way. Many more people choose to fly to Lukla due to time restraints; in our case, we thought it wise to conserve our energy for the Lukla-to-base-camp trek. The price of the package included our flights, a special airfare rate for Milan, plus Milan's services as a guide and porter. We were to pay for all of our accommodations and food along the way; Milan was responsible for his own upkeep in these regards. We parted with our money. October 17 was our departure date. (Not that we would ever be candidates, but an all-inclusive shot at the Everest summit from the Nepalese side cost anywhere from $30,000 to $65,000 US, depending on the route and the range of support with guides, Sherpas, food, tents, and group equipment.)

The very next day Rick woke up with a lousy, nasal-dripping, sneezing, coughing head cold. He did not see the humour in my comment, "It must be a stress reaction to the budget being shot to smithereens with our trek payment." What with the low prices for most things in Thamel, his budget phobia had been in remission. Well, we had a week for him to become shipshape, but why does this always happen after we have an excursion booked? There is no such thing as cancellation insurance on a Nepal trek.

The next five days were spent on leisurely pursuits. Scouring the shops, we hunted for wooden walking sticks, small day packs, and surround sunglasses (having been convinced by the shopkeeper that these were a necessary protection against the glaring sun reflecting off the snow).

Climbing aboard a rickshaw owned by a man named KC, who had been trying to cajole us into his rig for weeks, we enjoyed an hour-long ride around town. He often had to stop in traffic near the bottom of a rise, and start pedalling up the hill with the weight of the rickshaw plus Rick's and my combined 150 kilos (330 lb). I found myself clenching my teeth and holding my breath, somehow feeling this would assist him, as he rose to a standing position and ground down alternately on the pedals with every ounce of energy in his muscular 50-kilo (110-lb) frame.

Another day we took in the city zoo, even though our guidebook gave it a bad report. Although zoos are generally not beneficial places for animals, we have seen worse as far as zoos go. We came as close to a Bengal tiger as we would get on this trip and were astounded by their great size. We could have taken an excursion into a nature reserve, and safely on the back of an elephant hope to catch a glimpse of this elusive cat, but these jungle environs are also infested with mosquitoes. Since it was still malaria season and we had chosen not to take any of the prophylactic drugs, we decided to forgo this adventure into the wild.

One of our tiger balm buddies, Bhimsen, desperately wanted us to accompany him back to his village for the upcoming Dasain Festival. This most important celebration is dedicated each day to a different form of the mother goddess, Durga. It is a time for gift giving, feasting, and family reunions. Leery about bussing for six hours out into the Nepali backwoods with only Bhimsen's very minimal English, we luckily had the viable excuse of timing, as the 10-day Dasain festival would commence a few days before we had to leave on our trek. Goats and pigs are sacrificed for the goddess, becoming an intricate part of the feasting. Ritualistic slaughters can be watched at a particular place in Kathmandu, which KC pointed out on our rickshaw whirl. Rick was against going. I would have gone if it wasn't happening at 6:00 a.m. Before Bhimsen left for his village, we invited him for a Dasain festive breakfast of eggs, toast, potatoes, and bananas; he kept up his pleading with us to come with him right to the end.

* * *

Our much-anticipated day arrived. Rick's cold cleared just in the nick of time. Fifteen minutes after our alarm shrieked at 6:00 a.m., we were off and running to meet Milan at his company's office and then caught a cab to the airport. Our scheduled 8:30 a.m. flight lifted off at around nine. As our prop-plane droned its way to Lukla, I sized up the 20 passengers compressed into the small fuselage, noting we were a minority, being in our mid-50s. Milan called us mum and papa, explaining that it would be disrespectful if he called us by our first names.

This flight was not for the faint of heart. The dips and tilts as the plane was jostled by air currents sweeping through the Himalayan peaks destroyed our equilibrium ... and then there was the landing! A sudden swing to the right brought us between two mammoth mountain walls. At far too great a speed, the small craft aimed its nose toward an extremely short runway at a 30-degree angle up the side of a third mountain. Before I even realized I was holding my breath, the wheels thudded against tarmac, sending the small craft recklessly skidding and screeching to a stop just a few feet short of the rock wall at the end.

On mushy knees we collected our gear and wobbled up the stone steps at the back of the airport runway, then headed downhill to the hotels and restaurants along the winding main street. Lukla is a Sherpa village. Sherpas are the amazing mountain men who carry hefty loads for trekkers and mountaineers up and down the Himalayas, and also transport all matter of supplies to the lodges dotting the way along the mountain passes. Even with evolution on their side, the prowess of these small, agile men—being able to carry loads in excess of 60 kilos (132 lb) at high altitudes—is puzzling to scientists. Because they are paid by the kilo, the official load weight for Sherpas of 30 kilos (66 lb) is often greatly exceeded. We actually witnessed an undeniably gargantuan feat: the unstable and shifting load of a 67-kilo (148-lb) lady with a broken leg being carried in a basket by a 50-kilo (110-lb) Sherpa. We were not sure how far he had carried her, but it had taken him two days to get her back to Lukla from the place where she slipped off an embankment and cracked her femur.

It was soon apparent that past this point, the only other means of transporting goods over land was by yak. These burly beasts were tied to posts along the street, or were seen either leaving or returning with loads weighing over 90 kilos (198 lb). Milan told us that using helicopters as a means of transportation is not popular because of the expense.

Milan left us in the restaurant while he went to check on our room reservation. At this first supper, we were introduced to fresh garlic soup. Once we got past the dishwater consistency, we were hooked. The pungent aroma spiralled upward, making our noses run, and with each slurp our taste buds danced. Said by Sherpas and guides to be a good aide to acclimatizing, we committed to spooning it in at least once a day throughout the whole trek. Anyway, it sure beat the other available option: packaged dehydrated noodle soups with little flavour packs chock full of monosodium glutamate. Why go out of our way to kill brain cells?

After slurping our fill of the wholesome broth, we sat by the large windows overlooking the airstrip, vicariously reliving our harrowing landing as more planes screeched to a stop. The shuttle planes left again within minutes, with Kathmandu-bound passengers or cargo. During takeoffs, the 30-degree grade advantage was reversed: the steep decline was imperative for the needed momentum to become airborne. As each plane dropped off out of sight at the end of the runway, we waited with bated breath for the aircraft to reappear humming in the distance. Down from the airstrip, we watched helicopter beaters stir up clouds of dust from several landing pads.

Milan crossed the floor to our table.

"There is problem with room. Hotel gives rooms to pilots first, so we have wait and see how many come," he announced.

"How long will that be?" I asked.

"I keep checking, don't worry," Milan replied.

A young Nepali man entered the lodge. Milan bounded over to greet him, and they then sat down at a corner table, seemingly to catch up on news. After a time they approached our table. Milan acted as interpreter for the fellow, who was trying to convince us to hire him to carry our bags.

"Hey, Milan, you know we paid you a higher rate to help with our gear as well as being our guide," I reminded him.

"I know ... but my friend wants to carry also." Milan looked uncomfortable, but kept translating his friend's pleas. After a series of "No, thanks," and then plain "No," his friend finally gave up, leaving us feeling guilty, knowing the job situation in Nepal and being aware that locals believe foreigners have an unlimited supply of funds.

We had been super-cognizant of weight when we repacked for the trek. We only took the bare necessities and left most of our gear in a lock-up room at the Downtown Hotel. I would even venture to say by most peoples' standards of necessities, we had still less: a sleeping bag each, one change of underwear and socks, a Gore-Tex jacket, a few fleeces, long underwear, mitts and hats, minimal notions (I did not even attempt to squeeze in any makeup), and no other shirts or pants besides the ones on our backs and backsides. We considered what Milan had and split the loads into three, with Milan and Rick carrying about 10 kilos (22 lb), which left 8 kilos (18 lb) for me. Many porters hired by trekkers along the way carried obscene loads. One European couple, in particular, each had a large backpack plus a day pack straddled across their chests. Their porter strained under two large duffle bags and two hefty suitcases. They marvelled at how little we had. Pointing to their own load, the fellow tried to laugh when he uttered, "This was the height of stupidity," as all three continued huffing and puffing up the trail.

Pilots or not, by eight o'clock our patience was thinner than garlic soup. Just then, Milan waltzed over with a key. He was immediately called into the kitchen for a group meal with the rest of the guides and porters. Led by a hotel employee down to a basement room, the door opened to such an overpowering blast of mildew we could barely catch our breath. We stood momentarily in the middle of this dark, dank mushroom-incubator looking at each other, knowing we could not even stay in this room for a single night.

Up we trudged to the main level. Milan was nowhere to be found. "No more rooms" was the report from the desk. Handing back the key, we walked down the street and got ourselves a decent room at another hotel, had supper, and bedded down for the night.

Milan found us the next day. He was not pleased, as he was friends with the staff at the first hotel. The outcome was a better understanding of each other. Milan now knew there would be times when we would take things into our own hands, and we learned that his special guide rate depended on our staying at the same establishment (though it did not affect him this time).

The first day's trek was so easy I had a hard time not breaking into a jog. Breezing along for three hours from Lukla to the lower elevation of Phakding at 2,610 metres (8,563 ft), our path followed the startlingly clear Dudh Koshi (Milk River). Snow-capped peaks were visible beyond the lush green forested hills around us. Cool, crisp air and bright sunshine elevated our spirits.

"Hey, this is a lot of downhill," Rick commented. "You know what that means on the way back?"

Day 2 taxed our stamina: a mostly uphill trek over rugged terrain to Namche Bazaar at 3,440 metres (11,286 ft), tantamount to being on a Stairmaster for hours at a time. Ancient pines towered hundreds of feet above our heads, waterfalls crashed down the sides of lofty mountains, and aqua rivers roiled beneath our feet as we trudged across wooden bridges. Nestled in this magnificence, we basked in the sun for a whole hour at the small halfway-point outdoor café. Over a second cup of tea, we waved at trekkers who breezed by without stopping, but also noted that others who were there when we came were still lounging when we left.

* * *

"Yak attack!" I had to holler down to Rick so many times I was sure I'd be shouting it in my sleep. It is not hard to figure out who had the right-of-way along the narrow mountain paths. We caught on quickly that when jangling bells were heard, we should scamper up the nearest embankment while these Himalayan oxen—made extra wide by their bulky loads—passed. Several times the yaks decided to wander off the path and head straight for us trekkers, as we hung like grapes from the vine-like bushes on the embankments. Traumatic moments erupted until either the yak driver swatted the beasts back onto the path or pokes from a trekker's walking stick steered them away.

Once, as we were two-thirds of the way across a narrow wooden bridge, we heard a familiar jangle behind us. We turned and saw a yak six-pack come onto the bridge. Something spooked them and they charged, their crashing hooves rapidly reducing the space between us.

"Run, run!" Milan hollered. The bridge shook so violently it was like running on a trampoline.

At the end of the bridge we flew up the nearest rise, slipping and sliding on the loose gravel as the wildly agitated yak thundered by. Shouting drivers galloped in hot pursuit. Attempts to calm their animals failed until finally the yaks ran out of steam a city block away. We loosened our grip on the rocky embankment and assessed the damage to our scraped and bloodied palms; our knees, sticking out of our torn pants, hadn't fared any better. On our way again, we shuddered to think of the apocalyptic ending had we not already almost cleared the bridge when the stampede occurred.

Sherpas dotted the paths, their neck muscles bulging from the strain on their *naamlo*—the fabric belts around their foreheads attached to a *dhoko* (woven basket) heaped with cargo. They often stopped to rest by placing a stick under the load to support it, and then without disrupting the headband they leaned back just enough to transfer the weight of the load from their backs to the stick. It must have taken some practice not to dump the works. They were poorly dressed for the cold weather, and their footwear was beyond inadequate: most had only flip-flops, others wore broken-down shoes, and one fellow was barefoot. One Sherpa we passed had a swollen cheek the size of an orange; probably a badly abscessed tooth. When nearing a village, we saw their bonfires first, always in the most sheltered spot they could find—under a rock ledge or in a grove of trees. They cooked and slept outside. Even if the hotels had room for the Sherpas, they would not have been able to afford even the reduced rate given to the guides, who usually settled down for the night on the dining room benches and tables after the supper guests left.

We were ravenous when we finally trudged into Namche Bazaar. Settling on dal bhat, the energizing staple of porters and guides, we dug into heaps of lentils swimming in spicy sauce over a bed of rice.

Since the difference in elevation from Phakding to Namche Bazaar is 830 metres (2,723 ft), much more than the 300 metres (984 ft) per day recommended by mountain sickness experts, we spent a rest day in Namche Bazaar to give our bodies time to adjust to the new elevation. But even those few who choose to pay no heed to the altitude guidelines would probably not want to rush through this colourful Sherpa village.

As it was Saturday, the famous weekend market was underway. Nepalese people from outlying villages and Tibetan traders who had carried their goods many miles across the mountains congregated in the large central square, up the side streets, and anywhere else they could spread a blanket to display their wares. It had a festive atmosphere, with lots of bantering and bargaining going on. We bought a warmer pair of mitts for Rick, woolly socks for Milan, a handcrafted necklace for me, and celebrated our purchases by feasting on gooey cinnamon buns from the village bakery.

On Day 4 we made a four-and-a-half-hour trek to Shyangboche, at an elevation of 3,720 metres (12,205 ft). About two hours into the trek we came upon the Everest View Lodge. As the name implies, we caught a glimpse of Mt. Everest far off in the distance. Those who can afford it—and who do not want the exertion of a trek—fly in by helicopter. Milan said that the cost was $200.00 US for a night's stay to view Everest (through binoculars) from an overstuffed reclining chair beside a crackling fireplace with a hot toddy in hand.

From the Lodge, we were game for a one-hour side trip up to Khumjung Monastery, where Milan promised we would find a spectacular view of Mt. Khumjung. As we circumnavigated the lodge to find the upward path, we noticed a distressed group of four people huddled on a grassy knoll. One man was suffering badly from AMS (Acute Mountain Sickness). He was unable to even lift his head. They were waiting for a helicopter summoned for them by the lodge employees. Milan asked what had been done for him. Several remedial medications had been administered, but the only reliable method to halt the progress of AMS is to get the person to a lower elevation as quickly as possible and hope the damage is not past the point where it can be reversed. They were still waiting for the helicopter when we descended from the monastery to continue on to our night stay at Shyangboche.

* * *

While in Kathmandu, I had attended an AMS 101 seminar for a simplistic explanation of the two types of AMS. One is pulmonary edema, in which the lungs fill with fluid; the other is cerebral edema, in which fluid gathers around the brain. Oxygen deprivation is the sole cause of both. With the rarefied oxygen at high elevations, human bodies rally naturally by manufacturing more red blood cells to supply the body with adequate oxygen. Ascending faster than your body can adapt is dangerous. Even the most athletic person can succumb to AMS. In fact, the more trained the athlete, the more they tend to shrug off symptoms that should never be ignored—headaches, loss of appetite, nausea, light-headedness, or disorientation. The doctor conducting the seminar recommended Diamox, a diuretic, as a precautionary aid. I purchased a bottle, as well as a good stockpile of iodine tablets to treat our drinking water. Being eco-trekkers, we did not want to add dozens of plastic bottles to the Lodge's garbage sites.

Day 5: our goal was Tengboche at 3,860 metres (12,664 ft). After a three-hour trek, mostly downhill, we broke for lunch. It was a good thing we refuelled. The remainder of the day was a steady incline alongside miles of the world's largest species of tree rhododendrons (*Rhododendron arboreum*), which can reach up to 18 metres (59 ft) in height. During March and April, the national flower bursts into blooms of white, pinks, and scarlet.

Milan ventured out ahead to secure a room for us at Tengboche, which only has three hotels besides the renowned monastery. He made it there within two hours—compared to our five.

We ended up in the same lodge as a group of 20 other Canadians who were trekking to the Everest Base Camp with Peak Freaks, a British Columbia–based company that offers trekking and climbing excursions. This year's clients were of all age groups, including two families with children aged 10 and 12. Supper was an entertaining event with this boisterous group of people, two of whom were doctors who encouraged us to gauge the body's oxygen level with a monitor they had along. Rick's reading was 92–95 and mine was 91–94—both in the "very good" category, which was reassuring.

We begged for extra blankets that night. The farther up we went, the colder it got. We became acutely aware that our sleeping bags were not adequate, and prayed there would be a continuing supply of extra blankets along the way.

Day 6's trek was to bring us to Pheriche at 4,240 metres (13,911 ft). Up—as usual—at 6:00 a.m. (yuck), we were ready to leave at 7:45. The legendary Gurkha soldier training bases flanked the hill on the right as we ascended from Tengboche. As the hours and kilometres lapsed, the sparse and stunted growth heralded the end of the treeline. Admittedly, we were not the swiftest trekkers, so Milan again left us midway to book the night's lodging. After crossing a river, we faced an arduous three-hour climb. The land was increasingly arid; soon the scant vegetation barely reached our boot tops. We stopped dead at a junction with forks leading in several different directions. It must have been Milan who scratched an M in the dirt with an arrow pointing to the left ... at least we hoped it was Milan's handiwork. The icy wind bit into my forehead and cheeks, and there was no sensation left in my nose at all. I looked back at Rick through stinging, watery eyes and saw he was faring no better. As we crested the mountain, the velocity became so ferocious we resorted to doubling over and shuffling along so as not to be blown off the narrow ledge. *Oh, Pheriche, where are you?* Another seemingly endless quarter-mile around the ledge, the path turned downward, and we glimpsed miniature structures in the distance. Eureka! The gale-force winds dwindled. Leaning back, we let our body weight propel us down the mountainside. Near the village, rotund piles of yak patties stood like sentries. Nary a stick of wood would fuel the pot-bellied stoves; it would be dried yak dung mixed with grass from here on up. We hardly noticed the peculiar odour as the sizzling fire spread its rich warmth and a relieved Milan handed us a cup of steaming tea. He had been about to come looking for us. A bucket shower before turning in for the night was heavenly ... little did we know it would be our last for many a day.

* * *

A routine evolved: breakfast at daybreak, trek to the next designated spot, spend evening in the dining room to enjoy a much-needed repast, then relax, read or chat until the fire dies down. This popular roost was the only part of a lodge with any heat source aside from the kitchen. Most of the kitchens lacked proper ventilation and were smoke-filled. The kitchen staff and the guides who ate there seemed oblivious to the thick haze, which kept foreigners at bay. The dining room, though, was the happening place, where we trekkers congregated to swap stories, dry articles of clothing on the backs of chairs, and even engage in a few sing-alongs—a rewarding end to the day's exhilarating challenges.

The accommodations became more rudimentary the farther up we went, but the food was always flavourful (though lacking in variety). My favourite were *mo-mos*, which are tasty little meat or potato and garlic-filled dough triangles, boiled then fried, much like a variation on the perogies my Ukrainian baba used to whip up. Rick usually went with spaghetti (the other choice besides dahl bhat). Both supplied much-needed carbs. When the fire died down around eight, we all headed straight for our sleeping bags. We could see our breath in the bedrooms, and sometimes there was only a candle for light. From Pheriche on, we slept in all our clothes, as it was the only way we could keep warm (even with a scrounged blanket). Another advantage to sleeping fully attired was for the night treks to the outdoor squatter. There was no way to avoid it, as in high altitudes, the old bladder fills more readily. One clever girl shared her solution with us: an extra Nalgene bottle. Too bad we only had one each and no extras.

I would hold off as long as humanly possible before going out into the frigid blackness, praying there would not be a lineup. There were no lights in the outhouse, so cautious users took a few moments to allow their eyes to adjust to the dark interior, noting the logistics in order to aim right.

Some did not. Rumour has it that one fellow's leg disappeared down the hole in the floor, and he ended up burning his pants instead of laundering them.

If there was a worthwhile side to these excursions, it had to be the night skies. The diamond brilliance of stars in the black velvet of infinity and the low half-moon beguiled us with the promise of being able to touch her soft glow from the top rung of a fence ... If we dared to venture across the field in-between. Rick, who hated leaving his cozy nest even more than I did, ended up staying out the longest. His logic was that if he had to be out there anyway, he might as well enjoy this celestial extravaganza to the fullest.

The Pheriche dining experience was extra-special. Milan told us that he would be gone for a few hours to celebrate the ongoing Dasain Festival with the hotel owner, who was a good friend of his father's. He came back a bit tipsy while the fire was still roaring. A ghetto blaster appeared on the scene, and all those lucky enough to be present were treated to the Nepali men taking turns dancing to catchy folk songs. Our Milan was by far the best. His twinkling eyes and beaming smile captivated the audience as he spun and leapt around the room higher and faster than anyone else. He gladly obliged the chants for an encore. It was easy to wheedle the inebriated hotel owner into putting some extra yak patties on the fire. The festivities lasted until after midnight. Luckily, we would not be jolted awake by our shrill alarm clock at the crack of dawn: an extra day in Pheriche to acclimatize was in order.

Late the next morning, we climbed 300 metres (984 ft) up the mountain behind the village. We were following the "climb high, sleep low" method of acclimatizing. Allowing our bodies to experience a higher altitude for a short period, then descending back down for the night theoretically allowed us to climb even higher the next day with no ill effects.

After reaching our goal for the day, we sat for a while on the sun-baked rocks like kings on their thrones, nestled in the turrets of the mighty Himalayas. Milan let loose with the Nepalese version of our Bigfoot (or Sasquatch) tale.

"Keep your eyes sharp for yeti. Like very big, strong, and tall-size man covered with brown fur. While crossing Himalayas, many Sherpa see big footmarks in snow. Yeti does not like to meet with people, but many Sherpa see them standing in distance. Tenzing Norgay saw one." Milan stated this firmly, as if a sighting by this famed mountain man (who accompanied Sir Edmund Hillary on his 1953 climb to the summit of Mt. Everest) settled forever that yeti really existed.

Rick uncorked a thermos of sweet tea, which we rationed into three cups. The curling steam spiralled with my condensing breath as I sipped.

"One Sherpa is attacked by yeti so bad he went crazy with fear," Milan continued. "Another time a man is frozen and could not walk by himself and yeti carried him to edge of village where his people find him and he is saved. So you see? You can never tell what yeti will do. Remember: if you smell heavy garlic in air, yeti may be coming."

"Oh, oh, I smell garlic all the time," I giggled. "It's our own breath from our daily intake of garlic soup."

Yeti-less, we started our downward trek, the mystery of these strange creatures renewed. Fiction or fact? One vacillates, when sightings have been recorded by such notables as mountaineer Reinhold Messner—an unbeliever until he spotted one in Tibet in 1986.

Although it was more gruelling to ascend, Rick and I found it far more dangerous to descend. We had already learned the hard way to stifle the urge to charge back downhill; both of us had already wiped out on scree and felt the beginnings of the all-too-common development of shin splints. Also, the odd backward lean when descending is a killer on the old sacroiliac.

Still feeling spunky that evening, we decided to attend a talk on AMS at the Himalayan Rescue Association headquarters. The presenting doctor had a sledgehammer approach to ignoring the symptoms of altitude sickness, with descriptions of actual cases previously treated at the small rescue facility in Pheriche. Only weeks ago, a 22-year-old Australian girl had died of cerebral edema as a result of keeping up with her party of friends who were not adhering to the rest days. Rick and I had only experienced the normal body changes so far: somewhat reduced energy, increased urination, extra thirst, and now and then a heavy head.

Undoubtedly influenced by the AMS session, we convinced Milan (though he thought we were being overly cautious) to only go as far as Tukla the next day—a short one-and-a-half-hour trek. At 4,620 metres (15,158 ft), it has only a 380 metre (1,247 ft) gain from Pheriche, hardly more than our acclimatization climb of yesterday. Tukla has only two lodges, as being so close to Pheriche, it is usually only a lunch stop.

The climb was a continual uphill slope. Antagonists with us for the remainder of the trek made their appearance: frigid air with biting winds, and a halogen sun blasting through the thin atmosphere. Simultaneously these opposites played havoc with our exposed skin, a peculiar phenomenon. Starting out in the morning, we wore every piece of clothing we had along. Once on the trail, it was a juggling act to regulate body temperature. Fleece on, fleece off, on, off, more sun screen, hat on, hat off, on, off, always sunglasses ... eyes down to secure footing, stops to take in incredible scenery and catch our breath.

After arriving at Tukla, we stored our gear and ventured into the surrounding hills until sunset. Then, for the duration of the evening, we huddled around the fire at the Yak Lodge. Like-minded people filled the dining room to capacity. We met some very special people: Jenny and Dave from the States, and Steve from Canada, whom we found instant camaraderie with.

The owner of our lodge in Tukla was none other than Tashi Tshering Lhakpa, one of the Sherpas on the fateful 1996 Fischer–Hall expeditions, where eight mountaineers lost their lives the same day in a sudden storm—including the immensely experienced leaders, Scott Fischer and Rob Hall. We were honoured to meet this soft-spoken and distinguished gentleman, who told us that the 1996 Everest summit was his last climb; the catastrophic events caused him to abandon forever what had up until then been his life's work. Our fixation of late was reading about the human need to conquer the highest peaks in the world. We devoured several books on this 1996 disaster, all written by people who were on the climb. It was amazing to see the different perspectives on the same chain of events leading up to the fatalities. *Into Thin Air* by Jon Krakauer was the first book published (and later made into a movie). Krakauer subtly zeroes in on some actions of Anatoli Boukreev—a Kazakhstani guide-extraordinaire on Fischer's team—whom Krakauer believed made some poor decisions that contributed to the deaths. Anatoli Boukreev and G. Weston DeWalt followed with *The Climb*, wherein Boukreev justified his decisions to set the record straight. *Climbing High* by Lene Gammelgaard—who survived the ordeal—builds Boukreev's character as the main rescuer. We are left wondering whether Krakauer even knew Gammelgaard was along ... or was it because she sided with Boukreev that he did not mention her in his book, except in the list of names on Fischer's team?

* * *

We balanced our reading with the accounts of many sensationally successful Everest climbs. One in particular that gripped us was by Alison Jane Hargreaves. In May 1995, Hargreaves was the first woman to summit Mt. Everest with no Sherpa or canistered oxygen. I believe the body alone cannot master extraordinary feats such as this without the indomitable will of the human spirit. Sadly, in August of that same year after successfully reaching the summit of K2, Ms. Hargreaves was blown off the mountain to her death on the descent.

We were sleepless in Tukla (with none of the romance of *Sleepless in Seattle*). Our room was right off the dining room, in which a few old sots got into the whiskey. Though told to hush up by many of us who had adjoining rooms, they mindlessly kept up the roistering all night. An added ingredient to our insomnia was our teeth-chattering shivering, even with the extra blankets. How those two sat up without a fire, I'll never know ... lots of antifreeze, I guess.

On Day 9 we climbed to Lobuje at 4,930 metres (16,175 ft). The first half-hour was nearly vertical; a tough slog first thing in the morning. At the top of this rise we came to a wide-open area dotted with numerous stone memorials to people who had perished climbing Everest. Scott Fischer's was among them. Most were memorials to Sherpas. Statistics compiled in 2003—on the 50th anniversary of Sir Edmund Hillary and Tenzing Norgay's summit—report that of the 1,300 people to summit Everest from both the Nepalese and Tibetan sides, 175 died, the majority being Sherpas.

While getting ready to head off again, there was suddenly much excitement in the clearing. Binoculars were passed around as we witnessed 18 climbers summit Lhotse peak! At 6,700 metres (21,982 ft), Lhotse is the fourth-highest mountain in the Himalayas.

Another short-trek day. After lunch, we hiked up to a ridge above Lobuje to view Khumbu Glacier. What a chillingly magnificent sight! Crevasses of eons-old blue-green ice thrust through the layers of rocky sand, and pools of melted glacial ice shimmered like aquamarine silk. We would traverse a small part of this massive icefield the following day.

We entered our 15-person dorm at Lobuje for the night and slung our gear on the top double-bunk at the very back of the room, remembering that heat rises. The staff promised us a night fire in the dorm's potbellied stove. The double bed was $30.00 per night. Our other option would have been a room in the only other lodge for $65.00. Choosing the alternate lodge would have been a problem for Milan: he could sleep in the dining room for free at the cheaper lodge, provided we stayed there, but the same bonus was not available at the expensive one.

I read Rick's journal about that night and thought he accurately put it into words: "Everybody was hacking, coughing, snorting, sneezing, farting, or snoring. On top of all that I had to get up five times to piss." My most vivid recollection of that night was the stone-hard pillow. I would awaken every half-hour to slowly and painfully rotate my aching head while loud reverberations of Bob Seger wailing "Like a Rock" bounced around inside my cranium. I took off my fleece to roll up and use for a pillow until I began to shiver, as the cozy fire that had blazed when we went to bed was never stoked and had long since burned out.

When we went over to the expensive lodge's dining room for breakfast the next morning, we chatted with people who had spent the night there: they reported that it was "damn cold," so we did not feel as bad. The only real difference for the extra $35 was that they had had an indoor deep-freeze bathroom, while ours was an 18-metre (20-yard) traipse away to the outhouse.

Day 10: we aimed for Gorak Shep at 5,160 metres (16,929 ft). Rick was not in good humour this morning. Sleep deprivation never sits lightly with his constitution. We followed along the glacier for some time, then veered onto the sand-covered ice where our boots made a hollow crunching sound with each step. It was immense: like when swimming to the opposite shore of a lake, for the longest time our plodding along did not seem to bring us any closer to the other side, but eventually we stepped once again onto land. The terrain from this point on was the most rugged we had encountered so far ... or did it just seem that way? Halfway up a steep climb, Rick was ready to call it quits. Throwing up his hands, he adamantly stated, "You guys go ahead. I'm going back. This is like running on a treadmill and breathing through a straw." I knew he would never forgive himself if he did not go on when we were so close to our goal. With coaxing from Milan and me, we all made it to Gorak Shep.

* * *

Immediately upon our arrival, the warm sunroom built next to the hotel enticed us into its toasty fold, where we stretched out and snoozed on benches, well occupied by other snoozers. After our 40 winks, we just stayed where we were and watched the activity through the windows. Helicopters spun dust clouds as they landed or took off from a pad about 46 metres (50 yds) away. This was the highest conventional helicopters could safely go due to the thin air. Some super rescue helicopters have been developed. Eurocopter reported landing on the summit of Everest in 2005. The unmanned Alpine Wasp, developed by TGR Helicorp, has been in testing mode since 2007 and can technically operate up to an altitude of 9,000 metres (higher than Everest's 8,850-metre summit). Neither is in common rescue use, the challenge being that with air so thin, helicopter reliability can be drastically compromised by weather and other factors.

Trekkers approached the lodge from every direction, some with the worst sun and windburns I had ever seen: fiery red, blistered, and weeping skin patches. I planned to double my routine slathering of sunscreen.

Our attention was drawn to a man having great difficulty negotiating the steps to the lodge. There was a familiarity about him. He pulled off his hat. It was Steve, from Canada! We ran out to greet him. He had trekked from Lobuje to Gorak Shep, up Kala Pattar, and was now intent on returning back to Lobuje ... all in one day. His skin was drawn and ghostly pale. He said every cell in his body ached. Thinking something to eat would bring back his energy, he ordered a meal, but was unable to swallow a bite. We encouraged him to stay at Gorak Shep for the night, but he insisted on going back to Lobuje—where he had left his sleeping bag and all his gear. In addition, he expressed a driving need to just keep moving down. We then suggested he hire a porter to go back with him. The hotel staff tried to sway him in this direction also, to no avail. Telling us all to get off his back and that his mind was made up, Steve struck out by himself around 3:30 p.m. for the two-hour trek back to Lobuje. Darkness would fall before he got there. What if he slipped and injured himself or lost his way? Our imaginations ran amok with dreadful scenarios.

Turning in early that evening proved futile. Concern for Steve coupled with the plans for tomorrow's grand finale ran though our minds, and half the night passed before we fell into a sporadic sleep. Knowing that from the Base Camp the view of Mt. Everest would be blocked by the Khumbu Icefall, we would climb Kala Pattar for an unobstructed vista of the "top of the world." On the summit of Kala Pattar at 5,545 metres (18,187 ft), we would be higher than the loftiest Rocky Mountain peak in Canada (Mt. Robson, at 3,955 metres, or 12,972 ft) and above the highest Rocky Mountain peak in the United States (Mt. Elbert, rising to 4,444 metres, or 14,433 ft).

Milan was at our door at precisely 4:45 a.m. with glasses of steaming tea with milk. Breakfast could wait for our return. Filled water bottles left on a shelf overnight were mostly ice. We placed them between our layered clothing. Shortly after 5:00 a.m., swathed in chilling darkness, we began the gruelling ascent. Our breath condensed on our lashes and brows. Rick, still easily winded, told Milan and me to go ahead to get some good photos of Everest.

A thunderous roar of deafening proportions triggered heart-palpitating panic. "Avalanche!" Milan shouted, and pointed to a mass of snow moving down the side of Mt. Nuptse on the left, sending up voluminous sprays of powder. As the rumbling faded, we continued upward. The Base Camp was in plain view at the foot of the Khumbu Icefall to the right. Several crimson tents were perched on the trampled snow. On the periphery were used oxygen canisters and other refuse from expeditions.

Milan and I continued upward past the obstructing Icefall. Our eyes fused to the distinctive contours of Everest. Our boots crunched onto the summit of Kala Pattar. We were soon joined by Rick. With arms linked, we stood face to face with the highest point on earth, standing 8,850 metres (29,035 ft) above sea level. It is known as Chomolongma (goddess mother of the earth) to Tibetans, Sagarmatha (forehead of the sky) to the Nepalese; both are fitting. Our eyes scanned the panorama of surrounding Himalayan monoliths. Milan swelled with pride and love for this, the mightiest of mountains, straddling the border between his country and Tibet. I felt dwarfed and humbled by such an overpowering, daunting manifestation of nature's greatness. Rick's misty eyes and the broadest of smiles reflected his elation at meeting a lifelong goal.

Our extremities were pinched with frostbite, yet we stayed riveted as the sun, rising behind Everest, created a gleaming halo around its periphery, and the grey of dawn morphed into shades of blue.

We took turns in pairs beaming at the camera with an Everest backdrop to prove we were there, followed by high-fives all around before we started back down.

* * *

After a steaming hot breakfast, we set off for the three-and-a-half-hour trek back through Lobuje, Tukla, and Pheriche to Tengboche. We sure were speedier going mostly downhill. With all our extra red blood cells, I pictured us spinning around Tasmanian devil–style when we reached Kathmandu.

Spending the late afternoon at the Environmental and Cultural Centre at Tengboche, we gleaned some of the history of the area and learned about the fragile environment at these altitudes. In the early evening, we followed the tintinnabulations calling the monks to evening supplications. After the monks entered—along with many young boys who were being schooled in the monastery—we were ushered in around the perimeter of the prayer room. Once again we were privy to the mellifluous chanting of the sutras, many of which are believed to be the direct teachings of the historical Buddha.

* * *

From Tengboche to Namche Bazaar on Day 13 we trekked four and a half hours with no lunch break, with a lot of uphill considering we were going down in elevation. Rick gets testy without regular feedings, so halfway there I cracked out the Snickers bars and all was right with the world. I offered Milan a chocolate bar. He refused, saying he did not eat junk food. Very commendable; I passed him an orange while Rick and I almost swallowed our Snickers whole.

As we again approached the treeline, we revelled in the brilliant golds and russets of autumn now splashed amid the conifers on the mountainsides. Not even a breeze today. Definitely overdressed, we stopped every 20 minutes or so to discard yet another sweat-soaked piece of clothing until we were in T-shirts and had converted our zip-off pants into shorts.

Day 14 and October 31: Namche Bazaar to Lukla. We imagined our grandchildren raking in their Halloween loot and smiled. Eager to get back to Lukla, we chose to hike for seven and a half hours with a one-hour lunch break. I remembered Rick noticing the unbelievably long downhill route on the first day of our trek. We were now squinting way up at the same trail. A recent rain had left the trails slippery with mud. Milan had left us long ago to book our room. Thank goodness he was not there to witness our flailing: five steps up, slip back two. A monk going downhill passed us. As we made it up to the halfway point, we stopped for a congratulatory look backward for making it that far and saw the same monk gaining on us. He smiled and gave us a wan nod as the whoosh from his garments ruffled our hair as he sped past.

"Jeez, he's not even breathing heavily. He probably climbs this hill every day of his life," Rick wheezed. On quivering legs, we finally reached the top and gazed lovingly at the sweet haven of Lukla just ahead. I offered up a prayer of thanks that nothing had gotten in the way of our completing this extraordinary adventure. Then I envisioned what awaited us as we walked the last mile: a hot shower, a big plate of mo-mos, French fries, chocolate cake, a cup of tea, and a bed—preferably in that order.

* * *

November 1: we hoped to see the bright lights of Kathmandu by evening. We arrived at the airport early in the morning to see about changing our return flights, which had been booked for November 4 to allow some leeway time for us to complete the trek. Milan came back from talking to the powers-that-be and told us we were on a waiting list and would have to sit around for a couple of hours to see if we could leave later that day. I never did figure out the system, as even those whose tickets were for today had no specific flight number, and the aircraft shuttling back and forth between Lukla and Kathmandu were being filled with no strict adherence to the departure times stated on tickets.

What happened next had to have been more than just a coincidence. Who did we see walking around the corner, with a much stronger gait than the last time we had seen him? Yes, Steve from Canada.

"I can't tell you how many times I felt like just lying down on the path," Steve relayed. "I did not see a single soul along the way. Several times when there was a fork in the road, I would stagger off in one direction, and moments later a strong stab in my gut told me to go the other way. When I finally spotted Lobuje, I told my guardian angel she could have prompted me less intensely." Once at Lobuje, his sleep must have been comatose, as he did not remember even turning over for 16 hours. We were thrilled to see him alive and well and humorously reliving his ordeal.

Milan rushed over and told us we would be on the next flight. We hustled onto the tarmac and tucked ourselves into our seats, which happened to be close to the front. I tensed as I peered past the pilot to the nose of the plane, pointing down the 30-degree slant of the runway. The engine hummed and propellers whirred, making the small plane dance on the tarmac, before it jerked forward and roared down the runway to gain as much momentum as possible. Rick was the colour of skim milk. My stomach did somersaults and my heart fluttered as we dropped off the edge ... down, down, fighting against gravity. Suddenly the plane rattled, levelled off, and was cutting through the mountains.

* * *

Kathmandu looked exquisite in every way. Our room at the Downtown Hotel took on a five-star ambiance. Bishnue and Bobby welcomed us home. These fine young fellows manned the hotel desk 24 hours a day, making sure everyone's needs were met. For the next few weeks, we indulged in sleep-ins, eventually prying ourselves out of bed for a breakfast at Pumpernickel's: omelettes, cappuccinos, fruit, and the best cinnamon buns on the planet. We were welcomed back by our tiger balm buddies, who were still clandestinely marketing their wares. Our Kathmandu Granny blessed us each day—this tiny old lady who lived off the handouts of tourists was also in good with the Thamel restaurateurs, who often passed her a bag of food. Her missing teeth only made her broad smile more endearing as she held out her hands to clasp ours whenever she spotted us, hopeful of a coin, which we always had. Coming back to our hotel any time after nine in the evening, we would see her bundled up and sleeping in a squat position on one of her two favourite corners. One day an old beggar man entered her territory and she took after him with her cane, and no doubt some choice Nepali words.

Checking out the daily showings of pirated movies at five or six restaurants was a lark. The shows were the latest releases from North America. If we found one of interest, or sometimes even if the movie wasn't our usual choice, relaxing over a movie with supper was always appealing, movie buffs that we are. On significant occasions—like the first anniversary of our retirement on November 15, or special commemorations that we drummed up like "completion of our laundry and chores"—we would head to the plush ambiance of Helena's for a delectable veggie sizzler.

A special party was in order the day we finally obtained our visas for India. We could have walked the several kilometres between Thamel and the Indian Consulate blindfolded by the time we had our visas in hand. The scenario went something like this. First day: stand in a long line to get a form. After filling out the form, stand in another line to hand in the form and pay a processing fee. Not our lucky day! Just as our place in the queue of the second line was two bodies from the clerk, the office closed for the day. Back for the next day's lineup. After responding to questions, paying up and handing in the form, we were told to come back in two days for our visas. Another long lineup on the pickup day. When it was Rick's turn to stand in line while I read in the shade, he got to practise his French on the couple in front of him.

When I came to take my turn in the line, he asked "How long do you think this couple have been travelling?"

I knew by his intonation it had been an impressively long time, so I said, "Four years."

"Nope, not even close. Seventeen years!" This couple, in their forties, had chosen to travel for life. They had a large boat, which was now moored in Hong Kong. Their method over the years had been to choose a port, then travel overland to destinations they chose to see, then head back to their boat and sail on to the next port. When they ran low on money, they both worked for a time, and then went off on another adventure. Needless to say, they had no children and were not worried about a nest egg for their old age.

While we were engrossed in their captivating life story, the lineup dwindled, and at last ended with us tightly clutching our Indian visas. We headed straight to Rum Doodle's for a "success supper" of succulent steak. This restaurant and bar is a favourite meeting place for mountaineering expeditions. In fact, climbers eat free there ... but only if they conquer Everest first.

* * *

Our Nepali friends were getting ready for Diwali, the festival of lights (an Indian festival incorporated into their own longer Tihar festival). It is one of Nepal's most beautiful festivals, and is celebrated with great flourish in Kathmandu. Two deities hold top billing: Yama, Lord of Death; and Lakshmi, the goddess of wealth and good fortune. Yama is honoured with five days of rituals, while at dusk each day hundreds of tiny oil lamps and candles are placed in doors and windows to welcome Lakshmi. Electric strands have been added to the festivities by those who can afford them. Garlands of marigolds drape entrances. Many people sport a tika of red powder dotting the middle of the forehead. The first two days honour the crow and the dog. Dogs everywhere—with puzzled looks on their faces from the abrupt change in human behaviour—are tika'd, adorned with garlands of marigolds, and have food put out for them. On the third day, Lakshmi Puja, it is the sacred cows' turn to be swathed in garlands, tika'd, and fed. Young children go from door to door singing and begging for coins and sweets. The Newari New Year happens to fall during that time, giving rise to bands of young men caught up in much revelry. On the last day of the festival Bishnue and Bobby looked like walking flower shops. On this day, brothers are honoured with tikas and garlands by their sisters, who perform a *puja* (prayer and offering) for their brother's longevity. Sisters, even if they are married and living away from their family of origin, make a great effort to come back home for this ritual (unless they are pregnant, in which case they are not allowed to participate that year). Brothers reciprocate with tikas and gifts of money. The festival ends with much feasting.

Adhering to our new practice, we got out our camera to capture Bishnue and Bobby on such an important occasion, and later printed copies to send back to them. Not many people in Nepal have cameras, and we could just imagine the fun and pleasure they would have when they received the pictures.

David and Jenny, who we met on the Everest trek, were leaving for India the next day. At a farewell supper of veggie sizzlers at Helena's Restaurant, they told us about an interesting site we had somehow missed, which inspired us to leave the comforts of Thamel the next morning for a 4-kilometre (2.5 mi) walk to Swayambhunath (or the Monkey Temple, as it is commonly known). It was located on top of a hill; I started to count the stairs as we ascended. Midway up, we were watched over by brightly painted Buddhas 10 metres (33 ft) tall, surrounded by shrines to various Hindu gods—an example of how the two belief systems are interwoven in the Nepali culture. I spied my favourite Hindu deity: Ganesh, the beloved little elephant-headed god believed to be the "remover of all obstacles." I knelt down to have my picture taken with him. Probably mistaking me for a statue, a teeny monkey landed on my shoulder, leaping away instantaneously with a squeal when he realized his error and before I had a chance to react and outdo him with a feral shriek. Wild monkeys owned this hill. When a big male came sashaying down the wide stairway, the lesser-sized male monkeys screeched and scattered in all directions. It was even more amusing when humans, including us, scurried to the right or left of the path to stay out of his way. I saw a definite smirk on his face. After a total of 300 steps, our eyes fixed on a prominent stupa and a bustling commercial square from which we could see the vista of Kathmandu valley below.

* * *

Our stay in Kathmandu was coming to an end. We'd be especially sad to leave Bhimsen and Pundya. Both kept asking us if we could think of anything else they could do to make a living besides selling tiger balm. Bhimsen had two households to keep; that of his wife and children back in his village, and his temporary accommodation while he resided in Kathmandu during the tourist season. Pundya was a young, single fellow who sent money home to his parents, who also lived in a rural area. We came up with an idea that Bhimsen was not keen on, but Pundya thought was worth a try: noticing that the shopkeepers were stuck in their place of business for 12 or more hours a day, we suggested making tea (Nepali-style, with milk and sugar) and going around peddling it to these retail-prisoners. The Thamel restaurateurs would probably run him out for cutting into their business, but in the areas outside of Thamel where the locals shopped, this type of catering service seemed to be nonexistent.

Off we went with Pundya to shop for a dozen tin cups, a pot to boil the tea, tea bags, sugar, and the largest thermos we could find. With these purchases in hand we made our way to his home. Pundya pushed open a small, rather hidden door along a lengthy row of shops. A dark passage led to a courtyard, where a plethora of slum dwellings was unveiled—a raft of rooms on three levels, constructed of wood and appearing dangerously close to the verge of collapse. Following Pundya, we passed a central pump—the only water supply for drinking as well as washing for all the tenants. We climbed on all fours up a narrow set of stairs with a few boards missing. Pundya pulled out a key and opened a big padlock. Even before he opened the door we could see right into the room through the ill-fitting slat-walls, which did little to keep out the stifling heat of summer, the bone-chilling winter winds, or those intending thievery.

He was quite proud of the 1.5 x 2 metre (5 x 6.5 ft) room we entered. It contained a raised board for a bed (topped with a quilt for a mattress and one thin blanket), a propane camp-stove with two burners, a few cooking utensils, a water bucket, and one change of clothing hanging from the ceiling in the corner. He showed us a pot half-filled with rice and a few vegetables. Pundya explained how he saved cooking fuel by making enough at one time to last him a week (refrigeration being too out-of-reach to even be considered). I kept smiling, while my heart ached with the realization that this pot, filled to the top, could only hold what Rick and I would consume in one meal. He paid an atrocious rent for the room; gouging slum landlords are everywhere. He invited us to sit on the bed while he squatted on the floor, planning out how he would make and sell his tea. Soon several friends came to meet us and hear about Pundya's new business venture. Our investment of $18.00 set up this young entrepreneur.

With only a few days left before leaving Nepal, we thought we would not see Pundya again. On our very last evening we were thrilled to find him waiting for us outside our hotel with a wide smile on his face. Giddily he told us how he had raked in 175 rupees ($2.35) on his first day of tea-peddling, and 220 rupees the next. We will always wonder if Pundya is still selling tea.

That last evening, we made the rounds to say our goodbyes and to give away most of our winter clothing, extra day packs, and sleeping bags used on the Everest trek, as well as gifts of rupees. Milan, over a farewell coffee, gave us each a *khata*—a white Buddhist ceremonial scarf used for many occasions, this time for safe travel. Bhimsen presented Rick with a braided cloth bracelet and a cloth purse for me. We shook hands with our two favourite fruit vendors and the staff at our favourite haunt, Pumpernickel's. I found someone to translate to Granny that we were leaving the next day. She gave us a hug and we each expressed parting messages that neither could understand, but words were superfluous to the well-wishes in our hearts.

We left Nepal far richer in tangible as well as intangible ways. Our bodies were as rock-hard as they would ever get from our Everest trek, and endurance had taken on new dimensions. Our Nepali friends had imprinted their unique blend of attributes, cultural traditions, and genuine friendliness in our memories and on our souls. As we continued our progression through Asia, the crushing poverty was a rude awakening; to see the struggles to put a roof over a family's head, to put food on the table, to educate children, to obtain medical supplies and all manner of things we took for granted. It made our complaints and petty arguments seem nonsensical. The many heroes along the streets and in the hovels of Nepal commanded our deepest admiration and respect. Our perspective on everything we thought we knew was in flux; all we knew for sure was that we would never be the same. We were on a one-way journey in the evolving transition of travel.

Our Drawn-out Exit

We boarded an early morning bus for the Nepali border on November 26. A harrowing ride ensued as the rickety vehicle sped around mountain curves. We rumbled past steppe farming and fields stretching on for miles, water buffalo providing the source of energy to till the soil. Lush jungle began to replace the farmlands. We passed a total of four trucks and two buses overturned in the ditches along the highway. We were not sure if it was a misunderstanding on our part, or if we were given wrong information, but the anticipated four-hour trip turned into eight. At 3:30 we pulled into the border town of Sunauli.

Our backpacks were on a rack on top of the bus. Unknown to us until the baggage was tossed down, the fellow who had arranged them up there had attached the main waist clasp of Rick's to some other guy's pack, and not fitting together properly, they were good and stuck. The bus employees were trying to disengage them, yet no amount of fiddling released the buckles. Rick let out a yelp when one employee took out a knife: he was actually going to cut the packs apart! Did he think the buckles were just for show? Rick and the other pack owner took over and pulled and pried for another 10 minutes before achieving a non-damaging split.

Rickshaw drivers were lined up and waiting, sure of a fare, as the only way to get from the bus station was by rickshaw. A driver plunked our packs on the back of his rickshaw and told us to climb aboard. A quick calculation had us and our packs weighing in at 170 kilos (375 lb).

Rick said, "Too heavy."

The skinny little elderly driver grinned. "No problem, sir." He didn't even break into a sweat on the 5-kilometre (3-mi) pedal to our hotel. We instructed him along the way to stop at the travel agency holding prepaid tickets for our bus and train for tomorrow. The agency also changed the remainder of our Nepalese rupees into Indian currency. This all went smoothly, as did the requisite stops at both the Nepali and Indian customs and immigration offices in the middle of Sunauli.

A well-known saying is that even Nepalese and Indian travellers don't stay in this border town one minute longer than necessary. Grime! Unparalleled grime! The Indian side was by far the worst. It was like walking into a garbage dump with reeking piles of rotting debris. Dust swirled in the air, adding a shadowy murkiness to shapes and forms; unfortunately, it was not thick enough to obscure the sight of men responding to the call of nature by the roadsides. To this I would soon not even raise an eyebrow.

Our concern soon became focused on swarming mosquitoes. By dusk that evening, we were being eaten alive. Sunauli is in the Terai region, which was once a malaria-infested jungle. Since the mosquito eradication efforts in the 1950s and '60s, people from the surrounding hills of Nepal have settled in the Terai flatlands to farm and for industry. Jungle areas still exist in nature reserves such as the Royal Chitwan National Park. Though much improved, there are still outbreaks of malaria.

Our supper was a hurried affair in the hotel dining room, which was open to the elements on one side. It would not have helped even if it was totally enclosed. Swatting mosquitoes with one hand, we shovelled our meal down as quickly as possible with the other.

All we wanted was to sleep ... Instead, our room could have been a set for a B-grade horror movie. Upon entering our room, we first undertook the chore of killing the multitude of mosquitoes planning to share the room with us. Our scent frenzied the little buggers. Under siege, we were so busy swatting mosquitoes landing on our exposed skin that we were unable to string up our mosquito nets. Where were they coming from? We had already covered the gap above the door with newspaper held by band-aids. We hunted for other entry points—aha! They were filing in through an ill-fitting window in the bathroom. More paper and the last of our band-aids sealed it off. As a final touch, I sprayed the paper with repellent. Finally, we were able to set up the nets and crash.

We rose with the alarm at 6:00 a.m., then headed down the street to Baba's Restaurant for breakfast. Enough flies buzzed around inside the display cases that collectively they could have easily picked up a pastry and flown it over to us. We decided to forgo breakfast, settling for a dubious-tasting cup of tea instead. I tore next door to buy anything to fill our stomachs; two types of cookies would have to suffice.

The bus was already full when we boarded. After we showed the driver our tickets, he instructed a couple of men to move out of some seats, indicating that these were for us. The recently displaced sat on the ledge of the raised engine compartment. People kept boarding until every inch of the floor was covered with squatting bodies. In the end we counted 57 people in a 30-person bus. It seemed all the latecomers were paying the driver in cold hard cash, which he transferred to his pocket. We were the only Westerners on the bus, and I was the only woman; absolutely no one spoke a word of English. Our faces were numb and our necks kinked from returning smiles and nods. The bus pulled onto the highway to Gorakhpur.

Last but not least: we left with our Nepal budget averaging a mere $62.00 per day (including our Everest trek), which Rick thought was sweet.

Chapter Six
India

The highway was swarming with bikes, rickshaws, cars, trucks, ox carts, and just as many peregrinating goats, cows, and people along the shoulders. The bus jostled from side to side to avoid collisions. Fields of sugar cane and banana, coconut groves, grain crops, gigantic haystacks, and pens of water buffalo stretched outward from the road as far as the eye could see. The air through the open bus window was like a revolving door of scents, ranging from fresh-cut grass to burned stubble, foul manure, and choking dust.

Three super-sensory hours later, our bus pulled into Gorakhpur, one of the main switching points between the borders of Nepal and India. Trains and buses leave from here to major cities in India. Historically, and still today, it is a major military centre. The British used it as a recruiting base for Gurkha soldiers from Nepal, but that is not where the name Gorakhpur originated. Founded in the 1400s, this city's name was derived from Goraknath, a Hindu saint.

Checking our watches, we saw that the train to Calcutta was due to arrive at the Gorakhpur station in two and a half hours: time enough to add a more solid meal to the cookies we had hastily purchased before boarding the bus in the border town of Sunauli. Most of the eateries near the train station were canopied extensions of little shacks with open fronts where big vats of food bubbled, dispersing savoury aromas. Scouring the street, we spotted the most popular spot: the seats were filled and another half-dozen customers were waiting in line; a good sign the food would be fresh.

When it was our turn in the cafeteria-style lineup, we pointed to various dishes and a ladle-wielding man heaped them onto our large tin plates. Galloping to a table that people had just vacated, we dove into the variety of vegetables in sauces, rice, and chapati bread. My throat and esophagus became an inferno, robbing my lungs of the oxygen sucked in with each panicky breath. With eyes cascading a waterfall of tears and nose flowing like the Ganges, I gulped and gasped for air. I frantically grabbed for the glass of water on the table. Rick hollered "No!" and passed me the little bit of purified water we had left, though I would have wagered there were more than adequate spices and peppers in that sauce to instantly kill any micro-organisms in the local water. I stuck to the rice and chapati after that. Rick did minimally better, managing two or three spoonfuls of the fiery concoctions before calling it quits.

Next item on the agenda was to find a toilet. The waiter pointed down the street. I ventured out first while Rick stayed with our bags. This simple function became complex when a gigantic bull came between me and my goal. I stopped. Locals passed by, oblivious to the menace in his eyes. In order to distance myself from El Taurus, I looped onto the roadway. A vehicle screeched to avoid hitting me. The beast began to move forward! I broke into a run. It was a huge relief when a shoulder-check showed him moving in the opposite direction.

A block farther down the dusty road, I finally spotted "the facility." I should have known—a row of three men sat behind a table out front, charging for entry. I pulled out my pocket linings to show they were empty and said "I'll be back" in my best Arnold Schwarzenegger impersonation (though it was lost on them). Refusing to be deterred in my emergency, I briskly walked past them to the squat stalls.

Rick trekked the block next, then I went back a second time with coins in hand to do my part to show that travellers are people of their word.

* * *

With about an hour until departure time, according to our tickets, we decided to move along to the station to get our bearings. There was no information desk, but we easily found the correct track. Just to be sure, I showed our tickets to the armed guards at a security desk. They spoke no English, but confirmed with gestures that we were on the right platform.

We slumped down on our backpacks for the wait.

"Will you take a look at that?" Rick said.

Several cows were wandering down the middle of the railway tracks.

"Wonder if they know the train schedules?" I jested.

"They don't need a schedule. The cows here know their holier-than-thou status. See?"

The shrill whistle of an incoming train hardly budged their scrawny bovine hinies; when they were good and ready, they veered off at a leisurely pace to allow the locomotive to pass.

The platform began to fill with passengers. Even so, we figured there would still be a wait, as the locals lounged on their luggage in a relaxed mode. Women in a rainbow of colours tended gaggles of children under the scrutiny of ogling men. Full course meals appeared as if by magic from rucksacks and suitcases amid chatter and laughter. A lot of eyes looked our way with head-bobbing greetings. We were the only Westerners in the crowd that day.

The throng continued to thicken until hardly a square inch remained unoccupied. Rick, getting antsy, left the immediate area to pace. I snuggled down further on my backpack lounge and turned my face toward the mellow evening sun.

People began to stand and organize their bags. I took this to mean our train was nearing the station. Rick noticed the change in activity and quickly returned. For the umpteenth time since arriving at the station, we checked our coach and seat numbers.

The crowd moved en masse to the platform edge as a long train approached. As it passed slowly, our eyes scanned the coach numbers, which didn't seem to be in any particular order. The train came to a complete stop. Hampered by our packs, we awkwardly jogged toward the end of the train, jostling the bodies rushing in all directions. We came to the last coach and still no corresponding number. How had we missed it? With mounting tension we started back toward the front of the train.

"Look for a train employee. Where the heck are they?" I shouted at the back of Rick's head. About 6 metres (20 ft) away, we both eyeballed a fellow in uniform with a clipboard. We pushed our way toward him waving our tickets. Yes, an agent, and he spoke English!

"Your coach is two back," he said.

"Why is the coach number different than on our tickets?"

"That sometimes happens when you don't buy your tickets here. You should have checked in at the office down the street." We were slightly miffed that our Nepalese agent had not told us this and immensely relieved to have found our coach.

I suddenly saw movement in my peripheral vision. It was our train ... pulling away. I glanced at the platform. It was bare, with the exception of those waving goodbye to their friends and loved ones, now tucked safely on board. Even the agent had disappeared. I began to panic. We charged toward the nearest coach. Several teenage boys rushed past us. They were vying for the same car. They beat us to it, and by the time they all swung aboard, the train had gained momentum. I latched onto the vertical handrail. The train was now moving at such a speed I could hardly keep up, with the poundage on my back and my small front day-pack exasperatingly hitting me in the face as I bounced along. Finally I managed to swing a foot on the bottom step. I tried desperately to hoist myself up, but my body was like a chunk of lead.

"Get up (pant, pant) get in (pant, pant, pant) Irene, move it!" I saw Rick's head bobbing over my shoulder as he sprinted alongside.

With one fell swoop, Rick caught the handrail, gave me a shove upward, and swung himself onto the bottom step. I landed with a splat in the entrance way to the coach with Rick leapfrogging over me. I raised myself up on all fours, then to a standing position with the aid of several people who were stuffed into the coach entrance.

An instant replay spun through my mind. What had we just done? As the adrenaline rush subsided, disbelief set in, followed by hysterical laughter. We had actually been dangling from the side of a moving train. What would our kids and grandkids say if they knew of this tomfoolery? I knew my own old, well-worn lecture would erupt from our children's mouths: "You have not acted responsibly."

After this bizarre introduction to India, we had a feeling our motto "Expect the unexpected" would be taxed to the limit during our three months of travel here.

When we were finally able to contain ourselves, we passed through a few coaches to the one with our assigned seats. There were three numbers on the back of each of two benches that faced each other. Our designated numbers—41 and 42—were filled with a man and a teenage boy, with another man in 43. Three men sat on the bench across. After we pointed first to our tickets and then to the two seats by the window, the three occupants scrunched over to make room the width of one of Rick's butt-cheeks.

The train stopped just then at some junction and the train employees got off for some reason. Rick turned on his heel and marched off the train. Stunned, I ran after him shouting above the din of a car stuffed with chattering people, "Where are you going?" He moved with purpose and said, "Back to the station! We paid for a berth, and now we can't even sit down?"

A familiar face was in the cluster of men. Before Rick could even sputter a word, the agent who had previously directed us to the right coach said, "Where are you going, sir? I told you which car your seat is in."

"There are people sitting in our seats who won't move, this whole thing is just too much chaos."

"Go, go sir, back on the train, and I will be there soon."

Rick and I climbed back on the train. I again showed our ticket numbers to the fellows sitting in our seats. Before the agent came by to sort things out we had the matter settled ... India-style, meaning we shuffled bodies until we were all wedged in. The son squished in beside the three men sitting across. His father squeezed toward the man in number 43, and he invited us with a flourish to sit in reduced versions of 41 and 42. Our backpacks were pushed into the only place left: under the seat on the dirty, sticky floor.

Not one of the six males spoke English, so we were not sure who was instrumental in evicting the extras, but at around seven in the evening only two of the men in the seat across and Rick and I remained. They took over and transformed the two seats into four bunks by releasing the hinged boards near the ceiling. I didn't know how they figured it, but they indicated that Rick and I should go on the top bunks. After being brought a sheet, blanket, and pillow by a steward, we all commenced our bed-making for the night.

We had no sooner gotten settled when Rick remembered reading in our guidebook that thefts occur frequently on trains and insisted we retrieve our backpacks from under the bottom seats and put them on our top bunks.

"What? There is hardly enough room for us up here," I lashed out, but then agreed, as I now also envisioned waking up to gaping cavities where our packs once were. We ended up propping them behind us and leaning back into a half-sitting position. Before I could count to 10, I was out as if I'd been drugged.

At 4:00 a.m., I awoke and looked over at Rick. Priceless! Digging out my camera and trying to hold it steady while stifling peals of laughter, I captured my six-foot husband folded like an accordion into the remaining four feet of his bunk. His head, only inches from the ceiling, was slung back over his pack; his nostrils flaring in and out with each rumble. He had never, to my knowledge, snored before. It was still not as bad as the hard-seats in China.

At noon the next day, we arrived in Kolkata; India's largest city with over 13 million people. In 2001, the British name—Calcutta—was changed back to its Indian name, Kolkata. We picked a hotel from our guidebook, took a taxi from the train station, booked in, showered and aimed for the beds. It was dark by the time we came to again, so we ordered supper through room service. Tomorrow was soon enough to start exploring and hunting down cheaper accommodations.

This room in the Hotel Astoria, converted from rupees to $33.00 a night, didn't leave enough for meals, sightseeing, and transportation with our proposed budget for India of $60.00 per day (deduced from guidebook sources spouting how economical travel in India was). Rick, the budget control master, was fretting.

* * *

Stepping out from the hotel enclosure onto the streets bright and early the next morning, the congestion of both pedestrians and vehicles hit us like opening a blast furnace door. Our senses were buoyed to new heights. Heavenly incense and aromatic spices mingled with the miasma of rotting garbage. Blaring horns, screeching tires, vendors touting their wares, and the chatter of the multitudes going about their business pierced, bounced, and coiled on air waves. Movement in layers undulated in all directions; from the kaleidoscope of colour in women's saris to the intense competition for the gaudiest shop sign, to swirling dust and dirt. Pulsating life at its zenith—like no place we had ever been—and we loved it.

Our baby-step excursion was two blocks over to the Khalsa Restaurant. Perfect omelettes, crunchy brown toast and chai tea! After four cups of this steaming, milky, sweet, spicy brew, we still wished we had room for more. It was the best we had ever tasted ... and why not? Chai originated in India.

AUSTRALIA

The iconic Sydney Opera House.

Find the girl sitting at top right.
Devil's Marbles, south of Tennant Creek in the outback.

Koala appears innocent after repeatedly whopping me with a eucalyptus branch.
Nature World, Hervey Bay, Australia.

Outback humour.

Mail station in the outback.

CHINA

Photo by Rick Butler

Tempting aromas drew us into this 'Snack Street' off of
the famed Wangfujing Pedestrian Avenue in Beijing.

Photo by Rick Butler

Bikes, bikes everywhere—the flow of their zigging and zagging
like a harmonious melody in Chengdu.

The Great Wall.

Spirited young'uns at play. Giant Panda
Research Base outside of Chengdu.

TIBET

L to R: Carolina from Colombia, Irene, Ana from Mexico, Rick,
Julie and Eric from San Francisco. Roof of Potala Palace, Lhasa.

Potala Palace, once the spiritual centre, seat of
Tibetan government and home of the Dalai Lama.

Tibetans spinning prayer wheels to gain merit at base of Potala Palace.

Monks debating Buddhist scripture at Sera Monastery in Lhasa.

NEPAL

Rick, Bhimsen, and Irene at Pumpernickle's Restaurant in Kathmandu.

Everest Base Camp Trek

Yaks loaded with supplies for remote villages.

Saturday market at Namche Bazaar.

Lunch in chilly air with warm friends at the Yak Lodge, Tukla.
L to R: our countryman Steve, Rick, Irene, Jenny and Dave from the USA.

L to R: Irene, Yak Lodge owner Sherpa Tashi Tshering Lhakpa, and Rick. Lhakpa was a survivor of the fateful 1996 Everest expedition.

Rick and Milan in front of Khumbu Glacier. Mt. Everest in the background at top left.

Sadhus (Hindu holy men) that frequent the temples in Nepal. One had awesome dreadlocks that trailed on the ground.

Bishnue and Bobby, Downtown Hotel clerks, with foreheads tika'd and draped in garlands for the Diwali Festival.

INDIA

1,000 tiny cups are fashioned from clay each day and sold to tea vendors. City of Joy, Kolkata.

Patrick decked out in new, bright-yellow T-shirt for his 60th birthday bash at the Khalsa Restaurant in Kolkata.

Colva Beach, Goa. Locals enjoying sun and sea. No bikinis here.
Note rig to pull seadoos out of the water.

Boys carrying in the day's catch. Fishing village, Colva Beach.

Our camels and camel jockeys, L to R: Rama, Melchior,
Johnny, and Khristna. Thar Desert.

Taj Mahal in Agra, the jewel of India built entirely of white marble.

ITALY

St. Peter's Basilica, Rome. The crowd is gathering for the Pope's blessing.

Famed Ponte Vecchio (Old Bridge) from Arno River Bridge, Florence.

Tower of Pisa, the freestanding bell tower of the town's cathedral.

A waterway in Venice, the city that stretches across 118 islands in a marshy lagoon.

AUSTRIA

A brilliant player rules the giant chessboard in Domplatz Salzburg.

Rick discovered a hidden talent while in Vienna. He began to sketch!

HUNGARY

Budapest: Long lineup waiting to enter the Terror Museum,
which tells of Hungary's dark history.

The Royal Palace—now a museum housing a valuable collection of artifacts—dominates the skyline from the Buda side of Budapest.

SLOVAKIA

Rick in front of St. Elizabeth Cathedral in the main square of Košice.

A baba (grandma) in Košice on shopping day.

SWITZERLAND

Zurich: St. Peter's Church, with the largest clock face in Europe
in the background at almost nine metres in diameter (29 ft).

GERMANY

At the Marienplatz with our 'kids,' who met up with us in Munich.
L to R: Candice, Rick, Irene, Rob and Glenda.

Can you believe it? No tray! The Hofbraühaus in Munich.

Schloss Neuschwanstein from the window of Schloss Linderhof, two of the fantasy castles of Bavarian King Ludwig II.

Norman Foster's colossal glass cone in the Reichstag, Berlin's Parliament.

FRANCE

Musée du Louvre, the most visited museum in the world. Très magnifique!

UNITED STATES

New York: me, sneakily hopping on an NYPD motorcycle.

Caught red-handed by Officer Heartthrob.

New York's 102-storey landmark, the world's tallest building for 40 years.

Our second order of the day was to investigate other hotel possibilities. After viewing about seven or eight other establishments, we were not impressed. Like a Dr. Seuss description, they were too grungy, too cramped, too noisy, too rank, too creepy, too dank ... or had not enough security. The only two places passing our inspection which were cheaper than the Astoria were full. We decided to go back to the Astoria and see if our agreeing to stay 10 days would sweeten the rate pot, bargaining being deeply instilled in Indian culture. I would give it my best shot, although we had already decided to stay even if I was not able to negotiate a better rate. I pleaded my case with sycophantic nuances; they gave us a room on the first floor, with a private door opening onto the courtyard, for the duration of our stay, for $18.00 a night! I was Rick's hero.

Our viewpoint on what to do with any saved hotel costs, however, always differed. Rick's way of thinking was money saved on accommodations leaves more to spend on essentials. Mine was we have more money to blow on non-essentials. Or was it a difference of opinion as to what items fit into the category of essentials? We hit the huge market nearby. I came away with two "essential" salwar kameez. These long, loose-fitting shirts, worn over baggy pants of cotton, would be my salvation in the heat ... not to mention the modesty factor. My tight T-shirts were drawing male orbs like magnets, which I was finding disconcerting. Now I am not saying that North American males are any less fixated on female anatomy. The difference was in the directness of the ogling.

I was now set to walk the streets of Kolkata ... and walk we did, from one end of the city to the other. No mean feat, seeing that the city covers an expanse of 853 square kilometres (329 sq mi). Many monumental structures still stand as evidence to the city's colonial past under British rule. Victoria Memorial is one of the most prestigious. It is said to be a cross between Buckingham Palace's architectural design and that of the Taj Mahal, with its four minarets and dome of white marble. In fact, the marble came from the same quarries in Rajasthan used in the building of the Taj Mahal. A statue of Queen Victoria stands at the entrance to the impeccable grounds. The inside houses British war memorabilia. The whole complex seemed incongruous with its surroundings.

On we sauntered to the Marble Palace, which dazzled under the brilliant sun. Built as the private residence of a gold merchant, Raja Rajendra Mullick Bahadur, in 1835, its sumptuously decorated rooms are now a museum crammed with statues, pottery, mirrors, chandeliers, and fine paintings by renowned Dutch, English, and Italian artists. Thirteen different types of marble were used in the construction. The grounds evince the Raj's aspiration to cover all spiritual bases, with sculptures of not only Buddha, but Jesus, the Virgin Mary, and Hindu gods as well, plus six lions disparately thrown in the mix. The Mullick family descendants still live in a small back portion of the palace. We may as well have saved ourselves the trip to the WB (Writers' Building) Tourist Bureau to pick up free passes to the Palace, as we couldn't get past the front entrance guard without a specified amount of baksheesh, which turned out to be equivalent to the price of a paid ticket. The guides swarming us on each palace level also expected a tip.

Kolkata has a long history of being an art and cultural centre. India's most famous writers, painters, poets, intellectuals, and social and religious reformers are associated with Kolkata. We toured the Rabindra Bharati University and Museum. The university adjoins the home of India's most famous poet, Rabindranath Tagore—India's first Nobel laureate for literature. The Museum contains many of his paintings, poems, and prose, and traces the life history of Tagore and his family.

Having heard dreadful places referred to as the Black Hole of Calcutta, it was interesting to become acquainted with the origin of this expression. In 1756, local landowners—led by the governing Nawab of Bengal—captured 146 people from the East India Company. The prisoners were held in a small room with two small barred windows; packed in so tightly the door had to be forced closed. Left overnight without water in the scorching heat, 123 of them died of heatstroke, suffocation, or trampling. Morbidity drew us into the GPO (General Post Office) to stand on the exact spot of the infamous Black Hole. The GPO is in the B.B.D. Bagh area, which contains most of the city's historic buildings. Once called Dalhousie Square, this hub of Kolkata was renamed using the initials of three Bengali martyrs: Benoy, Badal, and Dinesh. The oldest church in the municipality, St. John's, is also there, as well as the famous Writers' Building, which was built in 1780 for clerks ("writers") brought over from England to keep records for the East India Company. It is now the seat of the West Bengal state government.

* * *

One can't just walk the streets of Kolkata: you have to jump, dash, stop, start, and weave along.

The ubiquitous and gaudy mustard-coloured taxis will run over the curb in anticipation of a fare. Kolkata is the only place left in India where rickshaws are hand-pulled. Those poor souls in bare feet or flip-flops brave the scorching pavement in summer, frostbite in winter, and flooded streets during the monsoon season while pulling their heavy loads.

The rich, the poor, and the destitute intermingled in the bustling streets. We stepped over or walked around sleeping bodies, especially if we were out after six or seven in the evening. People are born on the street, live their whole lives on the street, and die on the street. They use the public pumps to drink, bathe, and wash clothes. Fires in cans or small propane stoves cook the evening meals. To be able to eat each day is their principal concern. If a family member becomes ill, it is a major catastrophe, as a doctor and medicine are unaffordable luxuries. It was difficult to witness such abject poverty.

The hotel streets abounded with professional beggars. Signs in restaurant windows advise not to give them money, as this promotes a dependency on tourists. Running into some groups that volunteer services for the poor, we asked them their philosophy on the matter. Most concurred it is better to give to the houses that feed and clothe the poor than to the beggars directly. They added that if we were going to hand out rupees on the street, women in white are widows and are by far the worst-off. Often seen as a burden to the deceased husband's family, they are sent out to fend for themselves. Untrained and not looked upon favourably by employers, society has stripped them of most options other than begging and prostitution.

Some of the beggars were extremely aggressive, particularly a group of three well-dressed women who we soon recognized as regulars in our area. We watched them bypass younger travellers with barely a glance, while zeroing in on us. I had mistakenly given them some rupees the first day after we arrived, and now they laid in wait. On about day three, when I only had two rupees apiece for this trio, one lady said, "Is that all? Do you not care for poor people?" When I joined Rick where he was waiting across the street and shared their comment with him, he got his gander up. He marched over to them and I heard bits and pieces of his lecture mode raining down on them. From that day forward, they met us with smiles and "Hello auntie," "Hello uncle," "We do not want rupees, just to say hi." I still sometimes had rupees for them, but if I didn't, they no longer followed behind hassling us.

One day, when we were chatting with two of these ladies, a boy of about 10 came up and asked for rupees. I gave him a few.

He squinted up at me, saying, "Is that all?"

I don't know who was more shocked—the boy, Rick, or me—when one of the women swatted him on the back of the head, admonishing, "Just say thank you, don't say more."

Although we did understand the dependency issue, when a thin, tattered beggar held out a hand, and knowing a few rupees dropped into it would buy a banana, a piece of chapati bread, and a scoop of rice at a local stand, we could not turn our heads and walk by. I feel if it was not for the grace of God (or my reincarnation status this time round), it could be us on the streets of India instead of them, and although we gave to the homes, I also exchanged bills into coins to give out to individuals each day. That is our philosophy. In fact, our favourite breakfast haunt—the Khalsa Restaurant—kept a box of coins for just this purpose, making this our main exchange depot. And every evening upon closing the Khalsa, owners gave away all the remaining prepared food to the poor that lined up outside their door.

* * *

Most walks from our hotel involved wending our way along the Maidan, which was always entertaining. This very lengthy, green, mostly au naturale area was the scene of many cricket matches, which drew crowds of spectators. We witnessed union rallies in full swing, with workers voicing grievances, and once an organized strike march. Goats herded across the Maidan stopped for a nibble along the way. Mangy dogs ran loose. Mothers sat on blankets spread with picnic lunches. Fathers and children tossed balls and Frisbees. When we asked directions to anywhere in the city, calculations of distance were always based on the proximity to this landmark area.

It was a momentous day when we met Patrick. This mild-mannered, eloquent old gentleman, born of an English father and Indian mother, had been a tour guide for most of his life. His father had gone back to England while Patrick was a toddler, leaving him in India with his mother. He had been privy to an education at an Indian boarding school, spending his vacations with his mother, who unfortunately died during his teenage years; his father, being much older than his mother, predeceased her. One of Patrick's fondest memories was of the one time he had gotten to visit his father in England.

His current home was the remains of a partially torn-down building on Sudder Street. A cement slab, which appeared to be a foundation remnant, now functioned as his bed. About 1.5 metres (5 ft) above the cement base, a portion of old floor left from the second storey jutted out, which helped shelter him from the sun and rain. Two small bags hung from this makeshift roof: one for clothes and one for food storage. A blanket was neatly rolled up in a corner. A guard hired to patrol the back entrances of businesses in the area kept an eye on Patrick's possessions when he left the site.

Patrick offered to be our guide. We gladly hired him to take us to the slum, the subject of Dominique Lapierre's book (published in 1985) titled *The City of Joy*, forever melding our association of this area with Kolkata.

Patrick said he knew many people in the City of Joy, and he wasn't kidding. He led us through the streets waving and chatting to the occupants like a king in procession through his kingdom.

We stopped at a clay cup manufacturing shop in the small common yard between adjoining homes. Five men were busy transforming the clay into the tiny cups called *kullarhs* used for serving chai tea. Patrick told us they would then low-fire the unglazed cups, heap them on a wagon, and sell them to the chai wallahs (tea sellers) and open markets that use them. They toiled from five in the morning until seven in the evening, producing a thousand cups per day, which they sold for a mere 100 rupees ($2.25) to be split between five families.

A young woman appeared in the doorway of one of the homes carrying a pot of tea. We sipped the sweet brew with the added rich, earthy taste of the clay cup while the assembly line progressed. Two men formed the clay into uniform balls, which they passed on to the nimble fingers of two men working two small pottery wheels—one electric and one hand-turned—while the fifth moved the finished product into the sun to dry. We took several pictures of the artisans at work, and then we lined up the children who had been peeking around corners and giggling at us. Patrick wrote down their address and translated that we would send a copy of the pictures back to them. They told Patrick they had never had a photo of themselves. We sure hoped, when we posted them later from Mumbai, that they did indeed receive them.

On the streets again, we felt like pied pipers as the string of children following us grew longer and longer. While stopping to retrieve our water bottles from our day-packs for a drink, we were swarmed on all sides. Patrick gave them some details about us in Bengali. The children tried out their few English words. They all came up in turn to shake our hands. Soon some parents hovered to see what was going on. We asked the children questions about their families through Patrick. When we were ready to move on, the children stuck to us like glue. After almost tripping over a few, Patrick said something to the parents, whose few words instantly disbanded the entourage.

The citizens of the City of Joy, though impoverished, were more fortunate than those living on the street. They had a roof over their heads, no matter how crude the dwelling. We visited a family of six living in a 2.5 x 2.5 metre (8 x 8 ft) enclosure. Most adults in the city had some type of pittance-paying employment. We sensed a strong subculture even with our brief visit. Patrick concurred that there is a strong sense of community; all watch out for their neighbours.

Conditions were much improved from the time of Lapierre's book, which was based in the 1960s. Each corner now has a public well, though the sewer still runs in ditches on the sides of the streets. Young and old go about their day amid the cows, goats, and wild dogs poking around the fly-infested garbage. There is a passion for life despite the poverty. We were so wrapped up in all the activity and with acknowledging the friendly smiles and curious nods greeting us that we did not realize until later that no one, not even a child, had asked us for money.

* * *

By far the worst conditions Rick and I encountered were when we found ourselves alongside the canal slums during a walk. Desperate people come to Kolkata with just the clothes on their back in hope of work and a better life. For about a 6-kilometre (4-mi) stretch, makeshift hovels were put together with anything these families could find—cardboard, tin, tarps—and most were not tall enough to stand up in. Their only source of drinking water was from the polluted canal, which doubled as the only place for garbage and human waste disposal. They cooked over bonfires. It was total squalor. They probably did not get many foreigners frequenting this area, judging from the interest shown us. People waved and hollered "Namaste!" (roughly translated as "I bow to you," a semiformal greeting). Children feigned running by as if on some errand, though it was obvious that their mission was to get a closer look at us aliens out of the corners of their eyes. The haves and have-nots on this earth are worlds apart. We always come back very quiet from these excursions, turned inside-out and reassessing who we are in relation to this unfamiliar world.

A day later, we saw a Kolkata newspaper article stating that the canal area lean-tos would be demolished, as they were an eyesore and a breeding ground for malaria. There was no mention in the article of where those people were to go.

* * *

On our way to yet another breakfast at Khalsa's, a freaky insalubrious skirmish with a vehicle occurred. Hoards of pedestrians moved along both sides of the narrow roadway. Cars and rickshaws weaved around each other in the middle, with not enough room to pass side-by-side. Walking single-file behind Rick, I noticed a car creeping up from behind. A shoulder-check revealed that the driver was focusing on the centre of the road ... and not on me, walking on his left. I frantically attempted to move closer to a building, but two fellows carrying a large container suddenly came between me and the wall. As I twisted sideways to take up less space, the old rustbucket of a station wagon stuffed with passengers ran over my foot. I let out a yelp, and banged on the side of the vehicle shouting, "You dumbass, you just ran over my foot!"

"Irene, what happened?" Rick said, bug-eyed and perplexed.

"Oh my God, my foot." I stared down at the blood-red welts and sooty tire-tread marks covering my sandaled extremity. Then, like a thing deranged, I tore after the escaping vehicle. Hobbling alongside the passenger window, I pointed to my foot while shrieking, "You crushed my foot! Do you understand me?" Even if someone in the car did understand English, they no doubt thought staring straight ahead would make this ranting maniac vanish. The old beater just kept creeping away.

People gathered around to inspect the damage, which converted my anger into waterworks of tears.

The restaurant owner, who we were on first-name basis with, brought me a sympathy tea as we settled into our favourite booth. When I dared to do a wiggle test, I found that remarkably—aside from the fiery red welts—there was absolutely nothing wrong with my foot. Even more startling, I was now flooded with a clear recollection of weightlessness as the car was mashing my foot into the hard-packed road surface. An uncanny explanation sprang forth. Yesterday we had been to the marble sarcophagus of the great humanitarian herself: Mother Teresa. Her Missionaries of Hope (homes for the terminally ill) are now located around the world, but her body appropriately rests in Kolkata, the city where she first lovingly held the scab-and-dirt-encrusted destitute, offering them dignity in death. I was overwhelmed by her life's work as described on the wall plaques. Regardless of religious affiliation, anyone who dedicates their life to working on the frontlines in the worst slums of the world is a saint in my books. My parting prayer to this great lady had been to keep us safe on our travels.

I could hear her saying, "Lord, I'll be right back. These people are going to be high-maintenance," as she whisked down and lifted the weight of the car off my foot.

Needing to be pampered, we stopped on the way back to our hotel at Kathleens Confectioners for some Bengali sweets. The truth is that we never made it straight home without succumbing to the heavenly aroma of fresh-baked bread wafting out of Kathleens. This day I chose the most decadent treat, *gokul pithe*—little coconut and solidified-milk balls, fried and dipped in sugar syrup.

Being one to capitalize on Rick's commiserative mood, I insisted we take in a movie at an English cinema we had serendipitously come across a few days ago. I can't remember the name of the feature, but it was definitely two-thumbs-up with the locals, as the whole audience cheered and clapped when the hero made moves to trounce the villain.

* * *

Our second-last day in Kolkata fell on Patrick's 60th birthday. The day before, we had arranged to meet him for a birthday lunch at Khalsa's, where we had taken him once before. On our first visit with him, he had called the waiter over, speaking to him in Hindi while munching his toast with butter between sips of tea. That conversation resulted in an extra order of toast to go.

Patrick was waiting out in front of his home decked out in a new, bright-yellow T-shirt that had been a birthday gift from a soup kitchen he frequented. As much as we tried to persuade him to order a full meal, he insisted on his usual—but this time, along with his three orders of toast with butter (two for immediate consumption and one to go)—as well as tea, he ordered a bottle of ice-cold orange pop, which he downed within seconds followed by much lip-smacking.

He told us more of his fascinating life story: about the prankster he had been in school, and comical tidbits from his experiences as a guide for a large company. He told us about how when workers were doing repairs in his school's dorm attic, he stuck a small wad of paper in the door latch. To his glee he then had access to the attic and became the "phantom of the dorm" by stealthily entering at his whim to shuffle across the creaking attic floor.

His most disconcerting experience as a travel guide was when a shriek alerted him to a woman's sari caught in the door of the bus that had just dropped a group off. Though they stopped the bus prior to any physical damage, he blushed at the memory of her garb "unravelling right before my eyes."

Rick gave Patrick his fleece vest and long underwear, the last cold-weather items still left over from our Everest hike. Patrick put the vest on immediately, despite the hot day, stroked the nap every few minutes and said, "This will keep my back warm at night."

In our next batch of picture printing, we sent Patrick birthday pictures in care of a small store in the neighbourhood. We will never forget Patrick, and often wonder how he is faring as he grows old and is no longer able to fend for himself.

* * *

We were ready to move on from this amazing city, which is said to be the "worst and best" introduction to India. The poverty and pollution are severe, even for India. At the same time, being in Kolkata sparks a fascination with the culture with its unparalleled intensity. Some preconceived xenophobic notions were quashed. Before stepping onto Indian soil, Rick thought he would feel uncomfortable or unsafe if surrounded by a bunch of Indian men in an isolated area. I had thoughts of being in the wrong place at the wrong time and being the target of a Muslim radical venting hostility toward North Americans. All ominous feelings soon dissipated. Of course, in travels anywhere, street smarts are a must, and we were still learning. Luck was with us so far, even when we digressed from good judgment.

In mid-December, we left for Gaya by train. Opting for first class in an air-conditioned coach designed to accommodate four, the other two seats remained empty, leaving the whole compartment to us. Relishing the privacy, we leisurely gabbed, read, ate, and slept the seven hours away.

* * *

We arrived at our destination after dark. The Gaya night was chilly and blustery. The interior of the Ajatsatru Hotel was cold and uninviting. The desk clerk quoted the price to be 800 rupees plus tax (approximately $18), for a total of 856 rupees. I pointed out that the price was 550 rupees in our guidebook, but who was going to argue at this late hour?

We shuffled past walls marked by the scuffs and nicks of the myriad bodies that had made their way down these dingy halls over the years. We tried to avoid catching our toes on the random patches of loose floor tiles. After much key-jiggling in an ornery lock, we entered our room. One look at the paint-chipped furniture and beds with springs sagging so badly they resembled hammocks sent us marching back down to the reception desk. The fellow barely looked up as he slapped down another key. The next room was slightly more habitable.

Our next mission was to find food. The few small restaurants around the hotel were extremely grungy. The dimly lit street, being almost directly across from the entrance to the train station, was a frenzy of honking cars, motorcycles revving, and bodies scurrying. We ended up purchasing some pastries to take back to our room, ignoring the fact that the fellow serving us had to disturb a swarm of sugar-dizzy flies already sampling the sweets.

At about one in the morning, we bolted upright to hooting and hollering in the hall and someone twisting our doorknob. "Whaddya want?" Rick boomed. The slurring male voice on the other side indicated a harmless lad who did not quite know where or who he was. Some aspects of cultures seem universal—this was a troop of boys in their mid-to-late teens belonging to a team of some sort, taking advantage of being away from the confines of home.

Gaya was not a good experience; it was one of those places where nothing felt right. In retrospect, we should have hailed a taxi at the Gaya train station and taken the 30-minute ride straight to Bodh Gaya, which we did the next morning.

*　*　*

Bodh Gaya was like a breath of fresh air (well, a little fresher), with a much calmer quality about it. Upon entering the city, the taxi was held up by several water buffalo crossing the roadway, the one in the lead being ridden by a boy of about nine with a most engaging smile. Pedestrians outnumbered vehicles; those driving were courteous and did not drown the walkers in billows of dust. A slower-paced and more contented aura flowed around us.

Whereas Gaya's 45 shrines make it an important religious centre for Hindu pilgrims, its sister city of Bodh Gaya is India's holiest Buddhist city, and was built around the Mahobodhi Temple, referred to as "the Stupa" by Buddhists. Behind this temple grows the sacred Bodhi Tree, in the same location as the tree under which Buddha—Prince Siddhartha Gautama—received enlightenment in the sixth century BC. There are legends of how this tree is directly descended from the original. Towering over gardens and smaller shrines, the Mahobodhi Temple rises dramatically, joining the earth with the great beyond.

A walk in any direction from the Mahobodhi temple brought us to other houses of worship: the Thai temple, the Japanese temples Nipponji and Daijokyo, and the Tibetan and Bhutanese monasteries. A giant 25-metre (82-ft) stone Buddha—built by Japanese monks and blessed by the Dalai Lama in 1989—completed the holy sites at the end of a beautiful tree-lined road.

The busy season for pilgrims, students, monks, and tourists alike begins in September and continues throughout the winter. Lamas and teachers from around the world congregate, filling the monasteries that offer courses in meditation. A 10-day course has to be booked ahead, but daily meditation sessions are open to all. Several years ago, our son had immersed himself in one of the renowned meditation courses here, and he encouraged us to do the same. Had we known the difference between Bodh Gaya and Gaya, we would have stayed a few days, but it was too late. In our haste to escape the area, before leaving by taxi for Bodh Gaya at the crack of dawn, we had booked a train to Varanasi, which left the same evening at 11:50 p.m.

Oh, well. We had all day to happily wander in the warm sun and uplifting atmosphere. In the late evening we took a taxi back to Gaya, an hour before train time.

Lord Shiva's Domain

Varanasi (commonly known as Benares, or Banaras by locals, and also Kashi by the devout, meaning "resplendent with light") is the holiest place on earth in the Hindu religion throughout recorded time. Shiva, the destroyer god, reigns. He resides in every inch of the city. Over two thousand temples are dedicated to him. Every Hindu tries to come at least once during their lifetime to bathe in the sacred River Ganga (Ganges to Westerners), which flows alongside the city. The exuberance of life bursts forth as the 2 million people who call Varanasi their home are continually bombarded with tens of thousands of pilgrims and visitors.

Cremations are auspicious here. The dead are transported to the city in great numbers, and the funeral pyres burn day and night. The very old and terminally ill come to spend their last days here, as when one dies in Shiva's city, one is guaranteed moksha—liberation from the cycle of death and rebirth. We had been warned that we would never be as close to such an abundance of life and death simultaneously as in Varanasi.

Hailing a rickshaw from the train station, we piled aboard and gave the driver the name of our hotel, which—out of the ordinary for us—we had pre-booked. As he pedalled along, the rickshaw wallah suggested "better" hotels. Being aware of the commission he would receive for showing up with guests that had not pre-registered, we calmly repeated "No, thank you." He finally gave up and took us to our requested hotel, where we tipped him generously, since the fare was a pittance and he had missed out on a kickback.

The Ganga View Hotel was our gem of India ... so far. In fact, it had been a long time since we had stayed in such spotlessly clean, comfortable, cozy surroundings, featuring the most fabulous antiques to boot. The hotel dining room had a set time for a seven-course supper, for which we had to reserve our place by noon.

We took our first walk of many along the Ganges. All my life, my visions of India had included the Taj Mahal and the Ganges. It now seemed surreal to be on the shores of this holy river. I am invariably driven to dip my toe in every renowned body of water on my travels and have the event recorded with a photo. The Ganges was now added to my collection.

The ghats (steps leading down to the riverbank) stretch along the Ganges for miles. In some places, there are as many as 100 steps from top to bottom. The ghat names are in plain view, starting from Assi in the south to Raj in the north. They are the pulse of the city. Fascinated and mesmerized by the activity, we awoke each day eager to hang out at the ghats.

Early morning brought out the bathers; the Ganges is nature's tub, where locals spruce up for the day. It must take years of practice to become so adept at washing every nook and cranny while wrapped in a piece of fabric for modesty. The women are particularly skilled at undressing, bathing, and fully dressing again without ever exposing any skin between their neck and knees. We had seen similar finesse with the street people washing at the public water pumps.

Hindus from near and far came dressed in their finest garb to wade waist-deep into the holy river while performing soul-purifying rituals. Pilgrim men splashed about, stripped to their loincloths and heads shaven except for a tail of hair at the nape of their necks. This lock is something to grab hold of, if the gods show them immediate favour and sweep down to whisk them away.

The multi-functional river was also the main laundry facility. Women chattered above the irregular slapping and pounding of clothes against stone slabs. Considering the pollution level of the water, the clothing spread about on the steps to dry was surprisingly white.

Children at games of cricket manoeuvred up and down the steps as though they were on a level playing field. After being bashed by a backward runner intent on intercepting the ball, we learned to carefully circumnavigate all sporting activities.

Equally amazing were the kite-flyers. They ascended and descended the steps, eyes forever upward, without ever landing on a single patty. Each morning and evening cows, bulls, water buffalo, and goats came down the steps for watering, leaving a trail of dung and rank barnyard odour. When we read a study undertaken to measure the fecal particles per square inch, we did not need to see the computations to understand the magnitude. I must admit, we got pretty good at being able to walk upright and still miss most of the leavings; which, I might add, were never there for long. Soon after the animals left there was a competition between dung gatherers. They mixed the droppings with straw, patted them into rounds and placed the rounds out to sun-dry, thus transforming them into a common source of fuel.

While sitting and soaking up the setting sun one evening, we were jolted out of our reverie by a mite of a boy aged six or seven who was riding on the back of a water buffalo while overseeing four more rapidly hoofing down the steps. As the buffalo drank and lounged at the water's edge, the young fellow amused himself by prodding the other beasts with his stick in order to move them closer to the one he was perched on. He then grabbed the horns of the one alongside, and with great agility, swung onto the back of the next 2,000-pounder. A few times the burly animals made an impromptu move, leaving his scrawny body dangling with one hand still clasped to a horn between the potentially crushing girths of two, until he managed to hoist himself up again. Within minutes he had been on the backs of all five, and started the game over again.

"And we worry about the playthings of our kids," Rick quipped.

* * *

A cold snap was sweeping across northern India. We now had to pile on all our shirts at once under our Gore-Tex. A brutal change from balmy Kolkata left us thinking we had given away our heavier clothes too soon, but this did not deter us from our eight hours a day on the ghats.

Tour boats were rowed up the river and carried back down by the gentle current. The river was normally foggy each morning with the low temperatures. Boatmen still beckoned us, calling out dirt-cheap prices and promising a panoramic view of the ghats.

"Sir, boat. Only 30 rupees because you first customer."

"Sir, pay only 25 rupees—I am best price."

"Sir, you see things better from boat."

Peering out at the vague outline of the boats already on the water, we noted how the customers aboard were squinting toward the ghats, confirming our suspicion that the early fog was too thick to see through. When the sun broke through, the price quadrupled, business boomed, and the number of people filling each boat was sizable—or more accurately, cap-sizable. We counted as many as 20 adults crammed into a boat, appearing to be far beyond the safe capacity. Though our worries were probably unwarranted, being poor swimmers we decided to stick to dry land.

It was sheer bliss sitting and catching the warming rays of the midday sun on the steps of Dasaswamedh, the main market ghat. We watched the milling masses from all walks of life engaged in various undertakings: relaxing, visiting, meditating, begging, and especially negotiating. Little leaf boats filled with flowers and food for *pujas* (prayers to Hindu deities) were the most popular item for sale. The river was festooned with these floating invocations.

Lots of goods were on hand for mortals, too: food, drink, postcards, and the cherished Varanasi silks, which are considered a collector's item around the world. Haircuts, massages, and palm-readings were also going on, and *sadhus*—ascetic Hindu holy men—congregated in the busy market corners.

When our legs cramped from sitting, we climbed the steps to the old city. Hole-in-the-wall shops lined the narrow, winding streets. I would wager maze-planners taking in an aerial view of the paths behind the ghats would come away with a plan to baffle the best. It was not for the claustrophobic (which we are not, but my megalophobia kicked in at having to share space with large animals). I would start to hyperventilate as we flattened ourselves against the wall of a building as water buffalo were herded by. I could feel their bristles brush against my body, hear the sound of their trampling hooves, smell their rank breath, and taste the sweaty dust off their mangy bodies. Even worse were the times when cows came meandering down the path on the loose, with no master to hustle them along. The locals nonchalantly mingled with these heavyweights, giving them a swat if it was impossible to squeeze by. But to me, these were not the well-contented cows gazing at me with gentle eyes across a farmer's fence back home. These were scrawny scavengers, well aware that their lofty status gave them the right of way, and if two were intent on the same pile of garbage being dumped by a shop owner for their regal pleasure, the race was on, and I did not want to be in the way. Also disconcerting were the wild monkeys sailing from rooftop to rooftop above our heads.

Our mission one day was to find the Shanti Hotel within this labyrinth, to exchange American dollars for rupees. After taking an hour and a half too long to find the hotel, and then waiting for the exchange clerk to show up at the booth, it was dark by the time we began to wend our way home. Other travellers told us to be wary of walking in this area at night. I became skittish, brushing by groups of men lingering in the narrow alleyways, until I noticed how the shadowy forms were observing Rick. I had not realized before the visual impact of my usually clean-cut husband. Rick had not shaven since landing in Nepal. His beard was now bristling out quite grey—compared to his head hair—and with a density seldom seen. Bulky clothes for warmth added girth to his towering frame. His eyes completed the sinister mien; piercing, black, and glowing in the twilight. No one would mess with us.

We finally emerged from the old city only to find we somehow got turned around in the alleyways and ended up going in the opposite direction from our hotel; but at least now we could see our way on the open roads.

Ashes to Ashes

The traditional chant *Ram nam satya hai* (the name of God is truth) sent everyone scurrying respectfully to the sides of the paths in the old city streets. Four to six men from the Dalit caste (the lowest in India's class system) carrying a dead body on a stretcher above their shoulders passed at a moderate jogging pace. The deceased bumped along, draped in silk shrouds trimmed with gold tassels and strewn with strings of marigolds. We were told by a bystander that the colour of the shroud signifies the gender of the corpse—white for men and saffron for women. Male family members followed in procession. My heart raced each time a body passed by. This unaccustomed ritual no doubt prompted a flight (as opposed to a fight) reaction in me, with the added tension of not knowing which way to dash to clear the path. Rick often had to yank me out of the way.

The bodies were transported to the ghats reserved for cremations; Manikarnika Ghat is the most prominent, with many concrete pyre slabs. We counted as many as 12 cremations going on at once. Most families attending the cremations don't mind if there are onlookers, but at this main cremation ghat we saw spectators being told to move further back if they were standing anywhere but on the perimeter. Taking photos was adamantly prohibited.

The second most popular cremation ghat is Harishchandra. It is also busy, but does not have the capacity to handle as many pyres. This ghat builds its funeral pyres on a sandy area by the river's edge. It was here, from a raised platform, that we were able to watch three cremations from beginning to end.

The pyres had been pre-stacked with sandalwood, placed in a particular fashion for stability and good air flow while burning. The bodies were brought down to the water's edge. The covering shrouds were removed, revealing mummy-like figures bound in white cloth. Sacred water was poured over the head of the corpse from a vessel at two of the funeral gatherings. At the other, the whole stretcher was tilted and the head dipped directly into the Ganges. The tops of the bodies were doused with incense, and then raised—still on the transporting stretcher—onto the top of the pyres. Additional wood was placed on top of the bodies. The oldest son—or oldest male family member—walked five times around their deceased kin before igniting the pyre from an eternal flame.

Overhearing my comment to Rick about the absence of female mourners (as in Nepal), a Hindu man who introduced himself as "Satya—retired teacher," said, "This is so because to cry at cremation is considered bad karma."

The closest pyre was 6 metres (20 ft) from where we stood; the platform on which we were standing elevated us to eye level with the corpse of a tall, thin man. Our attention became focused on this mass of leaping flames. An unforgettable odour—pungent, yet sweet—filled the air: the scent of burning flesh partially masked by incense and sandalwood. We were unable to move, as if in a hypnotic trance. My gaze was transfixed. I thought of the extreme cultural difference surrounding death compared to our own; there was no camouflaging the "ashes to ashes" part here.

I wondered why no one was watching the corpse's left foot: the ankle was burned pencil-thin. "It's going to fall off," I whispered to Rick in horror.

The flames then seemed to shift to the right foot. It soon surpassed the burning stage of the left. My mouth dropped as it plopped onto the sand below. The Dalit attendant and one family member moved forward with long sticks and in unison, tossed the foot back onto the pyre. They then proceeded to push all other loose appendages toward the middle.

"A blow to the skull releases the soul, and on a more practical level, assures that the intense heat will not cause the head to explode," Satya matter-of-factly explained.

I was most thankful our new friend informed us of this pragmatic ritual before we witnessed it, or for sure I would have fainted as the Dalit delivered a swift crack to the skull with a resounding crunch, releasing plumes of sizzling steam.

The sombre atmosphere was punctuated by the antics of a couple of young Asian men beside us who were clumsily attempting to capture the event on their Nikon. They had their camera lens sticking out of a buttonhole in their coats that looked enlarged for this purpose. Satya, as well as a few other Hindu watchers, asked them to stop filming. It seems that in almost every crowd, there are always a few who think that the rules are for everyone but themselves.

Within three hours, the body was consumed and the ashes were sprinkled into the Ganges. What looked like minimal amounts of small pieces of bone were wrapped in a cloth and sent sailing down the river. After pouring a container of holy water on the remaining embers, the family departed.

Heading back to our hotel, we were still dazed but also amazed at our own impressions after witnessing this entire cremation at such a close proximity. We were not repulsed, as we had thought we might be. Instead we were flooded with reverence and felt honoured at being allowed to witness a family's funerary rites.

The very next afternoon, we were drawn to the river's edge by a large greyish object being carried by the current in our direction. Birds were pecking at flesh bobbing above the surface of the water. Those who can't afford the expense of a cremation, children under 12, and holy men are often placed straight into the river. As the mass neared, we determined it was a small water buffalo that had been in the water for a long time. We were relieved it was not a human body.

Wherever we turned, life and death were on an equal plane. The young, the middle aged, the old, and the dead were a part of every gaze up and down the ghats. Spirituality and worldly commotion intermingled, the fervour of religious ritual taking place amid whirlpools of mundane activities.

Shiva's city was truly a mind-altering experience.

* * *

The weather did not lessen its chilly grip. Temperatures ranged from 1ºC (34ºF) overnight to 10ºC (50ºF) during the day. I know it sounds harmless compared to our Canadian winters, but without proper clothing and central heating, those temperatures proved uncomfortable even for us. Our hearts went out to the street people. Though the days were sunny, it hardly made a dent in the temperature, and the nights fell to a dreadful, bone-chilling cold. The Indian media reported a high incidence of deaths due to exposure. Night bonfires blazed up and down the streets around our hotel with people huddled around. We started walking about later and later, as our hotel room was colder than the temperature outside. The hotel owner gave us extra blankets, so we were okay once snuggled down for the night, but by the time we hastily got ready to go out the following morning, our hands and feet were like ice-blocks.

What? The locals were actually putting sweaters on their goats. A green one looked dashing on a white goat. An oversized red-striped sweater was tied around the belly of a brown goat with twine to keep it from dragging on the ground. The cutest was a wobbly newborn kid with a fluffy pink sweater. As the comical fashion show expanded each day with more wool-clad goats, we knew it was time to leave. Our original plan had been to continue through more northern states and cities, but all we could visualize now were the beaches of India's southwestern shores.

We booked our train tickets the next day for Mumbai (formerly Bombay), from which—after a few days—we would go on to Goa.

A blast of warmth hit us as we stepped off the train in Mumbai, in climate and in atmosphere. The bright airy station was in the midst of architecturally prized buildings and bustling market streets. This city is known as India's most cosmopolitan; and we were ready for a little urban glamour.

In no time at all we were relishing specialty coffee shops, English movie theatres, bookshops, and white-linen dining spots, all within blocks of the neat hotel we nestled into. The Oasis was small and clean, its central location making it a choice spot for vacationing Indian families and businessmen alike.

The first thing I noticed when viewing our new abode was the peculiar plumbing in our en suite bath: a raised squat toilet. This oxymoronic facility was about the height of the toilet seats we vaguely remembered, but with a narrow lip of porcelain in the front and two foot pads with treads on either side. A dangerously high squat-perch, yet not at all comfy to sit on; however, sitting was more prudent, especially if you'd had more than one glass of wine with supper.

One day, exploring our new environs, we found ourselves staring up at golden arches, setting off a sudden frenzied craving for a McAnything. It felt like a little bit of home, which was odd because at home McDonald's is not on our list of eateries. As we stood in the long line to order and looked around at the packed tables, we thought for sure they must be giving something away, as McD's here was more expensive than all the surrounding restaurants serving local dishes. No beef burgers here, of course, but the chicken and veggie burgers went down well on our first visit and the many that followed.

* * *

The Punjabi restaurant on the corner of our hotel block became a good place to loll about and plan our Yuletide while the cook whipped up perfect omelettes (after we told him to hold the chili peppers) and alert waiters refilled our cups in a timely manner with sweet and spicy chai tea. It was now December 22. Our decision was to drop down to Goa within a few days, knowing we would have time to take in the sights of Mumbai at a later date because it was the city we would fly out of when departing India.

Hungry for signs of the festive season, our eyes devoured the few scrawny artificial pines decorated with bright red balls and silver garlands we saw in a department store window. On a nearby corner a young boy was putting the finishing touches on Santa: crayoned eyes looking out from above a beard of matted once-white wool pasted on a cardboard face; a straw-stuffed red plaid shirt with one sleeve cut off at the elbow, the severed piece fashioned into a cap; blue pants hanging below the body with a beat-up red runner placed below the right leg and a brown dress shoe below the left. Rick gleefully went over to pose with Santa and his creator. Within the nanosecond of me aiming and snapping the picture, a couple of men bolted out of the blue, one on either side of the boy and Rick to get their grinning mugs in the photo. They then walked off waving and howling with laughter. Giving the young lad—who spoke no English—a universal two thumbs up and a bag of chocolates, we danced away in high spirits.

In between the highs, we were experiencing pangs of loneliness. Homesickness gripped us as we visualized our family making last-minute Christmas preparations and the growing excitement of grandchildren counting the "sleeps" until Santa would come.

We had sent an e-mail giving each household a heads-up that we would be phoning them during a specified two-hour period on Christmas Day. We had also asked them to alert us if the time we set was not suitable, so we could make the necessary adjustments in our schedule. India was the only country where we could not obtain international phone cards, so we planned to make our calls from a long-distance service outlet.

* * *

At dusk on Christmas Eve, we headed out for our usual post-repast walk. For a change, we veered off onto a few side streets. We halted. Were our ears deceiving us? We heard the distinctive tones of cherubim and seraphim, sweet angelic voices proclaiming the birth of Christ. Following the melodious sound we came across a small, nondescript building with peeling white paint and swells of "Oh Come All Ye Faithful" floating through the open doors. Poking our heads inside, we saw that it was indeed a small Catholic church, complete with altar, crucifix, and statues of saints. The choir stopped practising long enough to invite us back for midnight mass.

When we arrived in our backpacker's best around 11:00 p.m., the church was already packed beyond capacity. We were touched by the welcoming handshakes and gestures and uplifted by the joyous service. How lucky we were to have come across this little church. Was it divine providence?

Galloping down to the phone outlet Christmas morning with ample rupees to make five 15-minute phone calls to Canada—as per our price-check of a few days ago—we started our first call. Immediately, we noticed that the time and cost gauges in the booth were adding up much faster than expected. Rick left the booth to inquire, finding to our chagrin that we had previously been quoted the wrong price. A dilemma! Our children were by their phones, so we could not possibly make it to the bank about 10 blocks away to get more rupees now, and the young staff—who barely spoke English—certainly would not have the authority to let us phone now and pay later. Our 15-minute calls dwindled to five minutes each, but we reached them all! It was wonderful to hear their voices and to share good wishes. We just squeaked by with enough rupees to pay for the calls by scrounging through our pockets for every last bit of loose change. I was initially upset by our rushed exchange of greetings, but began to feel better after we followed up with an e-mail message to everyone.

* * *

We rushed back to our hotel for our noon checkout, put our packs into the hotel storage room, and went off to fill our Christmas Day with outdoor activities until our train to Margao in Goa (from where we would make our way to Colva Beach) was to leave at 10:50 p.m.

Sashaying down to the Gateway to India—the triumphal arch standing guard over the harbour—we joined the crowds on the walkways alongside the Arabian Sea. We fought off a stream of touts selling knick-knacks and watched snakes being charmed out of their woven baskets, curiously weaving their heads to the melody of cross-legged flutists.

The Taj Mahal Hotel across the street looked like a great place for Christmas dinner.

Escorted by a smartly dressed attendant to a table in an almost empty, lavishly furnished grand dining hall, the maître d' exuberantly rushed to fill our water glasses and left a basket of breads and menus. It was a good thing we did not start munching on the bread while perusing the menu, as it was probably $10.00 a slice! Mumbai is known to be a city of insane extremes; it would have cost $200.00 for our entrées and a beverage each (sans hors d'oeuvres or a sweet morsel finale)! We exited when no one was looking and paraded down the street rolling with laughter, keeping our eye open for another restaurant.

Within three blocks we came across Leopold's and stopped in for a mock-traditional turkey and mashed potato dinner in the form of fried chicken and fries. We took in a movie, then picked up our gear in storage at the Oasis, then made the 10-minute walk to the station, which brought us close to train time and to the end of a most unusual—but enjoyable—Christmas.

* * *

Not stirring all night, we awoke refreshed as the train pulled into Margao. Whereas the slightest noise used to rouse us, with five months of Asian train travel under our belts we could sleep through almost anything. Our mates in the four-bunk compartment were two Indian fellows. Finding out that one lived in England and the other in Moscow was the extent of our conversation. My last groggy recollection was of three men snoring minutes after the train left the station.

A taxi from the train station deposited us along Colva Beach's hotel row, and the Colva Beach Resort fit us perfectly with a big bright room, en suite bath, private sun deck and friendly staff. Ahh ... beach bums for a month!

* * *

Goa immediately felt different. It has a unique history as an Indian state, never having been under the British Raj. Goa had been under Portuguese rule for 450 years, from the time Alfonso de Albuquerque colonized Goa in 1510 until Jawaharlal Nehru, tired of attempting to negotiate with the Portuguese, sent in an army, absorbing Goa back into India in 1961.

The long Portuguese influence is deeply embedded, especially in religious converts. Almost 30 percent of Goans are Christian. Old Goa is full of magnificent churches and cathedrals alongside Hindu temples. Even the smallest village has a one-room white-washed church.

Although St. Francis of Assisi—introduced by the Franciscan friars—is an important saint in Goa, St. Francis Xavier is Goa's patron saint. From the Jesuit order, St. Frances Xavier founded a mission in Goa in 1542. He is remembered for curing the sick with a little laying-on of hands. He went on from Goa to Sri Lanka, Malacca (in Malaysia), China, and Japan to spread Christianity through Asia. After dying off the coast of China in 1552, he was buried there. A few years later, his exhumed body was found to be perfectly preserved, even though lime had been dumped into the grave to aid in decomposing the corpse. Medical investigations revealed that the body had not been embalmed.

Eventually, the body was taken back to Goa, where it can be glimpsed through a glass casket in a mausoleum in the Basilica de Bom Jesus. Beginning in the 19th century, every 10 years the casket is brought out to the main aisle of the church, and pilgrims come for a close view and to touch the toe of the coffin. Travellers who were present for the last viewing in 2004 claimed that being among a million pilgrims paying their respects was a riveting experience; they also reported the extremely shrivelled condition of the saintly remains.

* * *

As well as the Christian heritage, another deeply rooted Portuguese influence is the blending of traditional Goan spices with the Portuguese love of meat and seafood. Pork-on-the-hoof abounds. It is the only Indian state where pigs outnumbered the cows at the roadside garbage dumps. Yet another legacy was the prevalence of alcohol—in the form of beer or *feni*, a local spirit distilled from coconut sap or cashews. Not even the two days of elections—in which Goa was supposed to be dry—put a damper on the public sale of booze. We were asked if we wanted "special tea" (wink, wink), which was beer served in a teapot and drunk from teacups.

Southern Goa's Colva Beach turned out to be a perfect choice for us. It was not nearly as dotted with resorts as northern Goa. Many of the northern spots are party centrals and draw a lot of the younger generation. Anjuna is known for year-round raves. Vagator and Arambol are close seconds for hardcore partygoers. There are other, tamer resorts in the north, but all are said to be busier than those in the south. Colva is frequented by Indian vacationers from all over the country, and by world travellers seeking a quieter retreat.

Our lives became uncomplicated, surrounded by miles of white sandy beaches, groves of coconut palms, the rolling sea, fishermen going out at the crack of dawn and returning with the day's catch, seafood shacks on the beach, small shopping stalls along the main streets, and homey restaurants—that was Colva in a nutshell.

A loose routine slipped in with a sultry languor: rousing ourselves at eight or nine or ten, we had breakfast or brunch, which was followed by a walk on the beach or a swim. Between noon and three, when the sun was scorching, we lounged in our room reading, crossword-puzzling, or chess-matching, or took an occasional stroll to the internet café. Later in the afternoon we took yet another long beach walk, jogged, or swam. Then, our most taxing decision: where we would have our leisurely sunset supper, and whether to stay for some local entertainment or nestle in our room watching a movie on one of several channels. Not in the least bit exciting, but so therapeutic.

One day, I insisted that Rick relax while I did the bakery run for the delectable cakes that had become our usual evening snack. My ulterior motive was to surreptitiously purchase two shirts for Rick's birthday on December 30.

My assumption that he would be delighted was correct, the shirts being the first new clothing he had donned in six months. He tried them both on three times, doing pirouettes in the mirror, unable to decide which one to wear to his birthday supper—the white one with OM written in black on the front, or the brown one with splashes of orange trim on the pocket and collar? The OM won out, and he didn't even ask me what I had spent when doing his daily budget.

The hours ticked toward the New Year. We rang it in Colva-style with a delectable seafood supper, after which we joined the crowds on Main Street for a gala parade of tacky homemade floats, boisterous singers, and a fizzle of fireworks. Back in our room, we dove into a large stash of gooey cakes, chocolate truffles, potato chips, and a bottle of wine while indulging in a TV movie-fest until the wee hours of the morning. What a life!

*   *   *

One Sunday morning in early January, we shattered our routine by opting to rent a motorbike and visit Old Goa to see the grandiose churches and mosques, some dating as far back as the 16th century. As we were getting ready to go, I felt a jolt of foreboding, but rationalized that it was only a lingering memory of my foot being run over in Kolkata. I quickly quashed it and focused on enjoying the adventure.

Rick was as excited as a 16-year-old revving up an engine for the first time. Mounting our Harley, we sped away ... okay, we really got on our rented Honda scooter and putt-putted down Colva's main street, looking for a gas station.

"Where the heck is this place? Did we miss the sign?" Rick called over his shoulder as we drove up and down the street for the third time.

We'll never know what alerted him, but on our fourth round, a man in coveralls ran out from a small shack hollering "Petro!" Silly us, we had been looking for a gas pump. The petrol-jockey had two one-litre pop bottles in tow. After transferring the gas from the bottles into the tank and pocketing our rupees, he sent us off with a smack to the rear fender.

Oh, the open road ... the elation of warm breezes ruffling our hair and kissing our faces. As we turned from the back road onto the main highway, we wondered what had made us think the traffic would be less insane in Goa than anywhere else in India. If we had not already known to drive on the left, we would never have been clued in by the helter-skelter patterns of carts, motor vehicles, animals, and people.

About three-quarters of the way to our destination, buildings popped up beside a crossroad, signalling the beginning of a village. Groups of people mingled by the roadway. Suddenly, a big white blur filled the peripheral vision of my right eye. My reflex action—to put out my hand—was met with the hard surface of the side of what I now discerned was a truck; I instinctively pushed outward to keep it at arm's-length. Rick realized that the driver of the five-ton truck was cutting us off to avoid an oncoming car barrelling down the wrong side of the road. His reaction was to ditch the bike to escape being mashed and dragged to oblivion under the sagging belly of the overloaded junky transport truck. The bike skidded on its side with us still straddling it. My whole right side crashed and scraped against the asphalt, as did Rick's.

Men rushed from the roadside and waved down the driver, who pulled over; a crowd surrounded us, blocking traffic on half the road. Most began dissecting and disputing the particular details of the accident, while several helped us remove our lower limbs from beneath the scooter and others ran toward us with cups of water.

In a daze, I observed my right elbow pulsing spurts of blood like water being pumped from a well. Rick tightened his bandana above my elbow as I snapped back to reality. Further assessment revealed that we were both minus a lot of skin on our right sides. An onlooker stepped forward and offered to show us the way to a hospital that he said was a few blocks in from the highway. The truck driver had not budged from his truck. We were told he would stay put until he knew our condition.

Remarkably, the bike was hardly scratched. We got back on the horse, as they say, and followed the good Samaritan to a small medical facility. Being at the rear of the bike, I had gotten the worst of it. Within minutes, my right hip and upper leg had ballooned out, almost splitting my cotton trousers, and I just knew my whole side would morph into an elaborate Technicolor display that would last for months. After the doctor swabbed and tweezed a pound of embedded gravel out of my elbow, he looped five catgut stitches through my flesh to close the wound. He then worked on removing another pound of gravel from both our right knees.

Back at the accident site, the big white truck was gone. Needless to say, we aborted our trip to Old Goa and headed back to our hotel. I could imagine old Mother Teresa saying, "Oh my dear God, these folks are a full-time job."

The hotel employee who had rented us the bike said he had no insurance, but I think he only lacked the proper insurance for rentals. Rick went with him to a repair shop for an estimate, and we paid for the small dent and scratches to the back fender.

There was nothing else left to do but pamper our aching bodies and be thankful we still had bodies that could feel pain. We spent a week lying around reading, eating ice cream, and rehashing the incident. Interestingly, when I told Rick of my unspoken feeling of foreboding, he also admitted to having had a strong sense to abort the ride, but didn't want to disappoint me. A strong case for acting on gut feelings.

* * *

Our beach walks resumed with a daily 3-kilometre (2-mi) stroll either north or south of Colva Beach. This was ambitious enough for us, but if a person had a mind to, they could walk along the beaches of Goa from the northern to the southern tip of the state—105 kilometres (65 mi) of almost un-interrupted coastline.

It was exciting to come across a fishing village just when the large wooden vessels returned with the day's catch. Women spilled out of palm leaf–thatched huts hoisting sturdy woven baskets that were soon filled to overflowing with small fish. They commenced sun-drying this bounty from the sea by spreading the fish over areas that had been made ready with a layer of dried palm leaves covered with burlap. A final touch was setting up net roofing, held in place by upright poles, to hinder swooping gulls from an easy meal. A snorting nose poked out from between two huts, followed by a lot of pig—blue-ribbon size. I waited for the pilfering to begin as he neared the banquet; instead, he sniffed and left, scuttling my notion that pigs will eat anything.

Away from the huts, proud men stood over large tubs, filleting larger fish with quick swipes of glinting blades. Piles of entrails were tossed back into the cleansing sea; circling gulls dived for the leavings. This was a good day for the village.

Brightly costumed women from the adjoining state of Kerala walked the beach. If we felt like purchasing a pineapple or mango, all we had to do was wave a hand and their gypsy beads clinked and their long dangling earrings danced as they ran over and whipped down the huge baskets of fruit from the top of their heads. Other Kerala gals enticed me with armfuls of jazzily patterned scarves. Rick estimated that my collection of the flimsy squares weighed 10 pounds.

Busloads of day trippers were dropped off at the beach in front of our hotel every day of the week. It was not hard to tell the locals from the tourists by their bathing attire. I could only imagine how obscene Western-style swimsuits looked to them. The men spilled out of the bus dressed in long-sleeved shirts and dress pants. Rolling up their sleeves and pant legs to plunge into the water was as undressed as most of them got. A few madcap 20-year-old males stripped down to their tighty-whities to dive into the rolling waves.

The ladies in saris pulled the material in the back through their legs, forming a pair of loose pantaloons. The ones in salwar kameezes rolled up their loose pant legs to frolic in the sea. At dusk, these happy waterlogged folks were loaded back on the buses for their trips home.

As in China, after a few weeks we had gotten into the homes of at least 50 Indian families ... by way of their photo albums. We were continually stopped while walking the beach and asked to pose with bunches of young men or women or whole families. I was not sure what the particular attraction was to us. It seemed the 20- to 30-year-old foreigners were not being asked. Maybe they were bypassed due to their scanty swimwear, whereas with our bruises we were mostly clad in walking shorts and T-shirts. Or maybe it was my sun-bleached tresses? It was probably Rick, however. He had started wearing a do-rag to keep the burning rays off his thinning top-knot. With his ever-increasing wealth of beard, all that was missing was an earring and a Harley (although being behind the wheel of anything ever again in India was out of the question).

* * *

January was drawing to a close, and we were getting itchy feet again, ready to move on to new adventures.

Rick decided to get his beard shaved off a few days before leaving our Colva nest. He was not about to tackle the steel-wool mass himself. I took a "before" picture of him sitting in the barber's chair, with the courageous barber willing to take on this feat at his side. One hour of dedicated work with a straight razor did the trick. A shave and a haircut: $2.00 for the works. I took the "after" picture, but nary a snicker escaped my pursed lips at Rick's raccoon look; suntanned upper face, and pasty cheeks and chin that had not seen the sun's rays for many moons. In all our favourite haunts I was asked, "Is your new man better than your old one?"

We left Colva with mixed emotions, knowing we would sorely miss the fresh salt air, the surf, sand, spectacular sunsets, and the many familiar smiling faces. A night train took us back to Mumbai, where we were to spend a few days before forging northward.

Our Best Shot at Planning Ahead

Tiring of the long lines at the station ticket counters, we decided to book our train travel for the whole month of February from Mumbai. Aurangabad was first on our agenda, which was a 10-hour trip into the interior northeast of Mumbai, still in the state of Maharashtra. With Aurangabad as home base, we would venture out to the caves at Ellora and Ajanta. After backtracking to Mumbai, we planned to travel to Jaipur in the state of Rajasthan, then to Agra in the state of Uttar Pradesh, then back to Mumbai, which would be our point of departure from India. As usual, though, there are pros and cons to everything. The downside of all this booking ahead meant keeping to a set schedule.

The ticket office of the Mumbai train station was gigantic, with purchase windows all around the sides of the 15 x 20 metre (50 x 66 ft) waiting area.

Taking a number and a form to be filled in with our destination particulars, we settled down for the long wait where we could watch the people watching us.

Bold signs on two pillars in the middle of the waiting area read "Seating for Ladies First." A long row of men sat between the signs, while the ladies stood scattered around the rest of the waiting area. Though the men sitting in the designated women's area were laughable, this brought to mind some serious human rights issues in this country. It is definitely still a man's world in India. Female infanticide is still practised, especially if the firstborn is not a boy. Dowries paid by the bride's family have been outlawed, but are still a fact of life in India. These dowries are often so large they have to be divided into increments to be paid over time. When the family of the bride cannot fulfill the promised amount, in-laws have been found guilty in courts of law for setting their daughter-in-laws on fire or doing away with them in other ways. Sati—the traditional practice whereby widows are voluntarily or forcibly burned on their husband's funeral pyre—is against the law, but is still highly esteemed. Elizabeth Bumiller, in her book *May You Be the Mother of One Hundred Sons*, documented an incident of sati being practised as recently as 1996. Stories of sati are still creeping out of rural areas today. Women are making some headway, though, and the next generation's impact will be exponentially more positive.

* * *

As the numbers called over the loudspeaker got closer to ours, we began to pay strict attention to ensure we wouldn't miss our place. We'd been waiting an hour and a half. Finally, 217 was called. The clerk worked from our form, asking the odd question. About 20 minutes later, we left with our wad of tickets ... but alas, back in our hotel room that evening, we found a major discrepancy. The date we were to leave Agra had been switched with the date we were to arrive in Agra. How had we missed this? So much for saving time in train stations. Back we went. We were told that the rule was if it was our error on the original transaction form, we would have to pay for the change, but if the clerk made the mistake, the change would be issued free of charge. Fair enough.

We were led down to the bowels of the station, where clerks sat in dingy, stuffy rooms piled from floor-to-ceiling with records. A veteran was assigned to find our original transaction slip. As he flipped through the stacks, he told us that he had worked in this very office for 25 years, having been with the railway prior to this in other capacities for an additional 15 years. He was looking forward to retirement in a few months. For a while, I thought we would be there to celebrate the occasion with him. After finding about 50 bundles with our booking date penned on a little piece of cardboard that was stuck behind elastic, he painstakingly leafed through them all. Scratching his head, signalling no success, he started through the same piles a second time.

"Never mind, we will pay for the change," we assured him.

"No," he responded, "I have one more idea." When we ascended with him to the ticket office level, he snooped in the drawers of the wicket where we had purchased the tickets. Aha! Our form was still in the drawer. The clerk had entered our data incorrectly into the computer, and then omitted adding the form to the day's bundle sent down to the record room. We *had* filled out the form correctly, and a no-charge ticket was issued.

* * *

Tomorrow, we were to leave for Aurangabad. After three days of bopping around finalizing our travel plans, we tucked ourselves in early and slept like babies ... until 2:30 a.m., that is, when a blaring voice and wood-splintering banging bolted us out of a sound sleep.

"Police check, police check! Open the door!"

My heart banged like a kettle drum being beaten by a maniac. As we released the lock, two men in uniform barged in with handguns cocked. A third officer, who was standing behind, waved the first two back. He shouted questions at us, scrutinized our passports and looked around the small room, and even stuck his head in the bathroom. Then, with a nod of his head, he backed out, banged our door shut and proceeded to batter the bejesus out of the room next door. Still shaking and in a cold sweat, we sat upright in the dark listening to the repetitive hammering, which slowly became less booming like a fading thunderstorm with the increasing distance of floors between.

The first thing we did in the morning was to pounce on the reception desk staff for an explanation.

"All the hotels in the area had a police raid last night. We are never given the reason why," was the clerk's casual reply, with the added no-brainer, "For sure they were looking for someone."

And that's all we would ever know.

* * *

Arriving in Aurangabad, refreshed from catching up with hours of locomotive-rocked slumber, we were looking forward to exploring the area's archaeological treasures.

We opted to start with the Ajanta caves: the oldest, and the farthest from Aurangabad at 100 kilometres (62 mi) away. All 29 caves are Buddhist *chaityas* (shrines) and *viharas* (monasteries). Hewn into the sides of a gigantic horseshoe canyon, at Cave 14 we could see the magnitude of the caves spanning out on both sides. The oldest excavation was carved in the second century BC, the last in the sixth century AD. After being occupied for 700 years, the Ajanta caves were abruptly abandoned for reasons unknown. At the height of activity, it is believed the caves housed 200 monks, as well as labourers to do the rough work, and painters and sculptors to produce the masterpieces. After being abandoned, they became overgrown until 1819, when a British officer discovered them while on a hunting trip for tigers. Being hidden for such a lengthy period had left the caves in amazing condition.

Almost all the Ajanta caves host a majestic, rock-cut Buddha. The vividly coloured wall murals are masterpieces depicting the Buddha's past lives with every imaginable background: forests, mountains, animals, ships, battles, streets, living quarters. The artists were skilled at depth perception and illusion. One 6-metre (20-ft) painting of the Buddha follows you not only with his eyes, but turns his whole body toward you no matter where you are standing. The delicacy and profusion of the work covering the walls is remarkable.

The Ellora caves are 29 kilometres (18 miles) from Aurangabad. Thirty-four in number, they consist of Buddhist, Hindu, and Jain shrines. The first 12 are Buddhist caves, which were excavated between the sixth and eighth centuries AD. With the re-emergence of Hinduism in the ninth century, Caves 13 to 29 are temples honouring Shiva and other Hindu gods. Caves 30–34 are devoted to ninth- and tenth-century Jainism.

The Ghrashneshwar Hindu Temple is a *jyotirlinga*, one of the 12 lingas or locations that hold the key to freedom from further reincarnations ... if all 12 are visited during a lifetime.

By far the most spectacular sight at Ellora was the Kailasa Hindu Temple. Chiselled out of a single rock, it is the largest monolithic structure in the world. It took 100 years to complete the interconnected shrines, galleries, and halls that comprise this great temple of Shiva.

Beyond the scope of the artistic masterpieces at both Ellora and Ajanta is the astounding fact that these immense caves had to be hollowed out of solid rock by chisels and hammers before the detailed artwork could even begin. The hardness of the rock at Ellora saved the structures from destruction by Muslims in the 13th century—mainly at the hands of Aurangazeb, who in iconoclastic fashion felt it necessary to ravage the religious images of those conquered.

Our next day trip was to Daulatabad, a 12th-century fort with an unbelievably complex series of defence systems: seven walls with asymmetrical entrances between, moats, folding bridges, and—as a last challenge to intruders—a maze burrowed through the mountain to protect the palace standing at the top. The last 150 metres (492 ft) of maze passages wind upward in pitch-blackness with pockets, once stationed with guards to ambush intruders. This is the most complicated protection strategy of any fort we have seen thus far in any of our travels. It is hard to believe its defences were breached four times.

* * *

From Aurangabad, it was on to Rajasthan, one of India's most colourful states. We couldn't wait to see what "more colour" meant, as what we had already experienced in this country was of theatrical proportions.

As the train rolled out, we began to think the other bunks in our four-bunk compartment would remain empty, when a gentleman dynamic in stature as well as apparent influence entered with great flourish. Following him into our small cubicle was an armed guard, who after stowing valises under the bottom bunk across from us, commenced to make up the bed. Peering over the book I feigned absorption in, I saw the guard-cum-attendant hold up a square of cloth while the VIP changed from his street clothes into baggy white *kurta* (pants and tunic). The sycophantic guard then motioned for the dignitary to sit on the bed, fluffing pillows around him before leaving the compartment. Only then did this rather rotund gent (probably in his late 50s from the furrows in his face and his shock of salt-and-pepper hair) acknowledge our presence with a terse nod.

The guard reappeared to take off His Nibs' shoes and socks and massage his feet. He then brought him tea and fruit and continued to come in every 15 minutes to see if any need had arisen. When the guard was not in the room, he stood outside the door.

Until late into the evening, each train stop brought a number of bigwigs swishing in and out of the room to pass pleasantries and offer baskets of food. Uniformed officials came in snapping to attention and rattling off reports. Though we heard this personage speak perfect English to his guard, all the conversations with the visiting entourages were in Hindi, leaving us dying of curiosity as to what status was commanding all this lavish attention. As if reading our minds, he at last looked down his nose at us and asked our names, introducing himself as the Inspector Deputy-General of Police for all of Rajasthan.

The armed guard asked at precisely 9:00 p.m. if it was okay to turn off the lights; who were we to object? The gist of his next statement was that we would be safely locked in with the old boy overnight, and if we needed to use the facilities we were to knock on the door. We were not sure from that point on if the guard would be outside the door all night, or if he slept nearby, or if he slept at all.

* * *

I awoke to a humming of "Ommm." A peek over the edge of my blanket revealed the Deputy-General sitting on his bunk in full lotus position. Though my bladder was bursting, I dared not move until he'd finished meditating and his eyes snapped open. After the guard aided the General with his morning routines, and we also had our morning preening out of the way, the guard brought in a big pot of tea and three cups. We ate our breakfast buns supplemented by all sorts of good things the General offered from his stash. He was a gracious host, and the new day brought out his gregariousness. He was most interested in how we lived in Canada.

"How many rooms does your home have?" he inquired.

"Three bedrooms, a living room, dining room and kitchen, two baths."

He: "How many children do you have?"

Me: "Five adult sons between us. It is a second marriage for both of us."

He: "Are your sons married?"

Me: "All but one, and we already have five grandchildren."

He: "How do you all fit?"

Rick: "None of them live with us, they are spread out all over Canada."

He: "That is like animals. If children do not stay in the home and take care of their parents when they are old, it is living like animals."

He must have anticipated my next question, as he added, "Even daughters who join their husband's family do not forget where they come from, and visit. They may beg assistance for their new family if circumstances dictate."

Me: "We have met many Indian families whose sons have left the parental home for destinations around the world for business and career opportunities. What do you think about that?"

He ignored that question, and started in on another subject.

"Do you eat meat?"

Rick: "We are mostly vegetarian, but do eat some meat and fish."

He, again: "That's like animals. Humans were not given teeth for meat by the gods. It is wrong to kill animals for food. It is immoral. No man should eat meat."

Me: "How about the people who live in circumstances where they do not have a choice? Canadian Inuit—the native people you might know as Eskimos—live in the far north, which is buried under snow most of the year, with summers too short to grow crops. For centuries the fish and animals they hunted were their only source of food."

He, emphatically: "Then they should move south."

How obtuse, I thought.

"We should always be kind and thoughtful, for God is in every leaf and blade of grass and creature, no matter how small," he continued.

I found this compassionate statement refreshing from someone who was in charge of enforcing the law.

"So, where does that leave your police officers, who sometimes end up killing people?" I thought I had him.

He: "It is always our right to defend ourselves, and it is the job of the police to defend others who are being victimized, and only to the extent to stop the perpetrator."

Another area that piqued his interest was why we travelled.

"The good thing about travelling to other countries is learning about other cultures. Different beliefs are not wrong, they are just different," I challenged.

He stated in ramrod fashion, "I have never left India. There is no need. We have everything here: mountains, plains, lakes, rivers, oceans, snow, desert, jungle."

While the guard fussed over exiting details, we left the General's world of black and white with ne'er a shade of grey between.

Rajasthan

We entered the land of the Maharajas, and the legendary cities built by these kings. Women passed by, richly adorned with *chudas* (arm bangles), *bichiyas* (toe rings), and lobe-stretching earrings, and men stood around sporting heavy moustaches waxed into flamboyant curls on each side. Vivid oranges, lime greens, brilliant reds, fuchsias, and sunflower yellows flashed before our eyes, not only in the women's skirts and head shawls, but also in the men's turbans—with up to 16 metres (52 ft) of material wound like coiled snakes, each colour signifying marital status, religion, caste, or occupation. It is a land copious in elephant mahouts and camel jockeys, where screeching wild monkeys are more of a nuisance than the ubiquitous cow. Colourful was an understatement; Rajasthan is psychedelic.

After arriving in Jaipur, we taxied to the Atithi Guest House and settled in. Early the next morning, we made our way to the Pink City. The mayhem potential of the main thoroughfares was by far the worst we had yet witnessed. Pedal and motor rickshaws, cars, motorcycles, taxis, oxen, camel and donkey carts, swarms of people, meandering cows, bullocks, and pigs all vied for space amid incessant honking, shouting, and fist-shaking, with the ruling denominator being size—yet miraculously, we did not see a single mishap.

The Pink City is partially surrounded by a high wall enclosing the oldest part of Jaipur and covering a large area that includes the City Palace, several museums, and numerous shops—all painted pink in 1856 to celebrate a visit by Britain's Prince Albert. The current Maharaja of Jaipur lives in part of the palace; the remainder has been turned into a museum with a rich collection of artistic and scientific treasures.

The Maharaja was out when we were there, but one can book ahead for a personal audience with His Excellency, which would have been a neat thing to do.

The largest pieces of silver in the world (according to Guinness World Records) are the two urns that stand in the palace's Hall for Private Audiences. Each urn, weighing 345 kg (760 lb) was built to hold 9,000 litres (2,378 gal) of Ganga water. They were hauled to England in 1902 when the reigning Maharaja Sawai Madho Singh II attended King Henry VII's coronation, as he did not go anywhere without the sacred liquid.

In the textile area of the museum, the clothes of the "fat Maharaja" are on display: the 249 kilograms (550 lb) heaped onto the 2-metre (6.5-ft) frame of Sawai Madho Singh I once filled the tent-like garments.

* * *

The day had flown by. Our feet were threatening to carry us no further, prompting us to take a rickshaw home. Just our luck: we got caught in rush-hour traffic with a teenaged suicidal driver taking harrowing chances, squeezing between and cutting off everything in his way at breakneck speed, including a big white truck (which will forever intimidate us). Keeping our fingers gripped to the rickshaw sides to buffer the zigzagging motion was out of the question, as he often came within a whisker of other vehicles, sometimes scraping their sides. As we swished like laundry in a tub with each hairpin turn, other drivers honked, cursed and pounded the air at his antics, while I became hoarse from hollering "Slow down!" In the cacophony, he either didn't hear me, or—more likely—was ignoring me.

At one point we were stopped dead at a jammed-up intersection. I took this opportunity to grab his arm and shout, "Look, if you don't slow down, we will get out and you won't get so much as a single rupee!" He did not say a word, but did curb his crazed wheeling slightly. Never happier to see our hotel, we descended on rubbery legs, and I made the driver listen to a lecture before passing him the fare. With a poker face, he didn't utter a word, but after his fare was stuffed in his pocket, he took off like a bat out of hell, turning the street corner on two of his three wheels. I hope he lives to see adulthood.

* * *

We chose a senior driver for our next excursion by rickshaw. This fellow was the absolute opposite of the speed demon. We now had to chuckle when everything on the road passed us as we motored up the hilly elevation to visit two of the garland forts 11 kilometres (7 mi) north of Jaipur.

Leaving our driver in the parking lot to chat with his cronies until we got back, we made our way to the lowest of the strongholds, Amber Fort.

It was built primarily as a residential fort for the Maharaja. We swirled our way through the amazing array of guest apartments, banquet halls, jutting balconies, spacious terraces, and, of course, the harem.

Jaigarh Fort, built for defence, was on the hilltop. After working up a sweat from plodding along the winding roadway, we welcomed the breeze at the top. The world's largest wheeled cannon, standing in the fort, had been rolled up this same steep incline, no doubt with great difficulty. The spectacular view looking down toward Amber Fort and the distant city of Jaipur was worth the climb.

The sun that had blazed all day disappeared behind the clouds on our way back home. Like a curtain-drop in a theatre, the air cooled instantly. Being back in the north of the country, and it being only February, I found the evening air as chilling as a witch's breath. Reason enough for us the next day to walk back to the flashy Pink City bazaars and purchase a pashmina shawl for little ol' me.

Along the way, we parted with some rupees for a bunch of miniature bananas from a fruit vendor. Still not India-ized enough to drop our waste randomly, we were soon walking along with a handful of banana peels while keeping an eye out for what we deemed an appropriate spot to deposit them. Noticing two cows about six paces to the rear of us, I tossed a peel over my shoulder and one of the bovine beauties quickened her pace and caught it in her mouth. Soon a calf joined in for the treats. We were soon rid of all the peels and the remaining four whole bananas. Two-thirds of the peels never hit the ground before being snapped up. I can't think of another place in the world where garbage disposal could be so unconventional. The small herd followed us for several more blocks before relinquishing the hope of more handouts.

Choosing an inviting shop, I undertook the monumental task of picking out a shawl. Heaping stacks of assorted shades and designs were unfurled before me by an animated shopkeeper, while I sat on cushions sipping the tea that had been graciously set in my hands. My eyes lit up at a rich taupe shawl with a wide cherry-red border interspersed by three bands of olive green and black right to the fringes. The light chatter segued into heavy bargaining until a mutually agreeable price was arrived at and sealed with a handshake. He threw the shawl around my shoulders as I covered his palm with rupees.

*　*　*

Three hours by bus from Jaipur is the oasis of Pushkar. Central to this small city is Pushkar Lake. Legend has it that Lord Brahma dropped a *pushkar*—or lotus flower—down from the heavens, and where it landed, the lake was formed. Pilgrims who bathe in the lake are absolved from their sins. Pushkar is also renowned as a starting point for safaris across the desert to various destinations.

We tucked ourselves into the Hotel White House and set off to explore on foot: the only way to go in this ped-town where no vehicles, including rickshaws, are allowed on the streets. The exceptions were a few motorcycles owned by residents. The silence was startling. No drugs or alcohol are allowed, and no public displays of affection (including hand holding) are permitted either. And not a morsel of meat can be found in this strictly vegetarian holy city.

This peaceful setting is disrupted in November each year with the annual Pushkar Fair, when the population swells by as many as 200,000 people and 50,000 camels. Camel auctions, camel races, contests, jugglers, acrobats, food stalls, and craft shops flood the grounds at the city's edge. Those who have been to the Fair contend that it is the most tumultuous festival ever.

* * *

Power outages are common in Pushkar, or so we were told when we came back to a frosty room from our first day of exploring. We were supplied with a charcoal heater, which gave us a couple of hours of heat. When we opened our eyes the next morning, we could see our breath. The power outage being over, the charcoal heater was exchanged for an electric stove element. The cord had no plug. The 11-year-old installer pushed the bare wires into the wall socket. The end going into the portable element was also broken and would not grip onto the prongs. He merely pushed some wood splinters into the socket to lodge it in. Wow. It was a wonder the White House was still standing.

Outside, a freak winter rainstorm with high winds swirled and lashed wet sand particles against our window. We huddled wrapped in blankets on the wide window seats and read the morning away with a steaming pot of tea and our mini-heater blasting (where we could keep an eye on it).

By noon, the sun poked through the clouds. Monkeys began landing on the corner of our balcony. Opening the balcony door, Rick snuck his hand with the camera through the crack and managed a few shots before they scattered, bounding from rooftop to rooftop.

Umbrella in hand, we puddle-jumped our way around the city. The goats and cows were gleefully drinking from pools of water left in the streets. Sun showers cast resplendent rainbows on the horizon.

Though many temples are only open to Hindus, we still had to pick and choose while temple-hopping the afternoon away, seeing that Pushkar has over 500. The most popular is the only temple in all of India dedicated to Brahma the creator-god. Brahma's two wives keep an eye on their significant other from temples devoted to them on the hills overlooking the city to the east and west.

No one really knows how many Hindu gods and goddesses there are. After checking several reliable sources with estimates of over 300 million, I had to finally concede this staggering number was not a typo.

As we sat on the floor in the back of one of the temples, I mused about the similarities in religions. An Indian theology professor whom we had met in Mumbai supported my view. Out of the multitude of gods, there are three main gods in the Hindu religion: Brahma, Vishnu, and Shiva. Many religions have a central trinity; think of the Christian Trinity: Father, Son, and Holy Spirit. All other Hindu gods are like Christian saints, in that we often pray to them for guidance or insight. There is an indefinite number of Christian saints. Butler's *Lives of the Saints* gives descriptions of 2,500; the *Dictionary of Saints* by John J. Delaney catalogues 5,000 major and minor saints, though some are not yet canonized. All formal religions have been interpreted and reinterpreted over the centuries, but theologians in general agree that in theory, all are aimed at fostering compassionate human beings. Seeing only the unfamiliarity in other's religious rituals along with additional cultural disparities translates into xenophobia, the cause of much mistrust, hatred, and conflict. Though circumstances differ, we are all spiritual beings on a human journey.

By the time we reached the 12th temple, we were famished. Oh, lucky day! We happened across the Omshiva Buffet: for 50 rupees each, we dove into the all-you-can-eat 30-item selection of vegetables in sauces, breads, sweets, and beverages. Smacking our lips, we agreed this would be our regular supper spot for as long as we were in Pushkar.

* * *

The next day dawned bright and sunny, perfect for a short camel safari out into the Thar Desert. In no time we were bobbing along, I on Rama and Rick on Khristna, with our camel jockeys perched on double saddles with us: Melchior (like one of the Magi) behind me and Johnny behind Rick. Over rugged hills of bushy and parched vegetation we bounced—not the undulating sandy dunes we had expected. The uneven gait of the camels attempting to find footing on the loose rocky trails had my buttocks screaming for mercy. I could not recall being so sore after a week-long safari on the Sahara years ago, with less natural padding back then. Whiny juvenile utterances escaped my lips, like, "Where are the sand dunes you keep promising?"

I was sceptical of Melchior's "Soon, soon," when suddenly we were traversing mounds of wind-rippled fine-grained flaxen expanses. Our guides stopped to let us off to run over the dunes and to sift the hot granules through our fingers. Johnny, the chatterbox of the two, told us that both he and Melchior had just turned 20 and had been lifelong friends, born only two days apart in houses next door to each other.

"Melchior has nine family members in his home," Johnny said, "and I have twelve." Giving his friend a playful punch, Johnny continued "His family will soon have more; he is to marry in one more month."

When we asked Melchior more about his future bride, he shyly responded "Her home is 250 kilometres (155 mi) from my home." I tried not to look too shocked when he added that he hoped she would "look nice," but he had never seen her; not even in a photo. As we jostled back home, my thoughts were of the young girl in this arranged marriage, whose life would be totally disrupted while Melchior's remained essentially the same. How traumatic it must be for her to have to leave her friends and family and everything familiar and hope her husband and his family would treat her well. Not fair, I say, although many of these arrangements seem to meet with success.

Agra

The next morning we were Agra-bound. Up until now, we had been sure Gaya won hands down for grime ... then we pulled into Agra. Every street we ventured onto was a mess of junk and garbage, save for the area around the Sheraton Hotel, which had taken on a turf war to keep the parks and streets around it clean.

The street outside our hotel, the Tourist's Rest House, was no exception. Auto mechanics worked on wrecks that would require nothing less than a miracle to ever be roadworthy again. Sidewalks were non-existent. We had to shoulder-check before weaving around old motors and pans of oil to avoid colliding with a wheeled or four-legged obstacle. We could always count on one granddaddy of a bull being sprawled like a lethargic sentinel near our hotel gates. But once inside the gates, we were quite satisfied with the stark but clean accommodation.

* * *

The mundane faded with each step we took closer to the greatest monument in India: the Taj Mahal. As we passed through the exterior walled gates, the hubbub of the city became muted. The mighty edifice appeared to be floating in a phantom mist above the shimmering central water path before it. The magnitude and sheer beauty was breathtaking; exquisite lace in white marble suspended against the sky. From all angles and distances, the pleasing aesthetics sent shivers down my spine. Hours seemed to evaporate. Our eyes could not get their fill of this extraordinary structure. The morning mist dissipated (though we knew it was really smog). Under the rays of the sun, a whole new persona of light and shadow was revealed in this architectural wonder.

Transported back in time, my mind dwelled on the love story behind its existence. I envisioned Mughal Emperor Shah Jahan in a state of despair. The year was 1631, and he had just lost his favourite wife of 19 years, Arjumand Banu Begum, fondly known as Mumtaz Mahal ("beloved ornament of the palace"). She had died giving birth to their 14th child, a daughter named Gauhara Begum. The emperor wanted her tomb to be one of timeless beauty. The first stone of the Taj Mahal was laid in 1632. Arjumand's body remained in Burhanpur, the city where she died, until the Taj Mahal was completed 23 years later through the efforts of 20,000 labourers working non-stop.

That was not the end to this bittersweet story. Emperor Shah Jahan's son, Aurangzeb, staged a coup in 1658. He fought his three brothers, killing one, and imprisoned his father in Agra Fort. Was it out of callousness that the prison cell of his father had a view of his beloved Arjumand's tomb? How he must have longed to be nearer to her. Shah Jahan's wish came true after his death in 1666, when he was laid to rest next to his wife. "A teardrop that glistened spotlessly bright on the cheeks of time" wrote Rabindranath Tagore, portraying this memorial of enduring love.

* * *

The next day was spent in an uneventful 24-hour trip back to Mumbai. Once again we were welcomed by balmy air as we stepped off the train. We were now ready to enjoy the delights of Bollywood, the home of India's colossal movie industry. Fourteen million people go to the cinema every day in India, and over 1,000 movies are churned out a year: twice as many as in Hollywood. The low budgets of Indian films are becoming a thing of the past with the public's increasing demand for settings in different countries—Australia, New Zealand, and Europe being most popular.

With time to meander through the glitzy cosmopolitan areas, we became fixated on the many beautiful women perambulating the streets who looked different—taller, more slender, caked with makeup, bright red lipstick, and inch-long false eyelashes. Welcome the hijra: the sub-culture of "in-betweens," the third sex found throughout India, though definitely more flamboyant in Mumbai. The hijra describe themselves as neither men nor women, but usually refer to themselves with female pronouns. Although most hijra start out as males biologically, and many are still castrated as in the past, others today retain functioning sex organs, or fit the bill as hermaphrodites, transvestites, transsexuals, or homosexuals.

Professor Gavaskar, who was spending a few weeks at our hotel with his family, enlightened us on some hijra particulars.

"In Indian society, if a male does not show heterosexual tendencies by puberty, he may be put out of the family and sent to a guru as a *chela* (student or disciple) to be socialized in this androgynous gender role. Others may have been forced into the hijra life, kidnapped from impoverished areas or sold by starving parents. One guru may have five or more chelas under his roof, and takes their income to support the household. They assume the guru's surname and consider themselves a part of his lineage." It was the professor's belief that although castration has been outlawed, this ritualistic emasculation is still performed in secret for more than half of newly debuting hijras as a culmination to their training.

We learned from the professor that the historical roots of this third gender mirror the androgynous Hindu deities, in particular devotees of the Mata mother goddesses; and it certainly fits the old adage "there is nothing new under the sun" when I thought of eunuchs throughout history. They are a part of Egyptian mythology and are recorded in the courts of Persia between 850 BC and 622 BC. The Roman Emperor Constantine (AD 272–337) had eunuchs to tend to his grooming. They were prominent in the royal courts of China during the Sui Dynasty (AD 580–618); by the end of the Ming Dynasty (1368–1644) there were as many as 70,000 eunuchs in the service of royalty. Their numbers dwindled until they ceased to play a role circa 1912, with the end of imperial rule. In Muslim countries, there were eunuch harem guardians, and currently in Muslim Bangladesh and Pakistan, tendencies toward this third gender are considered *Insha'Allah* (God's will).

This third gender has never held much status in the Indian caste system, but manages to hold the culture at ransom, as a wedding or birth without the singing, music, and dancing of a hijra would be lacking in good luck and fortune. Besides entertaining, they beg or earn a living through prostitution.

One day we came across a wedding procession on Mumbai's main street. A dazzling hijra danced in front of the prancing white stallion carrying the groom. Clashing cymbals, she twirled and dipped, warbling in her deep, lusty voice. As I had read, the hijra may use their mysterious legendary powers against those who are rude or refuse to pay them, so when she took note of us watching and gestured for a donation, I handed her a wad of currency.

Mumbai's zest was contagious. Walks in the salty breeze along the Arabian Sea were exhilarating. In the bay in the southwest of the city, we came across the fishing village of the Koli people, descendants of the original inhabitants of Mumbai. The hard-working Koli fisherwomen were at the wharf peddling the day's catch. We had been warned that they are known to holler, curse, and even chase onlookers who are not buying their fish, especially anyone who stops too long to gawk or insults them by holding his or her nose to block out the reeking fish smell. Luckily, they were too busy to pay us much heed, although we did a lot of mouth-breathing instead of scrunching our noses against the strong stench just to be on the safe side. Bellowing out prices, their sinewy arms swung great baskets of fish, some still flapping, onto canvas tarps as swarms of customers poked and bargained, though I had a feeling the most miserly customer knew better than to overly test these "grrrrls."

The inner city was equally rousing. Book vendors line the main streets for four long blocks. Every subject and language can be found there, especially a wealth of English books. The outdoor markets near the central train station boast gaudy displays of brightly coloured clothing, tawdry jewellery, notions, and knick-knacks.

Many of our Mumbai memories are about the food. The tantalizing aroma of peanuts and chickpeas roasting wafted through the air from steel mini-roasters on wheels. As we waited in the line of locals, our mouths watered in anticipation of the popular *pao bhaji* (batter-fried balls of potato spiked with chilis), and *bhelpuri* (fried pastry shells for scooping up a spicy sauce concoction). After three months in India, our digestive tracts had developed a worthy lining. But if the day's snacks happened to still be too fiery, we dashed into queue at the sugar-cane juice stand for a cooling potion to set us right. A favourite supper spot was a small vegetarian restaurant that left us planning what delight we would partake in the next time we stopped by: ample servings of beans, tofu, and vegetable combinations smothered in perfectly spiced sauces, complimentary side dishes of cucumber and yogurt to cool the palate, or the best banana lassi imaginable?

Over one of these delightful suppers, a heavy-duty discussion ensued, one we could not put off any longer. It was time to set our date to leave the country: February 25 would be our departure day.

It was hard to believe we had been on the road for eight months. Our anticipation of new horizons was interspersed by waves of melancholy, for India had stolen our hearts and was a boon to Rick's budgeting, coming in at $54.00 a day. Chaotic at every turn, the disorganized confusion took on a rational flow the longer we were exposed to it. The mass of humanity, renegade vehicles, and free-roaming animals was insidiously bewitching. We became acutely aware of India's inner political strife with so many minorities vying for recognition in this, the world's largest democracy; but unlike China, there was no lack of opinions being voiced. The people possess a winning charm, a wheeler-dealer propensity, and a sparkling sense of humour. We will forever grin from ear to ear in recollection.

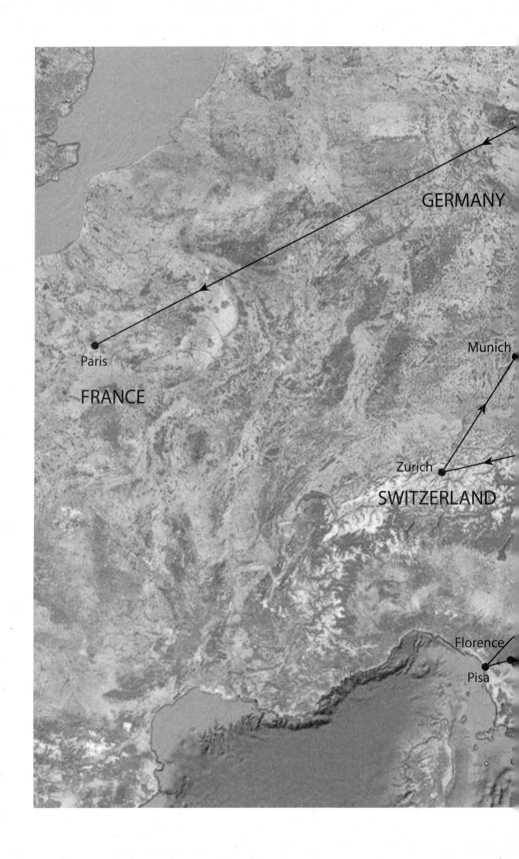

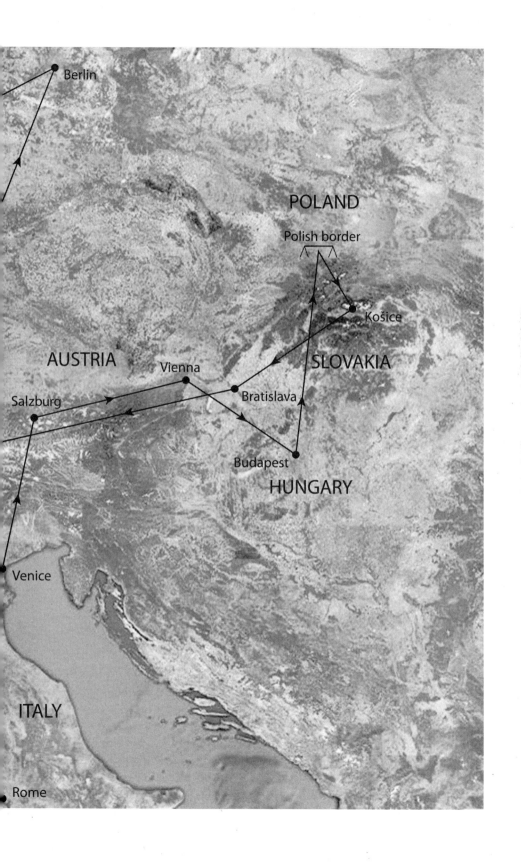

Chapter Seven
Italy

Ahhh, Roma! At last! In a fugue of sleep deprivation, we robotically followed passengers exiting the plane to the baggage claim, then headed out of the terminal to embrace volumes of crisp air and dazzling sunshine. After we rose early on our last day in Mumbai, 17 hours ticked by until our red-eye special left at 3:30 a.m. for London—a nine-and-a-half-hour flight. A seven-hour layover in London plus the two and a half hours to Rome put the finishing touches on our bedraggled state. We still had to make our way from the airport to a hotel bed. An angel was sent to us in the form of Pierre Luigi, who had arrived on the same flight and must have noted our look of bewilderment as to which direction to go in.

"Is this'a your first visit?"

After our affirmation Pierre zealously filled us in on the wonders of Rome, but more importantly, he led us to the train that would transport us to Termini Station, just two blocks from the accommodation we had checked off in our guidebook.

The route from Termini Station was a tad confusing, but after a bit of backtracking we spotted Everest Pensione, plus several other hotels in the same old city block just in case our first choice was full. We were welcomed by bella Theresa, who single-handedly ran the Everest, and soon were locked away in our haven, our Eden, our Olympus. The gleaming white marble bath was as tempting as Eve's apple. Steaming hot water streamed over our bodies. We patted ourselves dry with three fluffy pure-white towels ... each! And oh, the bed! So accustomed by now to foam rubber the width of my hand over a narrow board base, we were in awe of the spectacle before us: a king-sized, foot-deep mattress of perfect firmness; four huge, downy pillows; pressed sheets heaped with another foot of duvet, all in snowy white as pristine as a fresh snowfall. We hoisted ourselves up, almost needing a stepladder.

"What if I fall off?" was my last utterance—to no one in particular—before drifting off; a bed so far off the floor being only a faint memory. For 12 hours we floated on this cloud, oblivious to all except the total enjoyment of so much luxury. La dolce vita!

When we could sleep no longer, we still could not easily come to grips with leaving our nest. We had to gently remind ourselves a vibrant city awaited us. Eventually making our way down the three flights of stairs and into the late afternoon sun, we found a trattoria not far from our hotel entrance. When had we last eaten? I found myself salivating as we perused the blackboard menu: lattes, cappuccinos, pizza, sandwiches, pastries, beer, wine, and last but not least, good stiff drinks.

We sat at one of the little tables and dived into delizioso mozzarella-turkey panini and lattes. When Rick got up to settle the bill, I thought he was going to have a coronary.

"When'a you sitta down you paya doubla price'a on'a da menu," a patron translated the flow of Italian from the short, stocky, no-nonsense owner behind the cash register. Rick did a quick currency conversion and related that what we had figured would be an $8 lunch was now almost $16—the proprietor wasn't kidding. We learned the hard way why most customers belly up to the bar in the ubiquitous little bars and cafés throughout the city.

* * *

We headed out the next morning under an overcast sky to our first site choice: the mighty Colosseum, the largest amphitheatre in the ancient Roman world. It took three Caesars (which is a title, not a name) from the Flavian Dynasty to complete the originally named Flavian Amphitheatre (Latin: *Amphitheatrum Flavium*). Construction began under Emperor Vespasian sometime between AD 70 and 72. Three levels were completed by the time of his death in AD 79. The top level was added and the edifice completed by his son, Titus, in AD 80. Titus did not have long to glory in this achievement, succumbing as he did to a fatal illness a year later. His younger brother and successor Domitian's expansion of the amphitheatre included the underground tunnels for housing animals and slaves, plus a gallery to increase the seating capacity, before he was assassinated at the hands of court officials in AD 96.

As this iconic structure came into view, the sheer magnitude of it left me wonderstuck. Its elliptical form covers almost two North American regulation-size football fields in length, one and a half fields in width, and another field length for the vertical dimension. It is amazing how much of the structure is intact, as besides some major earthquakes, throughout the Middle Ages it served as a quarry for materials to construct other buildings. As we entered the inner sanctum, the roar of 80,000 spectators echoed in our ears through the long ages. We looked down into the pits from which the gladiators and wild beasts were hoisted up onto the (now missing) floor.

These gladiatorial contests were big business. Senators arranged them to demonstrate power and family prestige. They would deal with an agent who would advertise and negotiate with gladiator owners for the price of a gladiator. The losing gladiators could cry for mercy, for their lives to be spared. Their fate was usually left up to the crowd to decide; their decision was gauged by the most voluminous response in cheers to the current Caesar's hand gestures—thumbs up for life, or thumbs down for death. The gladiator's owner was no doubt relieved if mercy was granted since a gladiator was expensive to replace. It also became popular to have exotic wild animals combat each other or to pit beasts against gladiators. It is estimated that 500,000 people and over 1,000,000 wild animals died within these stone walls.

The Colosseum was also used for other public spectacles, such as executions, re-enactments of famous battles, and dramatic performances portraying gods and heroes.

Seating for the events was determined by rank. The sections of seating closest to the action were overlaid with marble for the senators and other nobility. These aristocrats also had the use of freshwater fountains and urine troughs with running water. "Standing" sections followed for the masses, consisting of platforms with several steps between each segment, the platforms continuing right up to the level where not-yet-invented binoculars would have been a boon. I didn't even want to know what these poor schmucks did way up there when nature called during events that usually lasted all day.

Corbels, in which wooden poles once were fitted, spanned the top outside wall to support a velarium. A special fleet of sailors had been on hand during the combats to roll this gigantic awning into place, if it was needed for protection against the elements. We wished this shielding mechanism was still in working order as the increasingly dark clouds burst open and sent their contents lashing downward on strong gusts of wind. We were glad the storm had the decency to hold off until we were done clambering to the far reaches of this ancient marvel. Nature's fury was short-lived, and the sun poked out at the halfway point on our walk back to the hotel.

Next on our list was the Pantheon, the best-preserved building of the Roman era. It was first built in 27 BC by Marcus Agrippa, son-in-law of the first Roman Emperor Augustus, then rebuilt in AD 120 by Emperor Hadrian. Michelangelo (di Lodovico Buonarroti Simoni, 1475–1564) felt it was the work of angels, not men. It possesses a perfect symmetry, from the 16 exterior granite columns to the abstract patterns of coloured marble tiles on the interior to the massive masonry dome, having a diameter exactly equal to its height—an architectural wonder of everlasting appeal.

Originally a pagan temple, now used as a church, the Greek name *pan* meaning "all" and *theon* meaning "gods" is fitting. Several Italian kings are buried within, and a shrivelled Raphael (Raffaello Sanzio, 1483–1520) lies in a glass-domed coffin. Inscribed on this Renaissance giant's tomb is the tribute (in Latin), "Here lies Raphael; while he lived, Mother Nature feared to be outdone, and when he died, she feared to die with him."

From there we ventured to the Piazza di Spagna and the Spanish Steps. These steps were built by the French in 1725, but were named after a Spanish Embassy to the Holy See. At the base of the multitude of steps is the square with a central fountain, believed to be designed by the famous sculptor Giovanni Lorenzo Bernini (1589–1680). Eighteenth-century models were known to hang out here, hoping to be picked and used in a painting. Centuries later, only the mode had changed. A professional photo shoot was in progress with a sensational-looking model strutting her stuff.

We were beginning to understand the saying: "All of Rome is a work of art." With the proximity of piazzas, churches, and museums, it is a city for wandering about on foot. But alas, post-China and India, we were finding our perambulations fraught with Asian-induced traffic paranoia, or possibly a full-blown phobia. Pedestrians in Rome have total right-of-way. The nanosecond a foot extends off the edge of a curb, all traffic comes to a lightning halt. Pedestrians do not even look left and right; they seem to be utterly confident that there's no danger of being hit. At each street corner, we found ourselves riveted as if on the brink of destruction, shrinking in fear of being flattened by the oncoming traffic. Cars that had come to a shrieking stop honked, and nearby locals on foot hollered, "Just'a go, don'ta be worry!", "What'a you wait'a fo?", and "Go, go!" Will we ever be able to trust anything on wheels again? Only time will tell.

It also took a while to realize there was no anger in these vociferous directives: another adjustment we began taking in stride. Italians are a loud bunch. Once when standing in a line for a purchase, a lady came up behind me and let loose in a high-decibel voice, making me jump out of my skin, then cower, thinking I had done something terribly wrong. It turned out she was just greeting her friend in front of me. We would often sit back, especially in restaurants, listening to jovial conversationalists competing to drown out the volume coming from surrounding tables; quite a cultural difference from us soft-spoken Canadians, eh?

Graffiti-covered walls and fences lined many of our walking routes. Of course, most was lost on us—being in Italian—but 90 percent of the English scrawl was American in sentiment, both pro and anti, such as "USA Rocks" or the cliché "Yankee go home." It never ceases to amaze us how in every country we have ever travelled in, people hold strong opinions about our neighbour to the south; whether positive or negative. We also find most foreign countrymen give little thought to Canada; in fact, its geographic location is often vague. After responding to the question "Are you American?" with "No, Canadian," the usual other tidbits known about Canada are tested on us: "Toronto? Vancouver?" Luckily, we can respond affirmatively to Vancouver, as mentioning anything in between these major east and west cities would be an exercise in futility. Though Canada is starting to make its mark, it is humbling to find that the "man on the street" in many countries knows so little about us.

* * *

It was with great anticipation that we made our way to the Vatican. In 1929, under the Lateran Treaty, Mussolini gave the Pope sovereignty over what is now Vatican City; rather melodramatic, as the Catholic Church already held power throughout Rome. Popes over the generations were often also the head of state, and even when they were not, the papacy influenced all matters. The nonpareil art in Rome (and in other Italian cities) was a direct result of the wealth of the Church. Each new Vicar of Christ commissioned the best artists, sculptors, and architects to satisfy their aesthetic indulgences and outdo the previous pontiff in quantity and quality.

During the Renaissance, Michelangelo and Raphael were at the beck and call of a succession of popes. Six rooms in the Vatican Palace contain frescoes by Raphael, whose prowess at bringing forth emotion in the faces of his subjects was unequalled. The profusion of work during his short career—from his mid-20s to his early death at 37—is credited to his proficiency at plotting schematics, whereby the background work and lesser characters were left to his School of Athens students, leaving him to focus on the central figures. Any works underway at the time of his death were completed according to his plans.

Michelangelo painted the ceiling of the Sistine Chapel while in his 30s. It took him four years to complete the over 300 figures covering the 644 square metre (6,929 sq ft) area (which was more than most artists could complete in a dozen lifetimes). I imagined this great master's face tilted upward from his self-designed scaffolding as he painstakingly incorporated techniques to make the figures appear correct on the curved surface from 21 metres (69 ft) below. Though Michelangelo was always a sculptor at heart, Pope Julius II pressured him into painting, a medium on which he was not particularly keen, yet even so he was compelled to strive for perfection; he had already earned the sobriquet "divine."

Hours went by with our eyes feasting on the biblical figures. In the central panel, an airborne grey-bearded Creator in a swirling cloak filled with angels channels His infinite energy through His extended index finger toward the outstretched index finger of a languishing earthbound Adam. This depiction of *The Creation of Adam* is one of the most recognized frescoes in the world and one that scholars, art historians, and theologians have puzzled over due to Michelangelo's known use of symbolism. Was this particular work driven by his philosophies, or perhaps by humour? Dr. Meshberger (Indianapolis School of Medicine) imposed an outline and cross-section of a human brain over a copy of the elliptical mantle of robes encasing the creator and cherubim, from which he deduced that Michelangelo was equating the gift of intelligence with that of the soul. Another theory is that the fresco is in the shape of a human uterus, suggesting Adam was born, rather than created; or indicating a cosmic egg from which all life emerges. The age-old desire to discern the motives of genius only adds to the enigma.

When our strained neck muscles refused to cooperate even a second longer, we moved toward the back wall. Twenty-four years after completing the ceiling, Michelangelo—then in his 60s—worked six long years to complete *Judgment Day*. This apocalyptic portrayal of a scene from the Book of Matthew is replete with both splendour and terror. The dead are heralded from their graves by trumpeting angels for the Last Judgment. To the right of a centrally placed Christ, glorified bodies rise up to heaven; on his left, writhing, anguished bodies fall to eternal damnation. Completed in 1541, controversy arose over the nudity of characters, and the shocking depictions of saints without halos and angels without wings. St. Bartholomew, at the foot of Christ, is holding a knife in one hand and a flayed human skin in the other; the agonized face frozen in its last breath is thought to be a self-portrait of Michelangelo.

We moved on to rooms filled with the works of almost every notable artist from the Renaissance and Baroque periods. Still other cavernous spaces saturated us with displays of ancient scripture, tapestries, elaborate papal furnishings, and Egyptian, Greek, and Roman treasures. Drawing on a lesson previously learned at the London Museum, we accepted the impossibility of seeing everything in a day, as the energy expenditure is enormous. We had to pat ourselves on the back for wisely plotting out a route for what we most wanted to see beforehand, and managing six hours of enthrallment before we collapsed into the chairs of a nearby café.

A few days later, after a humongous vitality breakfast, we took a bus back to Vatican City to delve into the wonders of St. Peter's Basilica. It stands on the site where St. Peter was buried. The first church was built during Constantine's reign. Work on the present church was started in 1506. It did without a dome for many years, as the foreboding size made it an architectural nightmare. Michelangelo took on the project in 1547. Although he died before completion, it was his ingenious design that capped the basilica in such a magnificent way.

Inside the basilica, we lingered over Michelangelo's *Pieta*. This sculpture of Mother Mary holding the dead body of her son is said to be the most perfect of all sculptures. Completed when he was only 24 years of age, it is the only work he inscribed with his name. There was a change of popes just as he was ready to place the sculpture in the church, so with the help of friends, he snuck it into its designated spot, fearing the new pope would reject it because it had been commissioned by his predecessor. Michelangelo clandestinely returned once more to inscribe his name on Mary's sash, in case in the confusion of the pope-shuffle he would not be acknowledged as the sculpture's creator.

Bernini's 29-metre (96-ft) bronze altar canopy is yet another heart-stopper. While admiring this mingling of sculptural and architectural excellence, we noticed a queue of people filing by and touching the feet of a particular statue.

"If you touch St. Peter's feet, he will remember you when you get to the gates of heaven," said the last lady in line. We immediately fell in behind her, figuring we should not bypass any means believed to facilitate ease of entry to the other side.

Next, we were enticed to climb to the top of the dome for a 360-degree view of the city; well worth the 522 steps (I counted, as usual) needed to get there. We left Vatican City exuberant and exhausted.

One would think that with all our walking, I would not have had to use up a whole spool of thread moving all our waist buttons over to the very edges. Our weight had not fluctuated much during our eight months in Asia, but we were now blossoming along with the spring flowers. The pastas, the sauces, the cheeses, the pastries, the lattes! Mamma mia! And the vino! So cheap you can drink it like water ... so we did. In fact, a big bottle of vino cost less than a small bottle of purified water in the supermarkets (the fabulous supermarkets!). It had been a long time since we had seen such stacks of tempting morsels, such a wealth of tantalizing nosh.

The restaurant pricing, however, was giving Rick's calculator a workout. The sky was falling—or so one would think, from all the upward eye-rolls of consternation as he penned the daily costs into his journal. A solution of no hardship was to purchase meats, cheeses, and crusty loaves every other day, along with a bottle of vino (of course), and picnic in a square, or dine at our exclusive table in our room at the Everest for our evening repast. And for girth control—great hardship, this time—we decided to cut out our mid-afternoon pastry stop.

* * *

For an outdoor venue, we wandered through the ruins of the Roman Forum; once the political, religious, and commercial centre of Rome. Julius Caesar once trod upon these streets; eerily, I felt the imprints of his ghostly sandals meeting the tread of our shoes.

"Beware the Ides of March."

"Et tu, Brute?"

"Friends, Romans, countrymen, lend me your ears; I come to bury Caesar, not to praise him."

"Not that I loved Caesar less, but that I loved Rome more."

Shakespearean dialogue sprang to our lips as we re-enacted Caesar's demise at the hands of his senators who conspired against him (we were surprised at how much we remembered from high-school English class).

The House of the Vestal Virgins brought to mind the Achilles heel of human nature. At any one time, six young priestesses lived in the prominent structure, chosen from the families of nobles for the honoured position of keeping the eternal flame burning. Commencing their duties between the ages of six and ten, they were to remain virgins until they were retired after a 30-year stint with a fat dowry. Those who did not manage to keep their vow of chastity were burned alive. The poor dude accused of robbing her of her virginity was flogged to death. One would think these harsh deterrents would put a damper on romantic impulses, but it appeared not, as many suffered the fatal consequences.

* * *

Bright and early one morning, we took a bus out to a part of Rome's history that lies beneath its soil: the 40 or so catacombs that circle Rome. San Sebastiano seemed like a good place to get a taste of one of these Early Christian underground cemeteries (though the oldest section, dating back to AD 50, contained the urns of Romans, who cremated their dead). Spread over several miles, workmen had dug passageways out of the volcanic rock; then professional gravediggers hollowed out the shelves for the Christian remains along both sides of the narrow passageways. As we shuffled along in the dim light, we noted that the norm was three or four shelves one above the other, with enough rock left between for support. A few areas had been reinforced, but the majority remained just the same as when they were hewn between AD 200 and 500.

Our guide Samuel said, "The Christians were soaked in oils—a kind of mummification—then wrapped in cloth before they were placed into the rectangular niches. Though now most are missing, a stone or terracotta slab then sealed each tomb." As we gazed upon the rows and rows of stone shelves, once filled with the bodies of men, women, and children of so long ago, I felt an uncanny presence as I pondered how they had lived: their mundane toils, their trials, their pleasures, and lastly, what circumstances brought them to their last breath.

"The catacombs became a place of clandestine worship, with Christian persecution being the order of the day," Samuel relayed. "Many historians feel the Romans turned a blind eye to this subterranean activity."

Samuel led us to the burial site of the third-century martyr San (Saint) Sebastiano, after whom the catacomb was named. He had worked toward becoming a member of the Roman military with the ulterior motive of alleviating the suffering of captured Christians. After his scheme was disclosed, Emperor Diocletian had San Sebastiano shot at by a line of archers, none of whom are said to have missed. When he miraculously lived through this ordeal, the Emperor had him beaten to death.

In AD 300, the bodies of St. Peter and St. Paul were brought here from other burial grounds for safety, as the emperor of the time was destroying sites of martyred saints. Later, the remains of St. Peter and St. Paul were moved to the two basilicas bearing their names.

Emerging again into daylight, our eyes squinted for the correct bus to take us near the train terminal where we would purchase tickets for our trip to Florence. Though we realized we had just made a dint in the wonders of Rome, we felt our choice of sites was well rounded and the time had come to move on.

In the train terminal, we came across a familiar symbol: the golden arches of a McDonald's restaurant. Upon entering, we witnessed an Italian adaptation of the American franchise: two old codgers swilling back beer in a corner booth, which prompted us to do a double-take to make sure we had come in the right doors. Easily persuaded to adhere to the expression "when in Rome, do as the Romans do," we were soon sloshing back brew with our fries and burgers. I found the droll peculiarity of a McD's pub hilarious. Rick is right when he says it does not take a lot to entertain me.

A perfect farewell to this great city was seeing sun rays glint off gods, steeds, and maidens frozen in white marble by Nicola Salvi in 1732. One should never rush when beholding the Trevi Fountain. The steps leading down to the cascading waters are an ideal perch for watching tourists tossing coins, enjoying a gelato, and just idling the time away. Rustling up some change, we joined the throngs in the traditional stance with our backs toward the fountain and airlifted coins over our shoulder, hoping the legend was true and this gesture would bring us back to Rome someday.

On departure day, a tap on our door made us both shoot upright out of a deep slumber. Had our $3.00 Tibetan alarm clock failed us? We had asked for a wake-up knock half an hour later than our 6:00 a.m. alarm setting, and I did not recall hearing the alarm go off ... but, yes, it was Theresa calling out "Buon giorno!" Blearily noting it was not yet even six, I opened the door to a beaming gran signora juggling a tray filled with puffy croissants, creamy butter, bowls of jam, and enough café au lait to caffeinate us out of our lethargy. What a send-off!

Florence

Rome to Florence (Firenze) was 360 kilometres (224 mi) in three and a half hours of velvet travel; memory came back to us from past travels of how Europe has the leading edge when it comes to riding the rails.

We were quite refreshed and flushed with excitement as we walked from the station to the Airly Guest House. Located close to the Ponte (bridge) Vecchio in the heart of old Firenze, this little pensione is cloistered within a small square, which shuts out the din of the crowded street. Owned and operated by a no-nonsense, bird-like woman, probably in her 70s, who spoke minimal English—but had a memorized speech about the rules that she imparted without so much as a twinge of a smile—"I need'a you passaporto. I give back when you go. Room 40 euro for night. Shower extra. Pay before. How long you stay?"

"Oh, about six or seven days," I responded.

"No! Exactimo."

"Seven," was my snap decision.

She lived in a suite surrounded by the five rooms she rented. The door to her unit was always slightly ajar in order to monitor comings and goings; we knew for sure there would be no partying to keep us awake at night.

Rick and I had a wager to see which of us could make her smile first. Rick won, the effusive charmer. He asked her how many years she had run the home.

"Since young girl." She patted the air at knee-level as one would a child's head.

"You are still a young girl," Rick said with a flirtatious grin, almost knocking me off balance by tugging me sideways to witness her pleased smile. I had to admit she was a gem in her own way. This spry little lady kept the place spotless, even to the point of swabbing out the bathroom after every shower. She dragged Rickie (as she started to call him) over to a stack of books left behind by other travellers while spouting, "Free, free!" I nuzzled in, finding several in English to swap for a few we had just finished.

It looked like in-house dining would commence again. The trattorias and bars in the area were even more expensive here than in Rome. We shared a sandwich that worked out to a whopping $22.00 the first evening. Some logistic work was needed to keep within budget. Price-checking other hotels, we concluded that the Airly was the best deal by far. Scouting out eating establishments farther away from the city centre, we came across some great places on Via Corso that had pricing we could live with, and after checking out the grocery stores, we were set to explore.

We started out early the next morning, cognizant of the possibility of contracting Stendhalismo. Once, a 19th-century French writer named Stendhal was so dazzled by the art treasures in Firenze he became faint and was unable to walk. A medical practitioner coined the term Stendhalismo (or Stendhal syndrome) for others similarly affected. About a dozen cases are still treated annually, and it is no wonder: Florence is the Cradle of the Renaissance. Many famous artists hailed from Florence, including Dante, Donatello, Brunelleschi, and Ghirlandaio. Michelangelo was born in the nearby village of Caprese, coming to Florence to study under Ghirlandaio at the age of 13.

If I had been born in Michelangelo's time, I think I would have stalked him. My obsessive passion for seeking out historical facts surrounding Michelangelo's life reached its zenith as I walked the streets, sat in the squares, and gazed at the churches he so loved.

I was also inspired to seek out an English translation of Dante's *Divine Comedy*, wishing that Italian was my mother tongue so my devouring of this masterpiece could have been in its original form of tertiary rhyme— which he invented for this work. Dante Alighieri (1265–1321) was indeed a radical. In his allegorical poem of one man's journey to God by way of hell's inferno and purgatory before reaching paradise, when elucidating mankind's sins against God, he had the gall to use the names of recognizable popes, political leaders, and the wealthy of his time as the transgressors. For defiling these powerhouses in his seditious works, he was sent into exile in 1301, and probably never saw his beloved Firenze again.

Only blocks away from the Airly we tripped across the famed Ponte Vecchio (literally "old bridge"). It was built in 1345 and is the only bridge in the city that was not demolished by German bombs during World War II. It is said the German commander in charge could not bear to bomb the bridge, and instead toppled buildings on each side to render it unusable. This rings a bit too romantic for a war story; the commander probably missed his mark.

During the 1500s, the bridge was lined with butcher shops. The butchers found the River Arno quite convenient for disposing of entrails and other refuse. The resulting stink offended the rich crossing the bridge en route to their offices, so the powerful Medici family kicked the butchers out in favour of gold and silversmiths, whose descendants are still there today.

* * *

As we carried on south of the River Arno, an elderly gentleman waved us over to chat; or more accurately, to practise his English. He was on his way to his church "Just up the hill!" and invited us to follow him. Why not? He put us to shame by floating up the steep incline as we breathlessly trudged behind him to the 1,000-year-old St. Miniato. After a prayer inside (and a rest), we left our impromptu tour guide to look around the church grounds and sizable cemetery. We had not seen better since New Orleans in Louisiana. There were rows and rows of elaborately decorated above-ground tombs and burial vaults encasing generations of deceased family members.

A shorter climb up from St. Miniato brought us to Michelangelo Square. A large bronze David presided over a smattering of souvenir vendors. After a few chilly days the sun was delightfully scorching, and the view of the city below was spectacular. We dallied until dusk.

The next morning it was on to the Duomo (cathedral) of the Cattedrale de Santa Maria del Fiore, with all its skyline-dominating immensity. Michelangelo once said he could not imagine how anyone could bear to be far from Firenze and unable to see the Duomo. Construction on this, the fourth-largest church in the world, began in 1296 and took 150 years to complete. It abounds with such treasures as Brunelleschi's enormous dome, Donatello's exquisite stained glass, and Domenico De Michelio's painting of Dante standing with a depiction of *The Divine Comedy* in the background.

Across from the main entrance of the Duomo is the Baptistery, built between the fifth and ninth centuries, where as an innocent babe Dante was christened. Along the side are Ghiberti's bronze doors, which took 27 years to complete and consist of 10 panels of scenes from the Old Testament. The Gates of Paradise was the name given them by Michelangelo at a tender age.

I could not miss the church of St. Maria Novella, which is filled with the works of Ghirlandaio. This was where Michelangelo, my demigod, began his apprenticeship. Wealthy families of the time often sponsored and owned private chapels in the community churches. The Rucellai chapel, belonging to Michelangelo's estranged grandparents on his mother's side, is in this church. The Rucellai family disowned Michelangelo's mother when she married his father against their will. I could envision a curious Michelangelo surreptitiously slipping into this chapel when left on his own at night to work, and I wondered what emotions these visits evoked in him.

In the centre of the city's main market district looms the Basilica di San Lorenzo (Basilica of St. Lawrence). It was once the parish church of the formidable Medici family, whose banking business was the largest in Europe during the 15th century. In the Cappelle Medicee (Medici Chapels), the principal members of their dynasty are entombed behind a stunning wall of green marble reaching from ceiling to floor. A second Medici Chapel, the Sagrestia Nuova (New Sacristy), was designed by Michelangelo and contains his sculptures *Night & Day* (Night is portrayed by a voluptuous nude female, and Day is a powerfully built nude male) and *Dawn & Dusk* (another non-clad pair, wherein Dawn takes the feminine form and Dusk the masculine). We stared at every limb, shank, buttock, and bulge looking for—but not finding—an imperfection.

That Michelangelo's mastery of human form is said to have been honed by dissecting human bodies to actually see the placement and interconnectedness of every bone, muscle, vein, and organ only added to our captivation. Knowing that the penalty for violating a corpse was death had not deterred him, but it had added caution to his quest for available bodies. Since the rich were interred in family tombs and the middle class were lowered in the ground amid rituals, only the homeless poor and those without families were relatively safe candidates. The church hospitals supplied free beds for the needy and—when the time came—an unceremonious burial. The largest of these in Florence was Santo Spirito, where Michelangelo had known the prior, Bichiellini. When Michelangelo blatantly told him what he wanted, the story goes that the prior stopped him in his tracks and warned him never to mention the subject again.

He did, however, invite his artistic friend to use the church library's resources on anatomy. After about the fifth meeting in the library, Michelangelo noted that the prior always used the same gold key to point out volumes, and as a bookmark. Could it be? After midnight that night, he tried the key in the mortuary. It worked! He laboured many a night between midnight and three in the morning dissecting corpses and bundling them again in their burial clothes, and thus came to know every part of the human body intimately.

* * *

While on the subject of human form: mine was not doing all that well. I was not sleeping soundly. Searing pain often woke me several times during the night. I had to sit up and slowly move my arm to get my right shoulder back in alignment. My posture was increasingly hunched over; I started to resemble Quasimodo, leaving me snarling and miserable. It did not help when Rick kept chirping "Straighten up." Also, my eyes were watery and red. Deciding I could not put off medical attention any longer, I found a clinic with an English-speaking doctor and off we went. The office seemed ready to close (if the receptionist tidying up papers with her coat on was any indication), although it was only three in the afternoon. After handing over the hefty 60-euro fee to the receptionist, I was ushered in to see the physician.

After explaining my two afflictions, he just sat stone-faced.

"Could it be Stendhalismo?" was my feeble stab at humour.

The doc frowned; maybe he had never heard of it. He peered into my eyes from across his desk.

"Conjunctivitis," he decreed. "Never rub your eyes with anything except your elbow. I will give you a prescription for drops." Go figure—I had gone through China and India wearing mostly contact lenses without any detrimental effects, and ended up with a problem in a much cleaner environment.

The doc became a pillar of stone again. I attempted to explain my shoulder problem in more detail.

As soon as I mentioned my backpack, he cut me off: "You're overdoing it."

I waited for more, then said "So?"

He finally lifted himself out of his chair and came around to poke my back a few times.

"You have pulled a muscle. I will give you a prescription for muscle relaxants." Scribble, scribble. He then went to the rack beside his desk for his coat. If I had not needed the eye-drops, I would have felt totally ripped off. I scrapped the prescription for muscle relaxants, but bought a trolley for my backpack and a big bottle of Advil and faithfully doused my eyes with the drops.

I had no intention of slowing down with so much to see, so it was on to the Uffizi, which holds more great art per square foot than any other museum in the world. We were enthralled by the Botticelli room; his *Birth of Venus* and *Allegory of Spring* are superb. Leonardo da Vinci's *Annunciation* took our breath away. After six spellbinding hours, an announcement reminded us it was almost closing time.

The Museo Nazionale Romano in the old fortress-like Bargello Palace holds Michelangelo's glorious *David*. We circled the 5-metre (16-ft) biblical king hewn from the whitest of marble, in order to see yet another angle of perfection in this well-muscled yet soft form of early manhood. David's body is tense as if mentally preparing to do battle with Goliath. We lost track of time. Had a gaggle of noisy students not swooped into the alcove, jolting us out of our trance-like state, we might have missed the other treasures the museum had to offer.

The Palazzo Pitti (Pitti Palace) was one last Firenze site that drew our interest. The present palace dates back to 1458 and was originally the residence of Luca Pitti, a Florentine banker. It was owned by the Medici family in the mid-1500s, then in the 18th century was used as a power base for Napoleon, and later as a royal palace for the newly united Italy. Its exceptionally decorated rooms with frescoed ceilings, silk wall coverings, and elaborate furnishings attest to the extreme wealth of the old dynasties over the centuries.

Our cup of masterpieces was overflowing upon leaving Florence.

Pisa

The next few days on our loose agenda were spent gaping at the Leaning Tower of Pisa (La Torre di Pisa). This renowned bell tower of the Pisa Cathedral still leans 5 metres (16 ft) off the perpendicular, but there is no longer the fear that it will tip over. The interior was closed to visitors during 1999 and 2000 while engineers finished a new support system.

Begun in 1173, it started to lean when only three tiers were completed by architect Bonanno Pisano. Construction was suspended for over 100 years—not due to the tilt, but because Pisans were in almost-constant battle with the cities of Florence, Lucca, and Genoa. Ironically, had this interruption not occurred—thus allowing the soil to settle before the addition of more tiers—it surely would have toppled.

In 1272, Giovanni di Simone again took up the task of adding the next four tiers, compensating for the tilt. Yet another almost 100-year interruptus occurred during the time the defeated Pisans were under Genoese rule. The final tier was not built until 1372, by another Pisano, Tommaso di Andrea. The sifting silt base has been blamed for the quirky tilt, which has brought fame and fortune. Galileo was born here, and supposedly dropped objects from the top in his experimentations with gravity. There are many world-renowned structures one knows of since grade-school from books. The Leaning Tower of Pisa is one, which for me added to the thrill of actually being there, just steps from its towering tilt.

Venice

A deluxe train whisked us away to the city that stretches across 118 small islands in the marshy Venetian Lagoon along the Adriatic Sea in northeast Italy. Venezia has been known as the City of Water, the City of Lights, the City of Bridges, and the Queen of the Adriatic. The famous Milan-born reporter Luigi Barzini, Jr., who wrote for two New York newspapers in the 1920s, described it as "undoubtedly the most beautiful city built by man."

The sum of these worthy descriptors lent an ambiance of romance to the caressing sound of the waters plashing the edges of the flowing streets, water-vehicles leisurely gliding along the canals (although their speed is regulated by law), and people milling about the walkways of the city (baby buggies being the only allowed wheeled conveyance).

We were soon giddily weaving our way along the winding streets and indulging in the array of quaint cafés serving up scrumptious *tramezzini* (sandwiches) and full-bodied cappuccinos, pasticcerias with sweets of such airy flakiness they couldn't possibly add a smidgen to our waistlines, and gelaterias churning out fresh ice cream—all aimed at inciting reckless passion in one's tastebuds. The only challenge we remember meeting during our week's stay was to lap up our succulent black-cherry gelato before the mischievous sun sent it running between our fingers. We looked forward to this contest every day ... sometimes twice.

* * *

After several days at the Hotel Minerva, we found ourselves dragging our luggage down the street to the Hotel Adua. We were accustomed to this downside of not pre-booking: being ousted by those who had booked ahead. We always rationalize that having double the experience is worth more than the inconvenience. Both hotels were bright, spotless, and located on Lista di Spagna in the Cannaregio area, close to the Grande Canal.

Not used to us gypsy types, the desk clerk at the Adua warned that if we were planning a trip to Venice during carnival week in February, it would be crucial to book accommodations ahead. Venezia's Carnivalle is as big as Mardi Gras in New Orleans. The whole town floods with costumed revellers partaking in open-air extravaganzas with blaring bands and stage shows, or exclusive masquerade parties for the 10 days prior to Ash Wednesday; the last fling before the 40 days of Lent in the Catholic religion. We took to browsing through the many shops that sell or rent elaborate carnival paraphernalia. We had a zany time poking and gawking at papier-mâché masks ranging from freaky to regal, feather-plumed headdresses, and apparel of exquisite lace, breezy tulle, shimmering satin, and glittering metallic fabric.

In our wanderings, I became aware of a difference in the behaviour of the beggars as compared with their kindred in other countries. They knelt in silence with bowed heads along the sidewalks of the busiest tourist streets. Like living-statue buskers, they remained motionless until a coin dropped in their cup, which prompted a brief glance upward at the giver and a "Grazie. God bless," before they once again became static.

And where were all the locals? Missing were the little old ladies buying plump tomatoes for sauces, old men smoking on benches, and teachers leading lines of half-pints. Besides the beggars, the streets seemed to be filled with mostly tourists. Shopkeepers and hotel staff told us: "It is too expensive for people to live here. Even most of the people working here travel back and forth each day from the mainland, Verona." The population has dropped to around 65,000—half of what it was in the 1960s—making it ever more dependent on tourist dollars to keep it afloat (pardon the pun).

Pollution is another major challenge. The canals used to be cleaned by the natural currents of the Adriatic Sea, but are no longer. Man had a greedy hand in the changing of the currents when, in the 1960s, a deep canal was dredged to allow tankers access to a refinery. This has since necessitated systematically cleaning the canals by blocking off sections and draining them so the gunk could be scrubbed away.

And then there is the well-publicized grande problema: Venezia is sinking. The foundation of the city is decaying. We saw evidence of this in the bowed-out walls of buildings, caused by moisture reaching where it once had not. A major flood in 1966 led to thousands of ground floors being abandoned. The water-lines up the sides of the buildings in the commercial areas told of past deluges, while on other buildings, the ground level was currently under a few feet of water, rendering the bottom floor useless. We could easily see why rubber boots are recommended during the winter season, when high tides flood the walkways in the low-lying areas.

Knowing the conundrums plaguing this phenomenal city only adds to its outstanding appeal: will it be here for future generations? We relished the winding streets—which fade into dark, narrow alleys then emerge again into other streets or squares—on our convoluted routes to as many museums as we could fit into our schedule.

The Gallerie dell'Accademia proudly displays the works of Venetian artists such as Tintoretto, Titian, and Veroness. Also, we could not be so near the Peggy Guggenheim Collection of modern art and not indulge. Finding that most of the works of Jackson Pollock had been removed to another location for a special exhibition was a tad disappointing; nevertheless, we did enjoy the few that were left, along with the oeuvres of Picasso, Miro, and Dali. Peggy was buried in the museum garden along with her beloved dogs.

Venezia's most famous church could not be missed: San Marco Basilica (St. Mark's) with its four domes and marble facade dominates the Piazza (square) San Marco. The large open square swarmed with people, pigeons, and seagulls outnumbering humankind 20-to-1. To get pooped on is believed to be good luck. A wealth of luck was being dropped from above, including a fortuitous bespattering of my right shoulder. Souvenir and food vendors were scattered throughout the square; cafés with shielding canopies flanked the perimeter. Brave souls, without so much as a newspaper to hold over their heads, filled the benches down by the water, languidly passing away the whole afternoon amid the swooping gulls.

On the eastern end of the square, Doge's Palace is connected to the old state prison by the Bridge of Sighs, named for the audible exhalations of lament once heard from prisoners being led into the terrible cells. Venetian-born legendary lover Giacomo Girolamo Casanova (1725–1798) once walked this bridge. The governing bodies of the city had long been after this libertine for his anti-establishment writings and scandalous carnal activities. After many trumped-up charges that did not stick, banned books of magic were found in his possession in 1755, for which he was given a five-year sentence in the Doge's prison. He escaped 15 months later and spent his remaining years staying clear of his Venetian inquisitors by spreading his versatile career talents and sharing his devotion to erotic pleasure with innumerable lovers throughout Paris, Prague, Vienna, Madrid, and various cities in England, Holland, and Poland.

We often skimmed the water up and down the Grande Canal on a *vaporetto* (water bus), a ride on which cost about the same amount as a candy bar. All nature of watercraft passed us by: delivery boats piled with merchandise, ubiquitous water-taxis, sombre funeral vessels, ambulances, police cruisers, garbage disposal boats; one type for every service normally provided on solid roadways.

And then there were the gondolas, as intrinsic a part of Venice as the pope is to the Catholic Church. Each day we watched the passing of these sleek black vessels with their raised front bows trimmed in chrome, their leather seats decked in fur and flowers. We smiled at smiling gondoliers serenading their smiling passengers. They were a sight to behold, smartly attired in their vertically striped shirts, the red ribbons on their flat-topped straw hats fluttering in the breeze as they dug long poles into the canal bottom to move their gondola forward. It was time to indulge ... What? $85.00 for a 20-minute ride? Our budget suffered a seizure, which we ignored as we surrendered to the charm and allure and floated down the picturesque canal while the rich baritone voice of our gondolier erupted in " 'O Sole Mio." There are some things in life that only come your way once.

* * *

Italy had been a luxury in every way: from the cities of architectural and artistic wonders to our pleasant, modest pensione abodes, the mostly sunny skies, the delectable cuisine (good thing we had not come across a scale), and the camaraderie of emphatic locals, which all combined to give this bellissimo country an exceptional rating. Our budget for Italy was on track at $132.00 a day. We were ready for other destinations.

Ciao!

Chapter Eight
Austria

The trip from Venice to Salzburg was a mere five and a half hours by rail. Crossing the southern and central Alps via Villach was spectacular. Several sketchpads were furiously being filled around us, and cameras clicked as we sped along. The crisply defined vista of colours and images has long aroused artistic inspiration. At eye level, the wild emerald grasslands were broken by quaint villages and manicured golf courses. In the distance, blue-hazed mountains culminated in snowy peaks with numerous ski runs. A spunky sun in an azure sky added the final touches to nature's canvas.

As our silver metal steed climbed higher into the craggy peaks, mountains of snow began to appear along the train tracks. While we were contemplating adding winter boots to our budget, the train's speed accelerated and we whooshed down the mountain into a snowless Salzburg.

From the central station, we found our way on foot to the moderately priced Pension Sandwirt.

"Grüss Gott (hello)! Ja, we have one room left. Breakfast included, goes from eight to ten," the owner Claudia melodiously sang out in her thick German accent.

And what a room it was! At least 5 x 6 metres (16 x 20 ft), and spic-and-span. My eyes zeroed in on the comfy-looking down-filled quilt and giant pillows as Claudia showed us around. Oddly, the shower and sink were in the room, and the toilet down the hall. The newly installed portable shower was hooked up to the cold water line and had its own heater. A pump drained the water into the sink drain. It didn't take us long to try out this nifty set-up.

We celebrated our arrival with a mouth-watering Wiener schnitzel and beer at the Gasthaus Wieserhof tavern, right outside the back door of our pension. We thought our innards would never fit around the generous portion of spicy, melt-in-your-mouth veal smothered in butter and herbs with delightful cheese oozing out the middle—plus a workingman-sized dollop of creamy potato salad—until we found ourselves mopping up the last bit of sauce with the crusty brown bread, thick with fresh butter. We refused dessert, but nibbled on some briny pickles. That was a mistake, as soon that dish was empty too. The sodium hit meant more beer. We staggered home very content, already planning our next meal. As we were losing our battle of the bulge, which had started in Italy, we would either need to invent some resistance strategy to deal with our partiality to the hearty Austrian cuisine or buy bigger clothes.

Early the next morning, after an outside temperature check, we put on every layer we could muster from our packs to insulate us against the frigid day.

"It is cold for the end of March," said Claudia. "It will go to seven degrees [Celsius] today." Our motto to "Follow the sun" was in jeopardy.

We headed for the main bridge over the broad Salzach River, which runs through the middle of Salzburg, and found that the 360-degree view from the centre accentuates how the city is cozily nestled in the snowy Alps. Across the bridge, the narrow streets of the old city are lined with four- and five-storey baroque homes in catchy bold colours.

The name Salzburg was coined from the salt mines (*salz* in German) surrounding the city. The mines were the key factor in the location of Salzburg, and although most no longer produce salt, they are open to visitors for their historical value.

Salzburg is Mozartland. Every souvenir is adorned with his well-known image. Liqueurs and chocolates are named after him. Mozart, born in 1756, was given the Herculean handle of Johannes Chrysostomus Theophilus Wolfgang Amadeus at his christening. The almost-empty rooms of his Geburtshaus—meaning "birth-house," where he came into this world and spent his childhood—echoed down the centuries with his high-pitched giggles as he raced about in mischievous pursuits. I envisioned his precocious chatter being stifled only when this child prodigy was at the piano, wrapped in the world of notes and melodies, as he was from the age of three. Mozart's first violin rests in a cabinet in all its well-worn elegance. The streets we looked out onto from his windows are said to be much the same as they were in his day, with many of the same shops lining the square.

Years later, his family moved to a more elaborate house several blocks away. Mozart's father, Leopold, no doubt purchased it from the proceeds of his son's performances. This home is filled with personal details of Mozart's life, such as the masterpieces he wrote here, and how from 1762 to 1766 Leopold set out on tours to 13 countries and covered 16,093 kilometres (10,000 mi) with young Mozart in tow. The poor accommodations and unsanitary conditions of road life were hard on his son's weak constitution.

At the age of 13 Mozart was made Director of the Archbishop's Orchestra in Salzburg. He moved to Vienna at age 25 at the command of Emperor Joseph II. He married Constanze Weber in 1781, and they were blessed with two children. His wife settled down, but it appeared Mozart could not. His frivolous spending, far beyond his means, on spirits and soirées kept them in the poorhouse. He craved approval from audiences, which turned into paranoia about losing his edge over competing masters. His last years were tortured by failing health and the frightening idea that he was writing his own requiem (he'd accepted a commission to write a requiem, and had become deathly ill while working on it). At age 35 he lay on his deathbed, afflicted with rheumatic fever. Too weak to write, he conveyed this final masterpiece to another composer, who completed the score. He was buried like a pauper in a common grave. Learning about the fascinating life story of this prolific genius who composed over 600 works was a fitting way for us to spend our first day.

The weather remained bone-chilling. On our sightseeing forays, we stopped for a steaming hot latte almost hourly. At a small café, which became a regular haunt, we took to noticing a frail prune-skinned lady of at least 90 always sitting at the same back table. It was difficult not to stare at the huge piece of chocolate layer cake oozing with a creamy filling that she habitually was engaged in consuming, sometimes ordering a second piece. When our "Ich spreche nur Deutsch (I speak only German)" server struggled over our order, a simple solution was to point to her plate, which brought a smile to her lips and a gleam to her fabulous ice-blue eyes. She carried herself—as well as at least a pound of bling—with a regal air. After about our fifth encounter we approached her table, dying to glean a little bit about her; but alas, our German was no better than her English. Just one of the many instances we felt frustration over a language barrier, though it simultaneously adds to the intrigue of foreign travel.

The giant chessboard in the Domplatz (Cathedral Square) was a place we stopped by almost every day. It took awhile to transfer the logistics of our 10 x 10 cm (4 x 4 in) travel-sized chessboard to the 4 x 4 metre (13 x 13 ft) board painted on the cement. The chess figurines ranged from two-foot pawns to three-foot kings. Neighbourhood men—who we began to recognize—took turns playing against each other, or with a willing visitor. The regulars were mighty sharp. I particularly liked to watch the strategies of a blonde "cutie" who was 40ish with a medium build and thinning shoulder-length hair. He would stand touching his chin or scratching his head while contemplating his next move. At first glance, he seemed quite ordinary ... until a sly smirk spread to his twinkling baby-blues, animating his persona, and he knocked another of his opponent's men off the board. This charismatic fellow, along with his cohorts, kept the surrounding benches filled. We wondered whether the many snack-cart vendors and shop owners around the square paid these local men to play, to keep the crowd from moving on too quickly, as inevitably the aroma of hot pretzels or pastries and the urge to rifle through the all-too-handy racks of souvenirs eventually became irresistible.

Easter Sunday was the day we were to visit the Dom (Cathedral). Having previously noted that the Easter Service would be at 10 in the morning, we arrived at 9:45. People were crowded in, almost spilling out the doors. Not about to let that deter me, I led the way. Sucking in our stomachs, we squeezed in against the back wall.

Only moments later the congregation stood and began hugging, handshaking, and wishing others what we guessed was an Easter blessing, then began to move toward the doors in a solid lump. We heard the last resounding chords pumped from the giant organ and the final strains of the choir as we were propelled en masse out the door. Halfway down the church steps, the parishioners began to separate. So much for celebrating the day with a church service. Where had we gone wrong?

* * *

The day was the warmest since our arrival in Salzburg, so we shed our layers of fleece for the first time. We lazed away the rest of the afternoon watching more chess and strolling through Schloss Mirabell's gardens while munching a big bag of chocolate Easter eggs.

Entering the breakfast room the next morning, we noticed that something was amiss: the room was empty of the usual chit-chat of munching patrons. Hmm ... the normally overflowing serving plates of bread, cheeses, and cold cuts only contained scraps.

Claudia appeared in the doorway with the coffee pot. "Vell, you are late. You did not see the sign that yesterday was the time change? Now it is already past 10 o'clock." Claudia retracted into the kitchen to scrape up a few leftovers.

That explained yesterday's church service being almost over upon our arrival. "It's a good thing we found this out now," Rick said, "or we would've missed this evening's event."

Dressed in our finest attire that evening and preening, we trekked up the hill to Festung Hohensalzburg (High Salzburg Fortress). It would be sacrilegious to leave Salzburg without indulging in a Mozart concert. Performed by a string quartet—two violins, one viola, and one cello— the Master's light and titillating compositions filled the 12th-century castle. Perhaps Mozart had played in this very room. We walked on air back down the hill; there could have been no better finale to our stay in Salzburg.

Vienna

The countryside during the three-and-a-half-hour train trip to Vienna (Wien) was full of farmer's fields being prepared for planting. The earthy palette of browns and charcoals was interspersed with newly sprouted greens and clumps of trees.

Even though we digressed from our norm and booked a room ahead for the Pension Laura, it took us about an hour and a half to finally shed our backpacks. The address we had for the Laura—77 Kaiserstrasse—turned out to be a huge, old building on a rather seedy street, containing many businesses and the Panda Hotel. We buzzed the Panda from an outside button-pad.

"Hello, who is this?" a voice responded.

"We have reservations for the Laura Pension, but have this address. Do you know anything about a reservation for Butler? We've already paid by credit card."

"No, I am just staying here, and I'm the only one here now. I'll let you in. Come up the stairs and I'll try to find something out for you."

After four flights we found the Panda's door.

"I've been trying what is supposed to be a direct line to the dorm caretaker, but no one is answering," the young lady said pointing to a wall phone. Finding we could not get an outside line from this phone, it was down the four flights of stairs again with us.

After walking aimlessly for about a block, thinking we had been scammed, we came across a phone booth and tried the contact number we had. A woman with limited English directed us to a restaurant to pick up the key for the Laura. The restaurant was in a nondescript building almost across the street from the Panda, at 72 Kaiserstrasse. We never figured out how these establishments were linked, but if that's the way it's done in Wien, who were we to judge?

Armed with three keys, we walked to another featureless building. One key worked in the outside door. That was good. After three flights of stairs, another key opened a door with a minuscule Laura sign on it, revealing a foyer, kitchen, and bathroom. Two more doors now faced us. The third key opened one of the two; I gathered that any occupants behind the other door—which our key would not open—would have to share the kitchen and bath with us.

Looking around our inner sanctum, we were glad we had booked for a whole week. The large bedroom was laid out like a mini-suite with a sitting area, desks, a table, and a double bed. It was bright, comfy, and warm (that last being the most important feature). Wien was in a deep freeze, and the rain being hurled by strong north winds was almost unbearable.

On the worst days, we relied on our stash of sausages and potato salad from the grocery store and stayed put. Just when I thought the other bedroom would remain empty for our whole stay, a key rattled in the suite door while I was in the kitchenette stirring a pot of soup. A honeymooning couple introduced themselves. We never laid eyes on them again, as they left before we were up and came back in the wee hours of the morning, so it was still like having the whole place to ourselves.

Once, when coming back to the Laura, we thought we had been robbed. The feeling that something was amiss washed over us the moment we stepped into our room. The next wave of realization was that the room had been tidied up, and thieves don't generally do that. Someone had entered our room mid-week to change the towels. A note was left on one of our pillows instructing us to place the keys in a mailbox when our days were up. We never did have any human contact with hotel personnel.

I enjoyed a good book on our stay-in days, and Rick discovered a hidden talent: he, who had never used his pencil for anything other than mathematical calculations and directives to his managers, started to sketch. First a wine bottle, then a stack of books, then a jump up to the human form. Naked women became his subject of choice. He copied voluptuous nudes from the Old Masters from art books we had collected along the way. He digressed occasionally from the female figure to sketch such works as Michelangelo's *David*. He was good. I was amazed. He was flabbergasted. Rick could not recall drawing anything in his life since grade school. It is remarkable how a long stay away from regular routine brings forth aspects of one's self that one had no idea existed.

We did venture out of our cocoon at times. Who could miss the chance of prying into the mind of the great Sigmund Freud? His office, thanks to his daughter Anna, is set up just the same as it was during his 47 years of practice in psychotherapy. The walls are padded and barred—seriously! Anna used an old photo to arrange everything, right down to the knick-knacks, in the exact same position as her obsessively neat father had always arranged them, including a small mirror behind his desk which he used to check his appearance before the next patient.

Freud (1856–1939) was born into a large Jewish family of nine siblings. Upon the closure of his father's company in Freiberg-in-Mähren (a city now in the Czech Republic, renamed Příbor), the family relocated to Vienna when Sigmund was three. His eventual career choice was to become a doctor, which was followed by his entry into the field of psychiatry. He married Martha Bernays and raised six children in the apartment across the hall from his office.

At age 29, he began experimenting with the effects of cocaine. His friend, Karl Koller, an eye surgeon, was using cocaine as an anaesthetic—one of the few safe uses of cocaine. Sigmund recommended it to friends and family as a "non-addictive" stimulant and analgesic, but later backpedalled on the addiction issue and quit using it himself.

Keying into the psychosomatic factor in illness, Freud developed and published his theories while delving into the human mind with psychoanalysis. His ideas were so revolutionary, he became world-renowned and rubbed shoulders with such prominent intellectuals as Einstein, Alfred Adler (a specialist in individual psychology), and Charles Darwin.

Sixteen years before his death he was diagnosed with cancer of the jaw and soft palate, which was no doubt a result of smoking 20 cigars a day. He continued puffing through 33 operations until he blew his last smoke ring at the age of 83 ... the man should have seen a shrink. A year before his demise the family fled to London to escape the Nazi invasion.

Anna often responded with humour to hyperboles around Freud's theories with this story: "In 1897, newspapers reported that our friend Mark Twain was dead, to which Mr. Twain responded, 'Rumours of my death have been greatly exaggerated.' It is to this same extent that the media exaggerates my father's theories." Following in her father's footsteps, Anna made major contributions to the world of child psychology.

After another day of cocooning in our Laura room with its belching heaters, we were ready to face the elements again. It was on to Schloss Schönbrunn (schloss meaning castle or fortress), where the Habsburgs vacationed during the family's 600 years of power. I had expected some excess, but was left stupefied at a summer home containing 1,440 rooms. The 40 rooms that were part of the tour were dripping with gold-leafed treasures, Bohemian crystal chandeliers, rosewood furniture, Persian rugs, Ming vases, and ornate white-lacquered walls.

We became caught up in the family's historical saga, which was documented in panels along the corridors of the castle. The castle became a part of the family's holdings when it was purchased by Emperor Maximilian II in 1559. It was destroyed during a Turkish invasion in 1683. During the 1750s, much of what can be seen today was completed by Empress Maria Theresa (Habsburg), Emperor Francis I, and their 16 children. Mozart enthralled the Empress and her friends in her marvellous Spiegelsaal (mirrored hall) at age six.

In 1809, Napoleon set up his headquarters here while his troops occupied Vienna. He must have taken the maxim "love your enemy" literally, as he married the Austrian princess Marie Louise. She blessed him with a son, who unfortunately died in the castle at age 21.

Another prominent Habsburg was Emperor Franz Josef, who ruled from 1848 to 1916. His wife became more famous than he: Elizabeth, affectionately known as Sissi, was a true beauty. Her thick, knee-length dark hair and slender figure were her trademarks. She rarely sat at the family dinner table. Obsessed with her 48 kilogram (105 lb) weight, which was distributed over a 177 centimetre (5 ft 8 in) frame, she lived on two oranges and a small portion of basic food such as potatoes each day.

In the Blue Chinese Salon, we saw the chair and desk where in 1918— after the defeat of Austria and Hungary at the end of World War I—Charles I signed his abdication from the throne, ending six centuries of Habsburg rule.

In 1961, the Grand Ballroom of the Schloss Schönbrunn Museum was the meeting place of President John F. Kennedy and Russian Premier Nikita Khrushchev for discussions on peaceful solutions to the Cold War.

* * *

After a guidebook review of "things not to miss in Vienna," we headed for the popular Kärntner Strasse, a pedestrian shopping street. The fashion boutiques, crystal shops, chocolatiers, casinos, cafés, and restaurants draw in the crowds, making it a people-watcher's delight. Most tourists are not aware they are sashaying down the same street the crusaders marched on their way to the Holy Land in the 12th century.

We stopped to see the Gothic masterpiece of St. Stephan's Cathedral. First built in 1147, it has survived fires and the damage of numerous wars to become Austria's National Church and a symbol of the country's freedom. The stone pulpit in the middle nave bears images of Saints Ambrose, Jerome, Gregory, and Augustine: the four Latin church fathers. A rare self-portrait of the artist, Anton Pilgram, hangs under a staircase; he is looking out a window with a sculptor's compass in hand. This self-portrait marks a pivotal point in art history, that of artists contracted by the church finally being acknowledged for their work, whereas before they had remained anonymous, their work dedicated to the glory of God.

The north and south towers can be climbed. We remedied the chill of the old stone structure by choosing the taller north spire and climbing up the 135 metres (443 ft)—divided into 353 tightly wound spiral stairs—for a breathtaking view (in more than one way) at the top.

Back out on the street, the sun had disappeared, and we could see our breath, which sent us scurrying to the warmth of the Kunsthistorisches Museum. The world's best collection of Peter Paul Rubens—Rubens being the undisputed master of 17th-century Baroque art—is housed here.

After rising to fame in Italy, where Rubens painted for eight years, he was appointed to the service of the Habsburg governor with some fine perks: a tax-free shop in Brussels, and gratis travel as diplomat for the country. As he spoke seven languages, he was perfect in this capacity. Rubens married a 17-year-old at age 52 and died happily shortly after ... just kidding; he actually managed 11 years with her, and she became the face and body of many of his works.

Rubens turned out more work than is humanly possible in a lifetime. Like many great artists before him, this feat was accomplished by hiring others to work from sketches on backgrounds and lesser figures in his Antwerp studio. For this purpose, Rubens hired Flanders' best. He would then breeze in to do the most prominent figures himself. Though the artist's intended message sometimes eluded us with his mix of allegorical figures, Baroque art was meant to move the viewer to the contemplation of moral lessons or emotions. His landscapes also depict moods. It was an education to see such a collection of works considered by many to be unrivalled in this artistic style.

* * *

Thankfully, there was no shortage of indoor activities in Vienna. Though we would miss the upcoming Lipizzaner stallion performance, we did catch a rehearsal at the Spanish Riding School. What truly magnificent animals! Being a rehearsal, we did not see many of the synchronized en masse moves that I associated with a dressage performance, but throughout the arena, proud horses and riders pranced through difficult routines individually or in groups of two or three.

Almost more entertaining was the banter of a couple of guys from North Carolina who seemed bored and intent on getting back at their wives for dragging them there.

"Now there is a guy who takes his job seriously. Look at that wiry little S.O.B. go," said one.

"Oh, ohhh! Is he going to get that one before it's squished?" drawled the other. They were referring to one of the two pooper-scoopers on duty down in the arena. What made their continued observations hilarious was that they were absolutely true. The fellow moved with the speed of light between horse buns, zigzagging across the arena and scooping on the run. As if possessing a sixth sense, he would often take off in the direction of a particular horse well before the "drop," reaching the horse with precision timing. It was easy to see why he was rail-thin. The other scooper, who by normal standards was fast, was left in the dust by his colleague.

With only one day left at our pension abode and not wanting to run the rigmarole of extending our stay, we made our way to the train station and booked our tickets for Budapest.

On the way to the station, we came across several blocks of closed roads and a multitude of police and military in the area around the old Habsburg Imperial Palace. This complex currently contains the offices of the Austrian president, as well as an international convention centre, a theatre, chapels, and several museums. We heard the approach of many voices chanting in unison. Over 10,000 people, mostly young, flooded the area with placards. Loudspeakers blared from the truck leading the mass of followers. Nazi swastikas with X's across them were the only signs we recognized. The demonstrators stopped before the large entry gates to the palace grounds. We approached groups of young people, asking if anyone spoke English, in an attempt to find out what was going on.

"The protest is against racism," one girl stated.

"Nazis are again joining forces in Berlin. I've heard they are about 300 strong. Right now, there is a group of Nazi supporters inside the palace grounds demonstrating against the historical information in the Arms Museum about Nazi military activity during World War II," said another.

A volley of passionate statements erupted around us: "History cannot be changed," and "The re-emergence of the Nazi mentality and supporters must be stopped."

The noise level was too great for us to find out specifically how the Berlin contingent wanted to change the documented facts, but we expressed to these young protesters that we agreed that the Nazi mentality should never be allowed to surface again.

We left for the train station. On our way back, an hour and a half later, the protest had become a combat zone. The Imperial palace gates had been broken and the police were using water cannons to back the protesters away from the gate. We were in the midst of a stampede of protesters hurling stones, pieces of wood from smashed barriers and broken fences, and any other projectiles they could find. The police were beating the protesters with billy sticks. The chanting had reached deafening proportions.

"The world is watching. The world is watching. The world is watching," a breathless, frantic voice repeatedly blared over one of the loudspeakers.

I was both terrified and horrified at the pandemonium around us. I moved back, hollering at Rick to do the same, but he remained riveted amid the turmoil. Right next to Rick, a policeman with a large German shepherd on a leash pursued a demonstrator who was running on the lawn of the grounds across from the palace. The young demonstrator cleared the 1-metre (3-ft) fence that surrounded the grounds. The dog flew over it with ease. The powerful canine landed and just kept charging, while the police officer— whom the dog's charge had horizontally air-lifted at an angle not conducive to regaining his footing—landed with a thud on his chest. Nearby protestors started to point and laugh. He went ballistic and started swinging his stick at anything that moved.

The crowd eventually began to disperse. Diehard demonstrators moved across the street. They were still taunting the police and military as we left the area.

We e-mailed our kids to see if indeed the world had been watching. Though it may have been televised in other parts of Europe, as far as they knew nobody was reporting on this demonstration in Canadian media.

Our days in Austria came to an end. After gathering our belongings and squishing them down to fit into our backpacks, we agreed that the bad weather in Vienna had turned out to be a good thing in some ways. It slowed us down, giving us time to reflect. Rick did a lot of contemplating as to what he would do when we got back home, but nothing seemed to fit. One of his missions for this year away was to find his passion (his newfound love of sketching aside, as he looked upon it as only a hobby). I took the time to coddle my right shoulder, which still pinched when I moved it a certain way, my most effective remedy being not to move it that way.

Austrians are in love with life, and this attitude is contagious. We left the cold of Austria with warm thoughts of the marvellous hot soups and lattes, toasty memories of encounters with locals, and our budget average of $121.00 per day, a smidgen over what Rick had allotted for the country.

Chapter Nine
Hungary

I felt like I knew Budapest before I even saw this marvellous city first-hand. Hungarian-born Eva, a good friend who had died of cancer a few years ago, had raved about the romantic atmosphere of the wide tree-lined streets with architectural gems from the past, and glamorous shopping and dining facilities that lent a cosmopolitan air. I was anxious to experience the city that had once brought nostalgic tears to Eva's eyes.

The three-and-a-half-hour trip from Vienna to Budapest whizzed by between glances at the ever-changing terrain and chatting with the young couple across from us in our coach. Hans, with his blondish no-nonsense brush-cut and determined jaw, was from Berlin; dainty Marika, with locks of flaming Clairol red, was from Budapest. They had met at a university in Paris and spoke French to each other. They spoke fluent English to us (it's common for Europeans to know several languages). Both Rick and I were born during a period when total assimilation was considered paramount in Canada and English alone was spoken in our homes, although older aunts and uncles knew our ethnic languages. We often wish we had learned other languages as children instead of having to struggle in adulthood, Rick with French and me with Ukrainian, knowing we will never speak these languages without an accent or as fluently as we would like to.

Out the window, the earthy hues of sandy browns ranging to rich black loams were interspersed with areas of newly sprouted crops, heralding spring.

"Eastern Europe, you will find, has lower standards than Western Europe," Marika warned. "The days under Soviet rule held back all Eastern bloc countries. It's hard to explain this to my friends who have only travelled in Western Europe. Don't expect to find as fancy hotels in Hungary," she said, giving us a few hotel names.

"We already have a small apartment booked with a fellow named Joe, who's meeting us at the train station." I told her the price Joe had quoted us, which was much lower than what Marika had said we would have to pay for a decent room. What have we gotten ourselves into now? I wondered.

The flat landscape transmuted into rolling hills and dense forest. I gazed at dark pines standing majestic and still. In contrast, the leaves of their deciduous counterparts fluttered gaily in the gusts of wind. Sunlight danced through the branches. Spun-cotton clouds hung suspended in an azure sky.

"Hey, Hans, did you hear anything about the protest outside the palace grounds in Vienna?" I chanced.

"Yes, I know something about it. In Germany, during Hitler's command, there was an SS division and a regular army. The exhibition inside the Museum portrays the regular army as being involved in Nazi crimes, and this is erroneous. The demonstrators inside the gates of the palace were against the way the exhibit blames the atrocities on the regular army, and the outside demonstrators did not agree."

"But was not everybody, including the regular German army, forced to do the bidding of the Führer?"

"Ja, but then it should be stated as such," was the opinion of this German youth.

Different slants and varied views on the same historical events—depending on what side of the fence you are sitting on—reminded me of a quote from Napoleon Bonaparte: "History is the version of past events that people have decided to agree upon."

* * *

We wished Hans and Marika well and parted with hugs on the Budapest train station platform, then scoured the crowd for Joe.

"I'll be the one in the baseball cap," Joe had told us over the phone. There was no chance of missing him, Joe being the only person in the throng with a baseball cap, and it being bright red at that.

"Hello, the Butlers. I'm Joe," he called out in a deep Johnny Cash voice as he stretched out his meaty hand for a firm shake. "Welcome to the best city in the world," he said with a grin, his mocha-coloured eyes twinkling. He hoisted both Rick's and my bag onto his broad back as if they were filled with goose-down and led the way to an older European-made compact car. Joe's back curled like a pretzel to fit in the driver's seat.

On the drive to the apartment, Joe gave us a much-appreciated guided tour along the way: "Look over there. That place has the best chicken burger in town. You'll find no better goulash than the restaurant we are now passing on the left. You must not miss the old section of town across the bridge. The bathhouse we are passing now is where the locals go, much cheaper. If there is anything you need to know, just call me."

We pulled up in front of a gate and entered a courtyard. A burglar-proof door of wrought-iron bars had to first be opened with a key in order to access the lock mechanism of the actual apartment door.

"Wow, Joe, this is unexpected," I managed to say as I took in the fully equipped kitchen; the bath with a shower; and the 4 x 4 metre (13 x 13 ft) room with a high vaulted ceiling, containing two sofas, two single beds, a table, and chairs.

"There's more," Joe said, pointing to a steep staircase. While Rick and Joe chatted, I climbed up to the loft, which covered three-quarters of the bottom floor-space, and counted three more single beds.

"This is an apartment that would fit three couples." I did not add: if they had a predilection for communal living.

There were no qualms about us renting this clean, bargain-priced place. We were glad it was suitable, as we would have had a hard time cancelling out on Joe. He was a genuinely giving soul. We paid upfront in cash for the Caterina Apartment. Joe said he would be doing check-ins at apartments he owned in various areas, so aside from his return the next day to deliver a working fridge to replace the one that had conked out, we would be on our own.

We finished off this eventful day by walking down the street to Simon's, a Joe-recommended restaurant, sinking into the puce velvet-padded seats of an ancient wood booth, and lapping up the quaint ambiance. The focus of our attention soon became succulent morsels of beef swimming in garlicky gravy alongside chunks of buttered potatoes, begging to be smooshed all together. After we finished off with fresh spongy bread to mop the plates clean, not even a CSI lab could have found evidence of the hearty goulash that left us totally contented.

Deciding on the loft for sleeping, we angled ourselves at a forward slant to climb the steep stairs—which also lacked depth, fitting only half of my size-7s and a third of Rick's size-10s. We pushed two singles together, away from the wobbly railing.

"Hope neither of us walks in our sleep," I said, looking down the 2-metre (6.5-ft) drop to the living room below.

There were more pros than cons to the Caterina, really. The little kitchen was great. We loved our breakfasts consisting of toast and jam and several leisurely cups of coffee. The apartment was also centrally located, close to all kinds of shopping and within walking distance of some major sites—that is, if one likes to walk as much as 5 kilometres (3 mi) to get to where one is going.

"Taking the waters" was a wonderful introduction to this city, which proudly presents 123 thermal baths and more than 400 mineral springs fed from 14 different sources. Some have separate sections for men and women; others schedule different times for different genders. In the one Joe recommended, the Széchenyi Thermal Bath, both men and women merged out of separate change rooms to bathe together. This bathhouse is known for its immense size, brightness, and cleanliness.

Thermal baths are covered by the medical system in Hungary. Rick breezed through to the men's change room and was in the pool within minutes, while I inched along behind about 40 women, each holding an official paper that had to be previewed by a clerk behind a little table in the hall before they partook of the therapeutic water treatment. When it was my turn to approach the clerk, I learned that cash customers can enter through another door, pay for a three-hour session, and go directly to the change rooms.

I finally made it to the entrance of the cavernous area around the indoor pools. Squinting at the battalion of bobbing heads, I spotted Rick wildly waving. He said he had almost given up on me. Together we waded and paddled through the pools of varying temperatures, trying them all out, including a minute's dunk in the most intense—a scalding cauldron reaching 44°C (111°F).

We proceeded to the gigantic pools outside. The day was one of glorious sunshine. I lowered myself into the soothing mineral-laden liquid. The healing warmth penetrated my very bones. When we became light-headed from the heat, we hoisted ourselves onto the ledge of the pool for a perfect mix of soft sunrays and cool air to counteract dizziness, and then slipped back into the aqueous elixir.

Rick's time expired long before mine, but there was no way I was going to leave before my three hours were up. He was sitting on a bench outside when I emerged, wrinkled and mellow. I was ready for bed, not the long walk home. But walk we did, stopping at the Joe-suggested take-out burger place on the way back to the apartment. We readily devoured our dinner plate–sized chicken burgers, which gave new meaning to the word "loaded." The "little rest" we curled up for turned into several hours of solid sleep.

Waking up refreshed at dusk, we decided to follow our map to a mall about five blocks from the Caterina. It was such a surprise to find this post–Iron Curtain, three-level, 400-store, upscale shopping facility rising out of the surrounding streets of tired shops. People strolled and browsed amid the latest European fashions, but few carried purchases, giving credence to the complaint of wages not keeping abreast with inflation. To help out the local economy, and to put my best face forward, I purchased an anti-wrinkle cream for $140.00.

"Geez, I only spent $2.00 on shaving cream," my frugal beagle complained. That evening, I noticed Rick had left his journal flipped open "accidentally on purpose"—as my mom used to say—with exclamation marks after my face cream entry. He was only being facetious. Although Rick still calculated each day's spending, he was no longer panicky about the money we had budgeted for our year away lasting.

* * *

The Hungarian weatherman was cooperative. On most days, we only needed a light sweater when soaking up the sights of the city.

Scanning our list of to-dos, we were next enticed by the Szépművészeti Múzeum (the Museum of Fine Arts). A truly great representation of ancient and European art is contained within its walls. Francisco José de Goya y Lucientes' *The Water Carrier*, rescued from a famous art heist, is here. As well as Goya's paintings, we scrutinized the works of Toulouse-Lautrec, Renoir, Monet, Cezanne, and Chagall from the broad Impressionist collection.

So far, we had stuck to the Pest side. It was in the late 1800s when the hilly residential Buda and Obuda areas were merged with the flat, industrial Pest area to form Budapest. Swelling to double the width—as in Vienna—the Danube River is a natural division between Buda and Pest. The city's long history of being destroyed and rebuilt is stupefying. From the 13th century right through to the 20th century, the Mongol and Turk invasions, the Turks fighting the Habsburgs of Austria, a revolution in 1848, World War II, and a 1956 uprising against the Soviet Union all took their toll. Once again the Baroque, Neoclassical, Art Nouveau, and Eclectic architecture has mostly been restored.

The Royal Palace dominated the hill on the left as we crossed the Széchenyi Chain Bridge over the Danube to the Buda side. Once across, we turned right, into the old town, where commoners lived during the Middle Ages. Our walk through the cobblestone streets lined with shops and little houses—whose owners do not object to curious heads poking through the gates at their attractive courtyards—was pleasant.

All of the so-called Castle Hill sits on 28 kilometres (17 mi) of caves formed by thermal springs, which were used by the Turks for military purposes and as air-raid shelters during WW II. It is said they can hold 10 thousand people. In calmer times, the caves are used as wine cellars. Our map led us to the entrance of a portion of the underground caverns off Uri Utca 9, which is collectively known as the Labyrinth.

We entered a mass of tunnels between 3 and 4 metres (10–13 ft) in diameter, which opened periodically into cathedral-sized caverns. Trickling water echoed in an otherwise-silent world. The rock walls shimmered with damp. We wrinkled our noses at the musty odours. The cold clammy air made goosebumps erupt on our skin. The lighting was poor; in some areas, we had to stop while our eyes adjusted to almost-total darkness.

In a cordoned-off area we came across a sizable glass case through which we gazed at footprints preserved in mud—Prehistoric, the sign read. Plaques on a nearby wall elucidated several theories of origin for these peculiar footprints, which had treads. Directing us from this display down a concrete path was an arrow and another sign saying, "This way to more puzzling relics."

"That imprint looks an awful lot like a cellphone," Rick said of the next one we came across. Leavings of a super-intelligent race who once visited our cavemen, maybe? "Look here. What? Isn't that slightly similar to a computer keyboard?" Rick questioned. Nonplussed, we rounded a corner ... and stopped dead in front of a man-sized Coca-Cola bottle carved into the rock. The farce was up. It was not that we hadn't been suspicious of the misfitting facts along the way to that point. Our gullibility was in part due to not expecting all the elaborate and expensive displays to end in a practical joke. Chuckling our way toward the exit, we were glad we had thought to bring sunglasses along for our emergence from the depths into the crystalline rays.

Back down on the Pest side again, we made our way to St. Stephen's Basilica—the city's largest church, with a capacity of 8,500 people—where we literally ended our day at the right hand of a saint. Within the cathedral, encased in glass and draped with strings of pearls, rubies, and gold, is the mummified hand of St. Stephen. It was strange looking at the shrivelled, flaking, mottled hand. It behooved us to learn how it came to rest in the vestibule of the church. King Stephen (the first king of the Hungarian state) became Hungary's patron saint on August 20 in 1083. As part of the canonization procedure, the king's body was exhumed. Upon finding his right hand as fresh as the day he was buried, it was detached and became one of the largest saintly relics in the world.

As we started to venture to sites farther away from the Caterina, another world was revealed under the Pest side of the city by our use of the subway system. The Budapest Metro serves 1,270,000 people on weekdays, with an average of 860,000 a day when weekends are included. In the event of a catastrophic occurrence, the tunnels are equipped to provide shelter, fresh filtered air, and drinking and wash water for 220,000 people.

The descending throngs on their way to catch a train are conducive to great business opportunities. The wide corridors are lined with racks of clothing and blankets, which are spread with everything from phone cards to puppies in baskets, all for sale. Restaurants compete with food stalls that do their cooking on camp stoves. Gypsy musicians and singers take up prime locations, pouring out a mix of vigorously spirited and eerily melancholy renditions. Corners are filled by day with the bundled belongings of street people who bed down here at night. Hawkers mill about with cardboard box trays attached to ropes looped around their necks. They bellow out the names of their wares and prices, hardly stopping for breath. One pint-sized girl selling knock-offs of name-brand batteries drowned out every adult around her. She marched right up to us with an effervescent smile and such determination we had to succumb. We bought a pack for future alarm-clock use.

* * *

Numerous walks down Hősök Tere (Heroes' Square) serendipitously brought our attention to an odd building, painted pitch-black, with cut-out letters on the roof overhang which spelled Terror. The line to get in was always two or three blocks long. Although we never came across an English speaker in the queue to satisfy our piqued curiosity, we did get the hours the place was open from a sign on the door.

We arose early the next morning to escape the predicted "unusually high temperatures"—not that we were complaining, only being in a queue surrounded by concrete is best while the sun's rays are still low. At least 20 people were already waiting for the doors to open, which would not happen for another 40 minutes. Aliz, an English-speaking university student, and her mother filed in line behind us and filled us in.

"This museum is about the horrors that happened during both the brief Nazi occupation and the Soviet occupation, which lasted many years. This is the actual building where these things took place," Aliz explained to us. "Most of the people who come are from Hungary, but we hope it will become known around the world."

The walk through the museum was sobering. We were supplied with an English tape-recorder to explain the pictures, trial rooms, meeting rooms, and prison cells. The Nazi occupation began in March 1944. The Nazis, using Hungarian authorities whom they had appointed, began capturing Hungarian Jews and other "undesirables" such as the Roma (gypsies) to be included in Hitler's Final Solution Program. The deportation trains began running. A placard in the museum read, "437,402 Jews from the Hungarian countryside were sent to forced-labour camps or extermination camps between May 15 and July 9, 1944."

On August 27, 1944, Soviet troops invaded Hungary. Hungary became a battlefield; 10 percent of the population was killed, and the country was in ruins before the German army was defeated and the last German troops were expelled in April of 1945. A month later Hitler was dead and Berlin surrendered, ending World War II.

The Hungarian people looked to start a new, free life and reorganize the country under a democracy, but this was not to be. Two political parties came to the forefront: the Smallholders Party wanted Western democracy, while the Left Bloc (led by the Hungarian Communist Party) felt the country's future would best be served by subordinating its autonomy to the Soviet Union. The Soviet-led Allied Control Council (the interim power leading the country during this time of transition) favoured the Left Bloc.

Information posters in the museum told of how in the 1945 parliamentary elections, 57 percent of the votes were cast in support of the Smallholders Party, while the Left Bloc received only 17 percent. Despite the unquestionable electoral victory, the Allied Control Council did not agree on the establishment of a government without the communists. With the help of the political police, the left wing used all measures it could to seize exclusive power, from political assassinations to terrorizing the population.

By 1947, the Communist Party had begun to introduce an open and brutal dictatorship in Hungary. The Iron Curtain fell, the borders were sealed, and Hungarians were swallowed in the reign of terror, losing political, religious, and individual freedoms. All those who were considered an enemy of the state were executed or sent to work out their days in the Gulag (a Soviet acronym for Chief Administration of Corrective Labour Camps). Millions died from guard brutality and the horrific conditions of 10 to 12 hour workdays of hard labour in sub-zero temperatures without adequate food, clothing, or equipment.

Any uprising by the people against the regime was quashed and although from 1987 onward various leaders worked toward democracy, it was not until 1991 and the end of Communism that Hungary totally escaped the Soviet yoke.

In the last room names and pictures lined the walls from floor to ceiling of men, women, and children who had been murdered during these horrific times. As people filed past tears flowed freely in sorrow and remembrance.

We left shaken. Reliving the horrors of this nadir of Hungarian history was a shocking and gut-wrenching experience. The unfathomable reality is that brutality, oppression, and genocide are still occurring today. It is a sorry side of our nature that allows these things to happen to our fellow human beings who share the same planet. We were appreciative of the opportunity to have been made so vividly aware of this part of Hungarian history. It is a part of understanding who they are as a people and how they see the world.

* * *

A note from Joe was stuck on our door when we arrived home, saying he would pick us up the following morning at 11 to take us to the train station.

This gracious fellow was right on time, and along the way he shared some parting words of advice: "This train is always full. It pulls in and starts to load up at around 8:00 in the evening. Since you'll be travelling all night, it is best that you are already waiting and get directly on so as to get a good seat in a non-smoking coach."

It was now noon. We would store our luggage in a locker for the afternoon. Our train was due to depart at 9:05 p.m.

We frittered away the afternoon, and found ourselves reminiscing about the locals who had adopted us, such as our grocery store clerk who broke out in a toothy smile when she saw us in line. Her exuberant "Hi!" was always followed by the singing out of the prices of each item in Hungarian as she punched in our purchases and collected our payment, then ended with "Bye-bye," leading us to believe these were the only English words she knew. Maria, a staff member at the internet café we frequented, ran to put an extra chair beside one of the computers as soon as we walked through the door. At another small café, the staff embraced us as regulars and began steaming the milk for our lattes as soon as we crossed the threshold. Needless to say, at the top of our list was our always kind and supportive Joe. Budapest was not only visually as beautiful as my old friend Eva had always said; its citizens were as unpretentious as Eva herself.

With our budget only slightly over at $111.00 a day and so much time to browse through nearby shops, we succumbed to temptation and each bought a new pair of shoes. I also splurged on a shirt, and Rick on a pair of jeans. Only a few weeks ago we had agreed to wait until we were back on North American soil before going on a spending spree to replace our well-worn clothes. We laughingly now modified it to mean from this day forward.

"Jeez, it's almost seven. We'd better high-tail it to the station," I said. "How many forint do we have left?"

"About 5,500 ... $33.00," Rick converted. "We'll never be able to spend it in an hour."

Neither one of us thought to go to the money exchange at the train station to get this currency changed into euros. What I suggested was more fun anyway: after stuffing some cash in a separate pocket for a food purchase at the station, Rick could barely keep up as I raced the cart around a grocery store. Hand lotion, toothbrushes, toothpaste, hair conditioner, cookies, shaving cream, and a few pairs of socks later, we tore into the station at 7:50.

The train was already in on Track 6. Making a beeline for the baggage check to retrieve our backpacks, we then charged back to our departure track.

"For Poland? Poland? Polski?" I breathlessly fired at a lady in uniform standing by the train.

"Igen, igen," she said, which I recognized as "yes, yes."

We boarded. Joe had been right: after walking through a half-dozen cars, we finally came upon one with room for the two of us, but not our big packs. We affixed them to the outside rail in the passageway, hoping no one would want to pass with wide luggage or boxes.

"Phew. I'm going to go out to find some food. The cookies we have are hardly enough for an appetizer," I said glancing at my watch. "It's 8:10."

Rick shouted "Wait!" and handed me his old-but-still-serviceable shoes to give to one of the less fortunate hanging around the platforms.

I spotted an elderly lady sleeping with all her worldly belongings in the entranceway of a store that was closed for the night. I showed her the shoes and questioned with gestures as to whether she wanted them. She nodded affirmatively and grinned. I charged off, glancing back to see her inspecting them.

Jogging to the first open food vendor, about another 90 metres (100 yd) away, I pointed to sandwiches, cinnamon buns, and water, paid, and darted back, stopping to give the shoe-lady my last few leftover forints along the way. I no sooner got seated again than the train began to pull out. Eight-thirty already? Rick and I exchanged glances. There were only Hungarian speakers in our cubicle.

"English? English? Does anyone speak English?" I asked, poking my head into compartment after compartment in our coach. Finally, I heard a "Yes."

The woman looked at our tickets.

"Not right train. You must to find ticket man," she said, pointing in the direction of the next coach.

I stopped to report to Rick, then walked through five more coaches before I saw a uniformed agent checking tickets and giving them the old hand-held hole-punch verification.

Producing ours, he pointed to the floor of the train and said "No," which made it clear we had indeed gotten on the wrong train. "Off. Miskolc," he said tapping his watch, "two hours." Then he continued, weaving his hand like a serpent, "Waiting. Right train coming."

Okay, that was as much instruction as I was going to get.

Rick and I swallowed our pride along with our sandwiches and cookies. We were utterly exhausted, but afraid to close our eyes in case we missed the stop.

Only a few other people got off at the small Miskolc station, and the ones who did soon vanished into waiting vehicles, leaving us all alone. A few lampposts shed the only light in the eerie blackness. Noting a single bench in front of the small ticket office—presently closed up tighter than a bank vault on a holiday—we huddled and waited ... and waited, and waited. I began to shudder with chills. Calisthenics were one attempt to revive our tired bodies. I seriously began to doubt that my interpretation of the agent's broken English had been correct.

At long last we saw a faint glimmer in the distance. How would the engineer know to stop? Relief flooded over us as the train slowed. An old man and two middle-aged women silently drifted out of the darkness to board the train. We got on and found a compartment all to ourselves.

The ticket agent came directly to our car and punched our tickets. Stretching out on each side of the benches, we fell asleep within minutes.

Slovakia is between Hungary and Poland. We were disturbed briefly when we crossed the border into Slovakia for a passport check.

The next thing I remember is being jarred awake by a thunderous utterance and squinting at a bear-like form in the doorway outlined by the pale light emanating from the passage ceiling. The train was not moving.

"Visa! Passport!" the shadowy figure boomed. "Need visa, passport."

I struggled to find my way back from the land of Nod. We apparently had reached the border between Slovakia and Poland. I glanced at Rick, who looked to be as unsuccessful as I was at shaking away the cobwebs.

The uniformed Polish customs officer reached for the passports, the light glinted off the metal of his holstered gun.

After looking them over he repeated, "Visa."

"We don't need visa. We are Canadian citizens."

"Must visa."

"Book says, no visa for Canadians." I waved my Lonely Planet.

The burly officer scratched his head and left with our passports. It was 3:40 a.m. I quickly flipped to Poland in my "bible." It did not state anything about visa requirements in the Polish section.

"Oh, shit!" we both exclaimed simultaneously as we flipped to the front of our guidebook and saw a check mark in the visa section for Canadians visiting Poland.

The officer returned with an armed guard who was toting a machine gun, no less.

"Must visa. Off," the officer said pointing to the door.

We commenced dragging our baggage past a dozen curious heads poking out of compartments. The nearest exit seemed miles away.

"Well, I've been kicked out of better places," Rick said, attempting a bit of levity. Stifling an inappropriate giddiness arising from nervous tension laced with disbelief and embarrassment, we were escorted off the train by the armed guards.

We were left standing in the middle of the platform in pitch-blackness save for a sputtering light bulb atop a lone power pole. I saw the Polish officer walking across the track, which triggered the realization that he had not given us back our passports. In a panic I sprinted after him.

I switched to my rudimentary Ukrainian: "Our passports. Menyi potreebney passporte. (We need passports.) De nashie passporte? (Where are our passports?)"

"Ahh, bring." He disappeared back into the guard station.

Surveying our environs further, I noticed that the ticket office (the only other building around) was closed. Several trains were in darkness on other tracks.

The officer appeared again and handed us our passports.

"Koodi mey yedemo? Cho mey robet? (Where we go? What we do?)" I asked, and put on my best sorry look.

He pointed toward one of the trains and said "Budapest," before turning on his heel and stomping away.

"Doosha dyakayou. (Thank you very much)!" I hollered after him. I had been told by my Ukrainian course instructor that 60 percent of all Slavic languages are the same. This was living proof: I had been understood.

As we walked toward the train, a conductor appeared in the doorway.

"So, you need go back to Budapest?" the conductor said, no doubt familiar with rejects. He invited us out of the cold starless night into the warmth of the most exquisite train car I had ever seen.

"We really don't want to go back to Budapest. What else can we do?"

"Why not go to Košice, in Slovakia? This train leaves in four hours back to Budapest, with stop at Košice. You can pay me now to go Košice."

"We only have American dollars."

"Seven dollars American is fine."

We counted out the money. A while later, the conductor hastened back. "Super-Conductor is coming to check. You must have ticket." He nervously asked for $3.00 more and issued us tickets. We actually felt bad that he never got to pocket the $7.00.

With our heads spinning from the whole incident, we stretched out on the seats, our vertigo and exhaustion dissolving into sleep. We were somewhat disappointed about not going to Poland, but quickly slotted it away in our minds for another time. What I found so comical was that only a few days ago we had a discussion about what seasoned travellers we had become. I guess we patted ourselves on the back too soon.

Our conductor pal woke us up in time to see the train pull into Košice.

Chapter Ten
Slovakia

Songbirds twittered a welcome from gently swaying trees, which were bursting with new greenery on our early morning arrival into Košice (pronounced Ko-see-chay). Following the path through the rich foliage between the train station and the city, we stepped onto a wide cobblestone street lined with small shops. Owners with pails of sudsy water scrubbed the sidewalks in front of their place of business. They thought nothing of leaning on their mop and chatting with their neighbours. Most of the men had a cigarette dangling from the side of their mouth, which interfered with neither their mopping nor their chatting. Hardly a vehicle passed by. It had been a long time since we were in a city as small as 250,000 people.

We located the Hotel Europa from our guidebook. It was closed for renovations, so we moved on to the Hotel Slovakia. It was over our allotted budget, but we probably would have voted unanimously to stay ... if they had a room ready right then. However, their first availability was at 10:00 a.m., and after our beastly night, a few more hours seemed like an eternity. Four blocks farther down the street, we found a room at the Akademia. Following the "breakfast included," we forced our bedraggled bodies a few feet farther into a spotless, well-priced room. Five hours of peaceful slumber transformed us back to almost-normal from the zombie-like state we had arrived in.

Since we were eager to set out, not even the ominous black clouds thwarted our bounding into the fresh afternoon air. Within a few blocks we were being splattered with a tepid rain. The wind started to blow in fierce gusts, playing havoc with our umbrella and successfully flipping it inside out just as the clouds split their seams. Within minutes of the deluge beginning, it became pointless to seek out shelter. Like giant sponges that could hold no more water, we sloshed and laughed our way to the Hotel Slovakia. Wringing ourselves out as much as possible, we went in for a steaming cup of coffee and *zákusok* (dessert). A hot shower upon our return to the Akademia was luxurious.

The still-dripping city was like a ghost town the next morning. Sunday was definitely a day of rest in Košice. In the town's Central Square, the Cathedral of St. Elizabeth stood in all its Gothic magnificence (it was built in 1345 and added to in 1508). Suddenly, the ornate wooden doors swung open and what appeared to be the whole population of the city spilled out onto the street, dispersing in all directions at the end of morning mass.

The streets veering off from the cathedral square were filled with charming old-world structures. A series of steps leading downward in the middle of an unusually wide street warranted investigation. To our stunned amazement, they descended to barred openings giving glimpses of the underground city upon which present-day Košice was built. We now knew the reason motor vehicles were prohibited along this stretch: to preserve the ancient roadways and walls of buildings still intact below.

By late afternoon, our wanderings had brought us full-circle back to the town centre. Sitting on one of the benches surrounding a fountain that seemed to be turned off in the park near the cathedral, we watched the last rays glint off the spire as the sun sank below the horizon.

A startling swoosh sent me flying off my seat. The gigantic fountain had come to life with a hundred fine jet sprays arcing into the air. Locals began to trickle into the square. Old folks chatted, lovers sat entwined, families kept track of children who could not stay put for a second. As darkness fell, an array of spotlights turned the fountain into a kaleidoscope of colour. The water gushed to varying heights in time to the strains of classical music, as if following the direction of a conductor's baton. With the ringing of steeple bells, the fountain stilled. The magical evening drew to a close; those gathered, including us, headed home in the shadowy glow of street lights.

The face of Košice changed with the beginning of the work week. Businessmen and labourers hustled about. Shop entrances were opened wide. Fresh fruit and vegetable stands materialized overnight. Women were on the move, armed with baskets and shopping bags. Monday was grand market day. Peasants from surrounding villages spilled out of trains and swarmed the town to stock up on goods. Extra-special were the babas; as wide as they were tall, their stoutness exaggerated by puffy blouses and dirndl skirts curving like mushroom caps around the thick stockings on their legs, each with colourfully patterned babushkas (kerchiefs) covering their heads. I felt compelled to capture these delightful elderly ladies on camera. Rick was my baba collection conspirator. When a baba hustled down the street and into camera range, I signalled for Rick to turn and pose, getting them both in the photo.

We were drawn into a shop when we heard English spoken by someone inside. Samuel, the shop owner who greeted us, said he hailed from Belgium but now owned and operated three clothing stores in Slovakia.

"What brought you to Slovakia?" we asked.

"It is a good time to be in business here. The middle class is growing and wages are ahead of inflation," he commented. "Tourism to Slovakia has been growing steadily. I am teaching my staff English. Not many people here speak it." We knew this only too well. Even the hotel and restaurant staff spoke English minimally or not at all. Whenever faced with trying to remember even simple phrases in a foreign language to make ourselves understood, I inevitably think of the immigrants who pioneered the Americas, the tribulations of being uprooted from everything familiar and arriving in a place where an unfamiliar language and customs must be absorbed.

Slovakia's history is one of strong masters. It was annexed to Hungary for 900 years. Bratislava, the capital city, was also the Hungarian capital from 1526 to 1784. After World War I, the Slavs joined the Czechs to form the state of Czechoslovakia. With control centred in Prague, problems of equal rights arose, moving Slovakia to become autonomous in 1938. With new promises, a second Czechoslovakia was formed after World War II, but dissatisfaction with Prague's power resurfaced. The Prague Spring reforms of 1968—proposing equal power between the Czechs and the Slavs—were never realized, as in that same year Soviet troops invaded Czechoslovakia. Nationalism flourished with the revolutionary wave against Communism that swept across Central and Eastern Europe in 1989, which led to the 1991 collapse of the Soviet Union. In 1993, Slovakia became the independent country that it is today.

Slovakia moulded to us like a teenage girl's jeans, and we had to see more. We boarded a train and were whisked through the gentle beauty of the Malá Fatra Mountains to Bratislava, a flourishing metropolis of half a million people. It is rarely swarmed by tourists, we were informed, except when "lots of Austrians holiday here in the summer."

A euro goes a long way in Bratislava, as it did in Košice. Food, transportation, and admissions are cheap. Accommodations are also cheap, if you check around. Borscht with dollops of sour cream and slabs of rye bread is a meal in itself. It did not take me long to remember how to say "bryndzové halušky," which is an irresistible traditional dish of tasty little potato dumplings smothered in crispy bacon and zingy feta cheese.

The Hotel Kyjev (Kiev) became our home. This imposing dull grey structure was built over 1972 and 1973 by the Communists for Soviet dignitaries and government employees. It was in a state of fading opulence. An enormous chandeliered lobby stretched out over the whole first floor. A spiral marble staircase wound its way up to a 300-seat dining room with sparkling white (but tattered) linen. The breakfast included in the price of the room was fit for royalty.

The downside of this establishment was the paper-thin walls, which transmitted each whisper, burp, and grunt of our neighbours to our ears.

No doubt they were purposefully designed to spy on those who were secretly plotting against the state, or to expose double agents in bygone days.

An exasperating night ensued when 10 German-speaking men in their 20s got into too much brewski. The songmaster counted off "Eins, zwei, drei!" before the group belted out another boisterous song, followed by the clanking of bottles and raucous laughter. Stale cigarette smoke bombarded us through invisible cracks. Our room phone to call the front desk was deader than a dodo bird. Rick pulled on his pants and banged on the noisemaker's door. They lowered their voices a few decibels ... for about a minute. The cacophony went on until the wee hours of the morning.

One of the culprits joined us in the elevator the following morning.

"Did you hear the racket all night from those inconsiderate jackasses?" I lashed out.

"Ya, ya, ya, it was terrible," the fellow with stale booze-breath and bloodshot eyes mumbled, then focused on his shoes the rest of the way down to the ground floor. I proceeded to the desk to demand a room change. Our dithering desk clerk told us they would be checking out that morning. Only then did I notice that all the desk clerks were being inundated with complaints from bleary-eyed guests over the night's ruckus. I figured there would be a fair number of grumpy tourists out on the streets today.

Speaking of streets: they were as impressively scrubbed and devoid of litter in Bratislava as they were in Košice. The air was surprisingly un-polluted, considering the high level of industrialization on the outskirts of the urban area.

We hunted down the city's cluster of monuments, redolent of the past. In the centre of the old town is Roland's Fountain (1572) and the old town hall (1421). Nearby is the Municipal Museum with its torture chambers. The Primate's Palace is stunning with its pale pink-and-white exterior, its roofline topped with marble statues and a huge cardinal's hat in cast iron (a symbol of the Archbishop, for whom the palace was originally built in 1781). The Hall of Mirrors in the palace was where Napoleon and the Austrian Emperor Franz I signed the Treaty of Pressburg (Bratislava's former name) in 1805, after the Battle of Austerlitz where 50,000 Russian, French, and Austrian troops were killed.

Bratislava Castle sits high on a cliff overlooking the city. It was once a post of the Roman Empire, later used by Hungarian royalty, and is now a historical and folk museum. All told, there are 180 castles and castle ruins scattered about the Slovakian countryside and in its medieval towns.

The traditional architecture stands in stark contrast to the long stretches of plain, bleak, grey apartments from the Communist era. This mass of rectangular shapes is reminiscent of a sombre Cubist Picasso. There is a standing joke among locals testifying to the monotonous layout of these structures: "If invited for the first time to a new friend's apartment, you never need to ask where the bathroom is."

A Canadian flag caught our eye, fluttering lazily in the breeze out of the second floor of an office building. We climbed the stairs to investigate the source. Canadian Bilingual Institute was emblazoned on a door that opened onto an energetic office. Henry, previously from our hometown of Vancouver, and his new bride from outside of Bratislava had opened this learning centre several years ago. They could not keep up with the demand for English courses. It was the second time we resisted trading in our backpacks for a closet and staying to teach. The world holds such a wealth of opportunity for English speakers to work abroad and to have a new home base from which to venture out to surrounding countries.

Every evening we strolled along the shopping streets around the Kiev Hotel. Most people seemed to be greeting and meeting friends rather than making purchases. Congregations of people stood in clusters. Ice cream in cones was definitely the most popular treat. Women young and old were fairly style-conscious—the babushka'd babas were scarce. Ruddy-faced, stocky men a bit on the shabby side sat along the ledges of buildings sipping from pop cans. When passing in close proximity, whiffs of a stronger concoction than Coca-Cola belied the true use of the receptacles. Roma (gypsies) serenaded the crowd for small coins. Sometimes with rhythmical handclapping, other times with violin and dulcimer, the performers spun their spellbinding webs of melodious folklore. We never tired of lapping up this quaint atmosphere.

Had we not fouled up at the Polish border, we never would have experienced Slovakia's Arcadian atmosphere and charming, good-natured citizens, who rolled out the red carpet for us foreigners. Rick approved of the $77.00 a day, which lowered our average thus far for Europe. We would go back to Slovakia in a heartbeat.

Chapter Eleven
Switzerland

The rugged Alps were the backdrop from our train window in the early morning light. Most of our long haul from Bratislava was spent in sweet slumber in our comfy sleeper coach. Peering out at the snow-capped peaks, I thought of several friends who had raved about their favourite ski chalets in this small country in which mountains make up 70 percent of the terrain. An hour descending toward Zürich brought us to hills dotted by grazing dairy cows munching the fresh carpet of green that had sprung forth after the winter snow had melted away. I had visions of their rich milk being churned into decadent Swiss chocolate as I dozed off again. We pull into Zürich, the largest Swiss city, at 6:27 a.m.

Flavours of German, French, and Italian are stirred together to form the unique seasoning of Swiss culture; 64 percent of its citizens speak German, 19 percent French and 8 percent Italian, the three official languages.

The five-block walk from the train station was invigorating on such a bright, crisp morning. As we neared the hotel area rife with bars we could have used hip-waders—the streets and especially the sidewalks were strewn with garbage. Beer bottles, broken glass, paper containers, scraps of food, you name it. Stale beer, wine, and other choking odours wafted up as the sun warmed the refuse. It must have been some party.

After about five hotel checks in our price range, it was apparent we were going to have to pay more than initially anticipated for a room. The amounts quoted in the guidebook were still in Swiss francs. The hotels had prices in both euros and francs. We questioned why the amount in euros converted into a much higher price in francs for the same darn room. We only got shrugs to explain the discrepancy until the straightforward owner of the Kran, where we ended up staying, was upfront with us about what was obvious: the hotels were taking advantage of the double currency.

"Both euros and francs are still accepted. When the price is stated in euros, especially for tourists, they are rounded up," he said.

"Yes, way up," I added with a dynamic hand sweep above my head.

"So, pay in francs to get the lower price," was his solution.

"Was yesterday a big holiday celebration? I've never seen so much garbage."

"The streets are like this every morning," he said. "Zürich is party central. Bar-hopping goes on until the wee hours. But it is all cleaned up by nine."

Indeed, the streets were being swept and hosed by the time we went to the money exchange to get a wad of Swiss francs.

Even though our guidebook stated that Zürich is the most expensive city in $witzerland and $witzerland is the most expensive country in Europe, we were not prepared for the exorbitant costs. After settling into the hotel, our next move was to eat breakfast, which consisted of a cup of coffee each and two minuscule egg-McMuffiny-thingies that cost us $24.00. It went downhill (or I should say uphill) from there.

Well, we at least planned to see the Heidis yodel and blow alphorns (alpine horns) before breezing on, Lucerne being the nearest place to see these wonderful traditions. Upon investigating ways to get there, we found out we could take a train, but unless we booked an exorbitant bus tour that included the entertainment, we would not be guaranteed a seat to see these performances when we got there. That was enough to make me yodel and Rick to expel enough hot air to blow any horn.

How about a tour of the famous Lindt and Sprüngli Chocolate Factory? It was free! ... Well, not exactly. Public transportation there and back came to $44.00 for the two of us.

Out of curiosity we price-checked items like clothing and appliances, which were as steep as the Alps. The cost of groceries had Rick proclaiming, "You even pay for the holes in the cheese."

We did enjoy our walks along the Limmat River, which runs through the city. The wide cobbled and brick walkways follow the gently flowing baby-blue waters. Shrubs and flower gardens adorn the edges. Pedestrian streets intersect the promenade in the old town with 16th- and 17th-century houses and guildhalls, which took us back in time. St. Peter's Church towered above the other structures. It boasts the largest clock face in Europe. At an amazing almost 9 metres (29 ft) in diameter, we could glance up from a great distance to check the precise time Swiss timepieces are known for. Water fountains abound, and the locals say all are safe to drink from. Though I did not try to count them, the official tally is 1,030.

The history and traditional architecture made our brief stay akin to smelling a rose while trying to avoid the thorns of high cost. "Pricing tempts people to get in and out as soon as possible," is a saying of travellers to Zürich. Rick's tally was $223.00 a day.

In retrospect, we should have chosen Bern, which is said to have a relaxed small-town atmosphere, or Geneva to sit beside the lake, or found a hostel in the mountains to hike and enjoy some of the most spectacular landscapes Europe has to offer. Next time.

Chapter Twelve
Germany

"Prost to München!" we toasted Munich, the big city with small town ideas.

Gemütlichkeit is what Germans call the convivial atmosphere of Bayern's (Bavaria's) capital. Even the uptight northern Germans come here to unwind in the vibrant setting of beer gardens shaded by giant chestnut trees, cavernous raucous beer halls, and endless eateries serving hardy, homey fare. On Sundays and holidays, most shops outside of the central area are closed. It is a day for locals as well as visitors to walk through gardens, take in some of the many museums, or stroll through the Marienplatz, Munich's most famous square. The special mix of cosmopolitan chic and old-city charm flirted with our senses on our first walkabout, swiftly blossoming into a love affair.

I encourage all non–beer drinkers, like myself, to try a *halbe* (half litre) of Bavarian bier. You will be converted and probably order a *mass* (litre) the next time around. It is easy to understand why Munich is known as the beer-swilling capital of the world. Like none other I have ever tasted! The sparkling, mellow, golden fluid glides over one's gullet, titillating the taste buds. Tiny bursting bubbles in the froth send up a delightful aroma, tickling the nose as one's head is tilted back for yet another swig.

The methods and quality of very specific ingredients have been handed down from generation to generation, regulated by the government since the 16th century. The Reinheitsgebot of 1516 (the German Purity Law) decreed that the only ingredients allowed are barley, hops, yeast, and water. There are a mind-boggling 5,000 varieties made by 1,300 breweries. Also, there are different brews for each season, as each specially grown grain crop ripens at different times. With preservatives not being allowed, certain beers are forbidden in summer, as they are more perishable in warmer weather. The alcohol content also varies. The Purity Law even set the price of beer in pfennig and hellers, which—if converted to today's currency—would amount to mere pennies, making this the only clause no longer adhered to in this venerable bible of beer-brewing.

We were beginning to think a park bench might be our accommodation for our first night after we arrived. Hotel after hotel was booked solid; there was a World Trade Fair on environmental technology under way. After an hour at the pay phone, one gentleman said he could give us a room ... for the next two nights only. We of course jumped at this offer. The centrally located Marie-Louise Pension was owned and operated by the Quality Hotel a few doors away. Stephen Leipold, one of the proprietors, greeted us at the Quality desk and gave us the particulars on our new abode.

"You must unfailingly hand the key in at this desk when leaving the room."

"With this three-pound weight attached, how could we forget?" I joked.

"You would be surprised," was his raised-eyebrow retort. Shuttling the key back and forth to the main hotel gave us many opportunities to chat with this interesting, kindly man. Stephen, who was perpetually on duty, started us off each day with restaurant suggestions, sites not to be missed, and a chocolate treat. We were delighted when he told us that if we were willing to change rooms for a few days then move back to the first room, we could stay there for the full two weeks we planned to be in Munich.

Our room at the Marie-Louise was certainly a "special edition" as far as hotel rooms go. Without exaggeration, it was the longest, narrowest room we had ever seen, measuring 5 metres in length and 1.5 metres across (16 x 5 ft). Two single beds, a table, chairs, and a sink were lined up in shotgun fashion along one side, leaving only a couple of feet to spare. Passing one another meant an extra (not unpleasant) squeeze. Rick thought it was extra-perfect. That it was less than half the price of a Quality Hotel room may have had something to do with it. The showers and toilets were shared with the occupants of six other rooms.

On our first full day in Munich, we hustled down to the Marienplatz in the heart of the Altstadt (old town) in time to see the much-photographed Glockenspiel in action. Every day at 11:00 a.m. and noon (and also at 5:00 p.m. from May to October), the carillon high up on the facade of the Altes Rathaus (town hall) is the focus for a 20-minute revue. Bells chimed out engaging tunes for the first while. Suddenly, figurines of ladies and gents began to dance, moving in and out of the archways, twisting and turning and dipping to the melodic pealing of bells. Just when we thought the pause of the figures was signalling the end, a miniature tournament commenced. Jousters on their steeds appeared from opposite sides, spears pointed at their opponents. One of the jousters was knocked off his horse; the other pranced in triumph past the arches. Two more jousters then appeared for the next competition. In a grand finale, the king and queen came out to bow, and the enamelled copper figures stilled as the musical bells wound down.

We dispersed with the crowd to the many outdoor cafés for some hardy Bavarian sustenance. The central area of the square took on a circus-like atmosphere. A talented fellow pummelled out wonderful tunes on a giant xylophone. Jugglers, break-dancers, and mimes picked their spots and instantly drew audiences.

Germans are formidable eaters, putting away three hardy squares plus a few snacks a day. Charles de Gaulle once made a statement about France in jest (or not) regarding the "difficulty in uniting and running a country with 275 varieties of cheese." How much more difficult would he have gauged running Germany, with its 1,500 types of wurst (sausage)? Meat and *kraut* (cabbage) are staples, along with the potato (which was first introduced by Frances Drake, the famed English explorer, in the 16th century). It took the Germans to transform the lowly potato to its pinnacle state: the *Kartoffelpuffer* (potato pancake). Other vegetables, such as peas and carrots, have not fared as well. Our "crisp is better" standard had not yet reached Munich, where restaurants boiled them until they were soggy.

Kaffee—a late-afternoon snack of coffee and cake to tide us over between the noon lunch and a late supper—was our favourite. The array of strudels and tortes was too tempting for most to resist, if the crowds at the coffee shops were any indicator. We took to lining up early so our favourites would not be sold out.

Craving some verdure and exercise after eating our way through the Marienplatz and the surrounding streets, the endless Englischer Garten seemed a worthy pick. A rapidly flowing river runs through the Garten, which is advertised as the largest city park in Europe. So tumultuous are the waters under the main bridge that inland surfers whipped back and forth riding the waves. Farther downriver, we saw people wade into the water and fall back into a sitting position to be swept squealing downriver by the strong current. One daredevil tied a bungee cord to a tree. After ploughing his way into the force of the current upriver of the tree until the cord was taut, he then released his foothold while simultaneously jumping onto a small surfboard. The double force of the water and cord propelled this human slingshot at rocket speed far past the tree he started out from.

Veering away from the river to the garden area, we suddenly found ourselves overdressed for our outing, and not due to the heat of the sun. Our path led us unexpectedly between long rows of nude sunbathers. Ordinary to extraordinary: there were both women and men, of all shapes and sizes. Many were oblivious to their surroundings, concentrating only on enjoying the spring rays in their textile-free state. Others had a double agenda. Three cheeky fellows strolling along in front of us were obviously gay-ly cruising; we watched their heads turn toward reclining non-clad males who if interested responded by putting their best side forward. The eyes of other male walkers were focused on recumbent women, who in turn were checking out the bodies of their choice of gender as they passed by on the walkways. A few scornful looks were shot our attired way. We had a good giggle over this bit of unexpected voyeurism.

* * *

Arising extra early one morning, we caught the S-Bahn train and then the 746 bus to Dachau, the first Nazi concentration camp, built in 1933. It was a creation of Hitler's top draconian thug, Heinrich Himmler, and served as a model and training facility for the many camps that followed.

A massive grey concrete wall strung with barbed wire along the top loomed around the perimeter of the large compound. As we looked about the still, bleak setting I became apprehensive about being in a place where such atrocities had occurred; yet like in Hungary's Terror Museum, we were drawn to know and feel and puzzle over the human capability to commit genocide against fellow human beings.

"Those who cannot remember the past are condemned to repeat it." These words of American philosopher George Santayana (1863–1952) are prominently displayed, expressing the sentiment behind the public display of Dachau against shoving the wrongs of history out of sight.

Our eyes instantly focused on the 2-metre (6.5-ft) width of grass separating the outside walls, the only spot of colour in the otherwise dismal expanse of dirt and gravel that was the central interior. Prisoners who had lost hope or could not endure more pain and suffering often walked onto the grass to be cut down in seconds by machine-gun fire from the guards keeping watch from the lofty stations around the complex. Arbeit Macht Frei ("Work makes you free") was inscribed over the entrance where new prisoners entered. For most, this freedom came in the form of smoke rising from the crematorium chimney.

All that is left of 15 of the barracks are wooden ties outlining the base. One stands reconstructed. Up to 1,600 men were crammed into the roughly hewn wooden structures meant for 200. The original shower building is still standing, complete with hooks from which prisoners were brutally hung from ropes tied to their wrists from behind their backs. This building was also the initial processing area, where people were stripped, sprayed with disinfectant, and robbed of all their possessions. Their lives became a blur of torture, beatings, starvation, and heavy labour.

For whatever reason, the gas chamber at Dachau disguised as a shower was never used. "Invalids"—those who became too sick or damaged to work—were mostly transported to the nearest gas chamber at Hartheim Castle to be done away with. The bodies of those who died in Dachau were hauled off to other Nazi camps where crematoriums, utilized to their fullest capacity, belched out smoke and fragments of human ash night and day.

"Between 1933 and 1945, hundreds of thousands of people from 34 nations passed through these gates," a plaque in the museum read. A map showing the locations of all known concentration camps throughout the Nazi-controlled countries was staggering. The death toll of the Holocaust was 6 million Jews, and another 5 million non-Jews who were also categorized as "undesirables" or *Untermenschen* (subhumans). This included clergymen, political opponents within Germany itself, and nationalists fighting for independence from the dozen or so countries that were invaded by the Nazis. Also targeted were homosexuals, the Sinti and Roma peoples (gypsies), criminals, and those presumed likely to perpetrate future crimes (such as the unemployed and vagabonds).

A salient memorial in the form of black metal bodies, twisted and contorted, with fingers and toes resembling barbed wire and mouths gaping in terror, is a stark reminder of the barbarism perpetrated against innocent victims.

It made us review our own racist propensities and prejudices lying hidden under the surface. At one time I would have bragged of not having a racist bone in my body. Many more years of living and a few psychology degrees have enlightened me to the prejudices incorporated deep in my psyche during early childhood, stemming from the racist attitudes of some around me, many of which were not necessarily even verbalized.

Our visit to Dachau left us shaken, subdued, and swelling with compassion for those who had suffered during the Holocaust and from all such horrific evils at any time throughout history.

* * *

It was a good thing that our Dachau visit was followed by an extremely uplifting event: my oldest son, Rob, his partner, Glenda, and Glenda's sister Candice (all aged 30-something) were now on German soil. They had been visiting Glenda and Candice's extended family by marriage in Beratzhausen and were currently on their way to spend a few days with us. The alarm rang at 7:00 a.m. (still the middle of the night for us night owls). We rushed around to make it out the door at eight bells in order to be at the station to meet the nine o'clock train.

"Grüss Gott (hello)," Stephen sang out as we approached the hotel desk to turn in our room key with its attached anchor. "Your relatives are not coming until noon."

"Oh, no!" I wailed, mentally debating whether or not we should go back to bed for a few hours. This idea was abruptly extinguished by Stephen's invitation to partake in the continental breakfast in the dining room, normally only included with the higher-priced rooms in the Quality Hotel. Waddling out onto the street a few hours later stuffed with delicious cheeses, succulent ham, hardboiled eggs, hunks of fresh bread, and half a dozen cups of black coffee sipped over the pages of a newspaper was definitely better than rushing to the station in the soggy condition we had woken up in, had our kin been on the earlier train.

What an exuberant feeling, to see these beloved smiling faces after being away 11 months! We got them settled in the room our dear Stephen had wangled for them. We had already lined up the places to go in Munich.

Our first supper together was at the Hofbraühaus. An oom-pah brass band could be heard from outside the enormous beer hall. It looked to be packed to the brim despite its gigantic rooms spread over three floors, which could seat up to 4,500 people.

Timing is everything. Squinting through the smoky, dimly lit atmosphere, we spotted a group getting up to leave and landed a table right in front of the bandstand. The musicians clad in their lederhosen and *trachtenhut* (feathered felt hats) kept the place rockin' to tunes that had patrons swaying, thumping, and joining in the chorus with gusto. Waiters' fingers stretched like octopus tentacles around the handles of six to eight steins of beer, not spilling a drop of the precious commodity as they dashed about trying to fill the demands of the full house. The average beer consumption of Germans is 250 litres (66 gal) of beer each year. Munich residents top that with an average of 350 litres (92 gal) per year. As foreigners, we felt it our assimilative duty to make our best effort to keep up. Ample portions of *Weisswurst*—zesty white sausages slathered with *süsser senf* (sweet mustard)—and heaps of mouth-watering potato salad at bargain prices disappeared from our plates at the speed of light.

This particular beer hall is often seen in documentaries and movies. The Hofbraühaus was the setting for the first meeting of Hitler's newly launched German Workers' Party in 1920. We had a more intimate reason to choose it: Tony, married to Glenda and Candice's other sister, Bea, worked here for several years after first obtaining his chef's licence. At a previous family gathering, Tony had told us that after being run ragged during his shifts, he would barely make it home before collapsing into a comatose sleep, waking up just in time to make it back to the beer hall for his next enervating stint.

Keeping up with the young'uns through the Neue and Alte Pinakotheks (fine art museums), the Deutsches Museum of Science and Technology—where we covered 13 kilometres (8 mi) of corridors over eight floors—the BMW Museum, and a trip back to the Glockenspiel at Marienplatz were notable achievements as well as a great mix of sites.

The day trip to Füssen (on the Austrian border) was our stepping stone to nearby Schwangau to see two of the many majestic domiciles of King Ludwig Freidrich Wilhelm II (1845–1886).

At Schloss (meaning castle) Hohenschwangau, we envisioned the growing years of Bavaria's future king. Originally built by the Knights of Schwangau, the castle lay in ruins from the time the order dissolved in the

16th century until Ludwig's father, Maximilian II, restored it from 1832 to 1836. It was within these Gothic walls that Ludwig met his lifelong friend, composer Richard Wagner, who deepened Ludwig's love of theatre, music, and mythology.

During his reign from 1864 to 1886, King Ludwig shirked political duties as much as possible. Castle-building became his obsession. To the many castles already accumulated by the Wittelsbach Dynasty, which had ruled Bavaria since 1180, Ludwig added many more.

Near the completion of his first extravaganza—Schloss Linderhof, in 1879—he had already started his next mega-project, Herrenchiemsee, isolated on Herreninsel, an island on the Chiemsee lake. A hall of mirrors lit by 2,000 candles and a Roman bath are but a few examples of the lavishness he achieved before he abandoned this second castle (where, by the way, it is said he stayed only once).

He leapt on and began what was to have been his prize undertaking: Neuschwanstein (the second castle on our tour, located near Hohensch-wangau, the castle of his childhood). We were awed by his fantasy creation, nestled in thick forest and misted by a waterfall high in the Alps—it was Schloss Neuschwanstein with its medievalist turrets that inspired Disney's fairyland castles.

Led by a tour guide, we revelled in the intricate woodcarvings, so intricate that the ones in his bedroom alone took 14 carpenters over four years to complete. Themes of the king's obsessions—swans and Wagner's operas—can be seen at every turn.

The royal coffers were continually being depleted by his ambitious endeavours. He became known as Mad King Ludwig. In 1886, the government had Ludwig examined by a medical commission, which proclaimed the King insane; possibly a stratagem to stop the eccentric King from continually bankrupting the royal family. Crazy Louie, as our guide dubbed him, was forced to abdicate. A few days later he was found drowned in a shallow lake. It has never been determined if it was murder or suicide. The interior of Schloss Neuschwanstein was therefore never completed; nonetheless, Ludwig did spend some time during the six-month period before his demise in the Lucullan theatrical sections that were finished.

Back in Munich, we spent a winding-down day with our family strolling along the promenade fronting the massive castle known as the Residenz. King Ludwig II entertained Mozart and Wagner under this same canopy of trees, though not often, as His Kingship hated city life and spent as little time here as possible, especially after he began his building sprees. It is ironic that he is laid to rest in the Residenz chapel. We whiled away the afternoon at one of the convenient outdoor cafés munching on soft, savoury pretzels and quenching our thirst with the country's national beverage.

We left Rob, Glenda, and Candice to play in Munich for another day while we boarded the "silver bullet" for Berlin. Though the whole European train system is of the highest calibre, the speed and comfort of the express between these two cities was unsurpassed.

Berlin

We arrived in Berlin and entered a no-nonsense, high-voltage, bracing atmosphere. Our impression while walking the streets was a city rushing: traffic and people were all in fast mode even doing what should have been more leisurely pursuits. Dog-walkers raced about challenging the shorter-legged canines to keep up, shoppers bustled about the 3-kilometre (2-mi) Kurfürstendamm retail area as if there was a fire sale. Joggers and power walkers filled the spacious parks, while the benches remained empty.

The disparity between this and Munich's easy-going tempo is not only due to Berlin's larger population of 4 million (compared to Munich's 1.3). Historically—and I mean waaay back in pre-medieval Germany—the country was divided into north and south, with the north dominated by barbarian tribes and the south controlled by the Romans. As the Roman Empire waned, the northern barbarians mingled with the southern inhabitants, but the Bavarians—as they came to be known—retained some features from their Romanized roots. Though further diluted over years of increased mobility, there is still a distinct difference between northerners and southerners in traits and mannerisms.

Religion, a common source of division in all countries, later reared its head in Germany. The German states were united under the rule of Maximilian I (crowned in 1493) and thus under the Holy Roman Empire. An Augustine monk named Martin Luther saw corruption in the church. He nailed his 95 Theses (complaints against Catholic doctrine) to the door of the church in Wittenberg in 1517, which resulted in the Protestant movement and the Reformation. The south of Germany remained Catholic while the north became Protestant. Though we have a ways still to go toward universal acceptance of all beliefs, in most countries the Catholic–Protestant rivalry is now a thing of the past.

Berlin epitomized the efficiency and organization I have always associated with Germany. Berliners are high on control in their lives. They are experts in compartmentalizing work, family, friends, and clubs and do not take it lightly when, for instance, work crowds into family time. Aggressive planning ahead is expected. Subscriptions and membership fees are renewed automatically, for example. It is up to the individual to let the business know three to six months in advance that he or she will not be renewing. If you forget, you pay. The life of being a perpetual clock-watcher is exemplified by the expression "das academische viertel" (the academic quarter-hour). It began with students feeling wronged by a tardy professor. If you are more than 15 minutes late, you had better be badly maimed or dead, as no other excuses will suffice. I liked the frankness of the German culture; there is no guesswork as to where they stand on issues.

Rick classified Berlin as one of the most photogenic cities. Contemporary skyscrapers are mixed with restored historic churches and landmark buildings. It is hard to believe this dynamic city was reduced to rubble during World War II. A purposely unrestored reminder of the war stands like a silent sentinel above the central district. The west tower church steeple of Kaiser-Wilhelm-Gedächtniskirche (1895) protrudes jaggedly into the sky; its damage the result of a British bombing on November 22, 1943. Our gaze fell on this world-famous landmark daily as we made our way to the very efficient subway system One day it took us to the much-anticipated site of the remaining Berlin Wall, which had surrounded the city for 28 years before being mostly dismantled.

At the end of the WW II, it was decided that Berlin would be divided between the Allies and the Soviet Union. Britain, France, and the United States controlled West Berlin, while East Berlin became a Soviet-occupied zone. West Berlin began to thrive economically. Passports, full rights, and West German citizenship were granted as soon as East Berliners resettled in West Berlin.

Uprisings were occurring in the Communist Bloc countries, including East Germany, with citizens demanding free and fair elections. Moves were made by the Communists to crush all visible resistance. Fortified borders were quite effective at keeping citizens from leaving the Soviet Bloc countries, with the exception of one evident gap: the city of Berlin. The drain from east to west increased; at one point, 8,000 people a day were exiting. It is estimated 2.5 million people leaked out between 1949 and 1961.

At the same time, the Cold War was in a deep freeze. The Wall was conceived of by Walter Ulbricht (General Secretary of the Socialist Unity Party, 1949–71), approved by Nikita Khrushchev, and constructed under Erich Honecker (who replaced Ulbricht as leader in 1971). Built to prevent the drain from East to West, the publicly announced reason was that it was to keep Allied troops from invading. In 1961, the 160-kilometre (100-mi) Wall—initially just a barbed-wire fence—surrounded West Berlin almost overnight, and was reinforced by East German soldiers. I can imagine the shock on both sides. The 4-metre (13-ft) high concrete blockade was erected with lightning speed, totally encasing the urban island of West Berlin. The only points of entry or exit were Checkpoint Charlie and the Brandenburg Gate.

Approaching Checkpoint Charlie—now a square shed in the roadway with a sign designating the spot—made for an explosive sensation. My insides seemed to be erupting like a volcano. As I turned 360 degrees, I visualized how during its operation two tanks would have faced each other here, with soldiers from both sides on alert for illegal crossings.

A museum in a nearby building filled us in on the hundreds of ways conceived by East Berliners to break into West Berlin, from the ingenious to the downright foolish. Ironically, some of the silliest ideas were successful, and some of the seemingly clever ones were not. It was hit and miss like Russian roulette—tunnels, modified vehicles with stowaways scrunched in fake seats or hidden trunk compartments, rope pulleys from east to west roof tops, ladders, hot air balloons, and homemade scuba gear to swim across the river were only a handful of the ideas we were shown.

The use of canines to sniff out bodies added to the extensive vehicle checks. Other measures to thwart escapes ranged from house-checks along the wall for suspicious activity to armed guard-towers to spiked wire grids (both on the roads and under the river).

An estimated 5,000 people made it safely across between 1962 and 1989; varying reports claim 192 to 239 were killed in their attempt. The tearing down of the Wall in 1989 was by far the most tangible manifestation of the crumbling Iron Curtain.

From here we went on to see the Brandenburger Tor (Brandenburg Gate), which was modelled after the entrance of the Acropolis in Athens. Gracing the top of the Gate is the Quadriga, a triumphant statue of a winged goddess of victory driving a four-horse chariot. This massive monumental arch, a symbol of Berlin, was the official boundary between East and West Berlin. When John F. Kennedy visited West Berlin in 1963, the Russians draped a gigantic red curtain across the entrance so there was no view of East Berlin.

We joined a line of people four blocks long, waiting to view the Reichstag, home of the Berlin parliament. The reunification of Germany was enacted within its walls on October 2, 1990 (within its impressive new walls, that is, as the old Reichstag was totally destroyed during the war). Architect Norman Foster's colossal mirrored cone looks down upon a central sphere, where placards tell the history from the original Reichstag (built in 1894) up to the present day. After reading our way around the sphere, we ambled up to the top of the glass-and-mirrored dome on spiral ramps and then down again.

New construction was evident throughout Berlin, but nowhere was it more apparent than in this area. The cranes were as thick as a flourishing garden of goldenrods shooting up toward the sun.

What was once East Berlin is still rundown compared to the cosmopolitan West. This was clearly evident when we walked down streets where we could see both sides of the previous division at once.

On Niederkirchnerstrasse, a 200-metre (656-ft) authentic stretch of the Berlin Wall can be seen, though it's in poor condition. The Topography of Terror, as it's called, runs along the south side of this Wall section for several blocks; the horrors of the past play themselves out in chronological order in the form of pictures and write-ups along a walkway that is only protected from the elements by a lean-to roof. This was once the location of the SS (Hitler's personal bodyguards) building, and then of Gestapo Headquarters. The buildings were bombed during WW II, leaving only remnants of the basement of the structure where torture took place between 1933 to 1945.

The street beyond—once known as Prinz-Albrecht-Strasse—no longer exists. The hotel where Hitler stayed and held many meetings was once located here, and Himmler's office was number 8 on the street.

The longest stretch of the Berlin Wall still standing is in a rough area west of Warschauer Strasse. We found the area frequented by drug users in a state of torpor and black-leather-and-chain punk types, but none of them bothered us. We proceeded slowly past all 300 metres (984 ft) of wall covered with messages of peace and hope from artists around the world. This, appropriately called the West Side Gallery, is a World Heritage Site, which explains its good condition.

The Holocaust and World War II still hang over Germany. Historians and politicians still haggle over how responsibility for the past should be attributed. The construction of a memorial for the victims of the Holocaust began in the summer of 2001 and is now completed next to the Brandenburg Gate. The Jewish Museum—designed in an irregular, jagged shape to symbolize a broken Star of David—attracts hundreds of thousands of visitors annually. Some of the most respected writers and politicians are speaking out on their theories on the traits that allowed this particular genocide to occur. A reparation fund has been set up by German corporations to compensate the victims of forced labour during WW II. A new citizenship law was put in place to integrate Germany's immigrants in 2000.

Visiting the historical sites of Berlin was a weighty experience for us. Though there is so much more to Germany, we were pleased with our polar-opposite choices of festive, laid-back Munich and electrically charged Berlin.

It was time to bid farewell to Deutschland. Keeping a tight rein on our budget during the first half of our year allowed us to loosen up a bit now, including treating our offspring in Munich. The budgeter announced that our 17 days in Germany had cost us $208.00 a day. We now booked our most expensive overland trip yet: first-class Berlin to Paris.

Chapter Thirteen
France

Several years earlier, we had made our first trip to Paris. All museums were on strike! I can still remember our outcry of disappointment. We vowed then that we would someday come back to see the Louvre. Wangling our Oneworld flight itinerary in order to depart Europe from Paris was our opportunity to do just that.

All our stops in other countries in the past year had been first-time visits. As our train rolled into the Gare du Nord (North Station), it felt neat to arrive at a familiar destination. The subway system was old hat to us. Refreshed from hours of dozing and reading on our nine-hour trip from Berlin, we galloped down the street from the train station to the Hotel Saint Quinton. Dog-walkers whisked along, pulled by half a dozen canines each. We remembered to keep one eye on the sidewalk to gingerly step around "le poo," a lesson in vigilance learned the hard way after a few slippery encounters last time round.

A soft summer breeze caressed our faces. We passed by restaurants and breathed the tantalizing aromas. People spilled out of office buildings. Horns honked at any vehicle that dared interrupt the traffic flow. We were steeped in joie de vivre.

As soon as we stowed our packs in our cozy hotel room, our mission was to join the multitude of diners flooding the sidewalk cafés. Rick's Canadian-accented French brought on a familiar condescending grimace from the server taking our order. It seemed like we had never left.

* * *

Early the next morning, we undertook the monumental task of touring the Musée du Louvre. I always think of it first as the home of Leonardo da Vinci's

Mona Lisa. This dynamic lady—contained in the relatively tiny dimensions of a 77 x 53 centimetre (30 x 21 in) painting—is as captivating today as she was back in the 16th century; not only for her enigmatic smile and missing eyebrows, but for the vast imagery of distant paths, bridges, valleys, and rivers behind her. Few other works of art have been subject to as much scrutiny as this one has in attempts to delve into the multi-faceted design and intent of its creator.

We found the spectacle of Michelangelo's unfinished slaves a compelling example of how Michelangelo chipped away at blocks of marble, releasing bit by bit the sculpture trapped inside.

It was surreal to be standing beside *The Venus de Milo*; fragments of both damaged arms were found separated from the body when it was unearthed by a peasant on the Aegean Island of Milos in 1820. The masterpiece, slightly larger than life, is believed to depict Aphrodite, the goddess of love and beauty, and is attributed to Alexandros of Antioch (an otherwise unknown Hellenistic sculptor).

We moved through the enthralling treasures of Oriental, Egyptian, Greek, and Roman antiquities, but for us, to be saturated with the paintings of the Old Masters was akin to spiritual enlightenment. Witnessing the genius of da Vinci, Raphael, Rembrandt, and Caravaggio in person was as close to heaven as we could be while still in a mortal state.

The Louvre has a fascinating history. The first building on the spot where the museum is now housed was the 12th-century Louvre Palace of Philip II, the remnants of which are still visible in the crypt. This palace was altered frequently by the kings of the Middle Ages. Francis I (reigning from 1515–1547) renovated the building into a French Renaissance–style residence, and it was during this time that he acquired the Mona Lisa.

By the mid-18th century there were proposals to turn the building into a museum, but it wasn't until during the French Revolution that it was finally declared a public museum, opening on August 10, 1793 with an exhibit of 537 paintings. The collection grew with the spoils of Napoleon Bonaparte's successful military campaigns. After his defeat at Waterloo, some pieces were returned to their original owners. The collection grew again under the reigns of Louis XVIII and of Charles X, and then through the Second French Empire ushered in by Napoleon III (Louis-Napoleon Bonaparte, during his reign, 1852–1870). Acquisitions slowed during World War I, and most of the valuables were removed and hidden during World War II.

Today the Louvre contains more than 380,000 objects and displays 35,000 works of art in eight curatorial departments, with more than 60,600 square metres (652,000 sq ft) dedicated to its permanent collection. It is the world's most-visited museum, averaging 15,000 visitors per day, 65 percent of whom are tourists. It was well worth coming back for.

* * *

Democratically it was decided we would each choose a site to fill the two remaining days of our stay. For moi, it was the Eiffel Tower that beckoned, although we did not take the steps or lift to the top this time.

I found it interesting that this iconic and striking piece of structural art was met with much public criticism and considered an eyesore when it was completed in 1889. Named after its designer, engineer Gustave Eiffel, it was built as the entrance arch to the World's Fair marking the centennial of the French Revolution. The metal structure is said to weigh 7,300 metric tons (8,047 US tons), and if the non-metal components are tallied in, the weight would be approximately 10,000 metric tons (11,023 US tons). Including the 24-metre (79-ft) tower, it is equivalent to about 81 storeys of a conventional building, making it the tallest structure in Paris.

But who can measure this symbol of romance in mere numbers unless one is privy to the aggregate of marriage proposals that have occurred here? Tom Cruise did it. So did Rod Stewart, as well as many others. (With the swinging doors of marriage-divorce, I should clarify: their proposals were to Katie Holmes and Penny Lancaster respectively.) Sitting in one of the tower's restaurants, gazing lovingly into each other's eyes, and sipping a fine vintage wine, or standing on one of the platforms looking down at the glittering city lights below, amour reaches a zenith of intensity.

A stroll down the Champs-Elysées, Paris's most prestigious avenue, was a Rick-favoured excursion, with no objections from me thanks to its delightful two kilometres of cinemas, cafés, restaurants, and luxury specialty shops. The Arc de Triomphe rises from the centre of Charles de Gaulle Place to the west. This monument was erected to honour those who fought for France, particularly during the Napoleonic wars. On the inside and top of the Arc are the names of generals and wars fought, and underneath is the Tomb of the Unknown Soldier from World War I. To the east is the Place de la Concorde with its landmark obelisk, a gift from Egypt. The square is backed by the Church of Madeleine with its 52 Corinthian columns and the grand Hotel de Crillon, where Queen Marie Antoinette (1774–1792) once came with her elite friends for piano lessons.

We indulged in a $22 mini-sandwich each. Mon Dieu! Quite digestible though, considering that rent on commercial space in Paris can top the scales at $1.5 million US for 1,000 square metres (10,763 sq ft). As we sat over a second cup of coffee, I thought how amazing it would be to be sitting here in July, when cyclists with thighs as thick as my waist would pump their way with jet speed down this promenade in the Tour de France. Since 1975, Champs-Elysées has been the finish line for this world-renowned 3,500-kilometre (2,175-mi) race through France and to a bordering country each year; the duration is approximately 23 days, broken into day-long segments or stages.

An evening at the Moulin Rouge was a risqué grand finale. Some of the scenes from the movie starring Nicole Kidman were filmed here. The scantily dressed, striking mademoiselles flounced, kicked, and sang their way across the stage. The dinner was as delectable as the price was exorbitant. Our daily costs averaged $190.00. Although it felt like we were splurging our way around Paris, trying to be free spenders, there was an unnerving undercurrent to releasing our deeply embedded travel budget, so we were not as free as perhaps we thought.

On our last day, we walked along the Seine and sat for hours on a bench looking up at the huge Notre Dame Cathedral. We were overcome with the bittersweetness of another farewell; this one was more pronounced than leaving any other country, as it marked the closing chapter of our travel abroad. At the same time we were filled with the sweet anticipation and excitement of once again being on North American soil. Our flight booking was set, and ready or not, the North Atlantic was soon below us as we winged our way to New York City.

Chapter Fourteen

United States

Landing back on North American soil, we experienced a rush of elation tinged with melancholy. I was totally unprepared for the dichotomy and depth of emotion that kept welling up. I did not know whether to laugh or cry ... so I did both. Rick was in the same space. The thrill of being back on our continent and the grief over the impending end to our year-long adventure tossed about in our minds like a piece of driftwood, at the mercy of the ebb and flow of the tide of our emotions.

This being our third visit to New York, we knew it would be the ideal place to appease our muddled mood. There is nothing quite like the neon sizzle of Broadway. After a traditional gorging at a New York deli, we were swept up in the sidewalk crowds. Seeing a New York police motorcycle parked in front of a shop, I raced over and pretended to get on while Rick aimed his camera. I only saw a glimpse of the uniformed officer as I was hoisted into the air and onto the bike seat and found a Stallone-sized arm around my shoulder and a seductive DiCaprio smile in my peripheral vision. I carry this prized photo to flash to my girlfriends, with a smug challenge: "Bet you can't top this!"

Our last sojourn in this fabulous city had been during the winter months. The smattering of white under bare branches in Central Park back then was now transformed into profuse greenery, from the thick carpet of grass to the canopy of leaves meeting the cerulean sky. Gardens in full bloom embellished the environs with a plethora of vibrant yellow, violet, pink, and scarlet shades. Sunbathers lay scattered here and there on the vast lawns. Children raced about in the play areas or splashed in the wading pools. The torrid sun eventually sent even the most ardent sun-worshippers to shady cover or for a refreshing dip in a lake. Baseball field bleachers were filled with fans cheering successful slides to home base. Pedestrian walks were interspersed with paths for bicycles and all other motor-less wheeled contraptions, including for-hire horse-drawn carriages. It was invigorating and uplifting to walk through this verdant oasis covering 341 hectares (843 acres) smack-dab in the middle of Manhattan.

And then the rains came; two days of solid downpour. Starbucks is a great place to grab a window seat and "umbrella-watch." Bright ones, gaudy ones, floral, striped, and black ones, some big, some small, many broken ones—as well as some poor sods without any—all paraded by. We were chai tea'd out by the time the torrents turned to showers gentle enough for my tiny blue paisley umbrella (purchased in Beijing) to manage. Rick's full-sized one had been tossed out months ago. Sharing my tiny one left us each with a wet outer side. Just as we were about to purchase a larger one, the sun came out.

Broadway is synonymous with theatre par excellence. We fit in as many productions as possible every time we visit. This time round, we saw *Hairspray*, which was great with its 1960s-style dance songs and poignant message about the injustices in parts of American society. *Hairspray* has infiltrated a large percentage of North American households with John Travolta's portrayal of the female teenager's chubby mother in the 2007 movie version. Rocking to *Mamma Mia!* was Abba-solutely marvellous, and *Lion King* was good for the soul.

On a previous visit, I had taken a photo of the World Trade Towers while lying on my back on the sidewalk. It was the only way I could capture the caption above the door and still fit in all 110 floors of the sky-piercing edifices.

This time our eyes were riveted to the construction at Ground Zero. A ramp had been built across the street from the devastation so the site could be viewed above the restricted area fences. For blocks around, the walls of the ramp and fences were covered with the pictures and names of loved ones, colleagues, and friends who had perished. Flowers, poems, banners, flags, and all manner of mementoes gave voice to all the lives touched directly or indirectly. The horrific act of terrorism shocked and saddened the nations of the world and will forever remain unfathomable.

It was time for the final leg of our journey. Our year away had come to an end. Our thoughts dwelled on getting back to a "regular" life—not knowing if we wanted to get back to a regular life, or whether we could even if we wanted to. We felt deeply ambivalent about our journey coming to an end. We bid our farewell to New York, having rid our account of $203.00 a day. As the plane reached high altitude, our thoughts soared to home and family.

Chapter Fifteen
Back Home

Our 767 touched down in Vancouver. I was tempted to kiss the tarmac, but felt that would be too Pope-ish. Rick and I exchanged tear-filled glances as we sailed through customs and hoisted our packs onto our backs one last time.

Our property manager, who was in possession of our condo keys, met us at the outside door of the complex. How perfect was it that our tenant's job relocation coincided with our return!

Stepping across the threshold of our new home, we found the brightness and layout as pleasing as we remembered it.

The following month was a blur. Our greatly anticipated motor trip across Canada to reunite with our five sons (between us), their wives and partners, our six grandchildren, and one great-grandchild sustained us through our settling-in period.

A whirlwind of shopping, cleaning, and painting ensued. I became extremely adept at painting trim with my left hand, while *sotai* sessions (Japanese balancing therapy) corrected the right shoulder imbalance that had plagued me since Italy. Through a series of manipulations and exercises to re-align my body, I could once again swing my right arm in a pain-free 360-degree rotation.

There was a year's worth of mail to be gone through, and then a truckload of belongings from storage. It was just like Christmas; everything looked new, and there was so much. Living lean for the past 12 months made us shake our heads at our old idea of necessities, especially in the clothing department. Fifty shirts seemed excessive after becoming accustomed to four; 25 pairs of pants were more than enough after only two. The garage sale we'd thrown before leaving was no match for all the chucking, dumping, ditching, and trips to Sally Ann that sprang out of our new minimalist credo.

While undertaking the physical labour of getting our living space in shape, our minds often drifted to events of the past year. We would call out to one another while unpacking in different rooms with, "Hey, we are only working six hours a day; a breeze compared to a chai wallah's job!" Or we would take a break from our scrubbing to express, "Do I ever miss the only major decisions of the day being where to eat and what to see." We'd roar with laughter at some comical incident from our travels, like the time we jumped onto a moving train in India. At times the reliving was so vivid we could almost smell, taste, hear, and feel a place brought to the forefront of our memories that filled us with nostalgia, such as wandering through the Saturday market of a Sherpa village.

We did a lot of debriefing on how meeting our original goals fared throughout our travels.

Rick was satisfied with our final budget results. By his strategic division of time spent in countries where travel is economical and those where it is not, our total spent during the year was $35,808.00, only slightly exceeding his pre-trip calculations. Kudos to Rick! (I even had a twinge of guilt over my evil intent toward his calculator.)

In the more expensive countries it became a challenge to find ways to keep costs low and still stick to our overriding motto: "We are not here to suffer."

As for our fourth motto, "Follow the sun": although we arrived in Europe before the balmy weather, and a few other times had to wear everything we owned to keep warm, for 10 out of the 12 months we basked in summery rays.

In the realm of expect the unexpected, the obstacles we encountered in China and India gave us a proficiency for adapting to plan changes. Not only were we ready to go on from a foiled plan A to B, but sometimes waaay down the alphabet sequence to E, or F-lexible as an Olympic gymnast.

Though we started out like Tasmanian devils in Australia, by the time we reached Asian soil we took on a more leisurely pace, with enough rest between excursions to maintain good health and not become stressed. When arriving at a new locale, we familiarized ourselves with the area around our hotel and found the most suitable eating places, parks, and shopping spots for necessities before undertaking historical and geographical sites.

Being together 24/7 was another bit of uncharted territory we waded into. Irritating habits are not so easy to ignore when they're in your face. Being jet-lagged, train-lagged, bus-lagged or just plain lagged was not always conducive to civility. After a few altercations for silly reasons, we both felt it imperative to count to 10, read a book, go for a solo walk, etc.—in other words, cool down—before broaching whatever was bothering us. We tried to follow our fifth motto: "Find ways to maintain our own breathing space." Sometimes it worked and sometimes it didn't, but we came out of this still lovers and friends, and with a greater acceptance of our foibles.

Our guiding principle of trekking the globe with gentle footsteps was lived up to for the most part (although we stomped on a few toes, mostly from our own ignorance of a culture). Using the same methods of travel as locals and staying where locals stay enlightened us in ways being under the umbrella of a tour or being enclosed in a five-star resort never could (and besides, it would take a billionaire's account to afford a year of such travel). The subtleties and complexities of a society can only be observed on the front lines, and as with anything, the more we learned, the more we realized how little we knew.

The common denominator of the peoples of the world is the desire to live in harmony and peace. Transcending oceans, borders, and cultures are these basic goals in life: to take care of one's family, and to provide them with food, shelter, medical care, and education. We saw first-hand how differences in political power, the degree of bureaucratic corruption, the havoc created by radicals, lack of social programs, and natural disasters without a rallying government are monumental obstacles—none of which we have ever had to face in our own relatively sheltered lives in Canada.

We could never go back to being who we were at the outset of our journey. In the vagaries of travel, anonymity washed away how others knew us (our personal and career accomplishments thus far in life), leaving us to continually redefine who we were in relation to each culture experienced.

Having tested the theory of travel being the perfect transitional setting, our year away certainly gave us time to reflect on our lives, where we had been, and in what direction we would like to go. It definitely broke old patterns, allowing us to see more clearly where to channel energies during the next segment of our lives. For us, this has come to mean continuing our gypsy propensities in roaming the planet—milling about ancient ruins, joining in local festivals, having tea with villagers, floating down famous rivers, and climbing mountains for breathtaking views. It means having the foreignness of each country fade as we slowly learn to see issues through the eyes of others.

Our year away after 35 years in the workforce was the best gift we could have given ourselves in many ways, and last but not least, it meant the satisfaction of having LIVED OUR DREAM.

RICK'S

Included: Accommodations, food, entrance fees, incidentals, and transportation

The Rough Budget was Rick's calculations based on guidebook prices, with no idea at the time as to how many days we would spend in each country.

Country	Days Spent	Rough Budget
Australia	32	$115/day
China	47	$80/day
Tibet	11	$100/day
Nepal	60	$60/day
India	90	$60/day
Total Australia & Asia	240 days	
Italy	29	$135/day
Austria	19	$120/day
Hungary	13	$100/day
Slovakia	13	(replaced Poland's budget at $100/day)
Switzerland	3	$190/day
Germany	17	$160/day
France	7	$175/day
Total Europe	101 days	
United States	14	$200/day
Grand Total	**355 Days**	

Budget

Not included: Oneworld air tickets

Our target cost for the year was $100 per day for the two of us. By staying in the less-expensive countries longer, we were able to realize this.

Actual Expenditure	Daily Average
$3,840 (incl. $1,198 bus pass)	$120
$3,807	$81
$2,574 (incl. flight out of Tibet)	$234
$3,720	$62
$4,915	$54
$18,856	$79/day
$3,828	$132
$2,299	$121
$1,443	$111
$1,001	$77
$669	$223
$3,540 (incl. entertaining offspring)	$208
$1,330	$190
$14,110 (incl. $1,941 of train travel)	$140/day
$2,842	$203
$35,808	**$100.86/day**

Irene Butler is an award-winning travel journalist. After 35 years of careers in education, real estate, and retail store management, her life now revolves around new travel adventures and coast to coast Canadian excursions to visit family, including her seven grandchildren. She lives in Vancouver, British Columbia, with her photographer husband and fellow adventurer Rick.

Irene is a member of TMAC (Travel Media Association of Canada), Federation of BC Travel Writers, and BCATW (BC Association of Travel Writers). She has degrees in psychology and gerontology.